CHOCTAW BY BLOOD

ENROLLMENT CARDS

1898-1914

VOLUME VII

TRANSCRIBED BY

JEFF BOWEN

NATIVE STUDY
Gallipolis, Ohio
USA

Originally published:
Baltimore, Maryland
2015

Reprinted by:

Native Study LLC
Gallipolis, OH
www.nativestudy.com

Library of Congress Control Number: 2020911767

ISBN: 978-1-64968-010-5

Made in the United States of America.

This series is dedicated to
Mike Marchi,
who keeps my spirits up.

CREEK CENSUS.

SECOND NOTICE.

Members of the Dawes Commission will be present at the following times and places for the purpose of enrolling Creek citizens, as required by Act of Congress of June 10, 1896:

At Muskogee, Nov. 8 to 30, 1897, inclusive.
At Wagoner, Nov. 8 to 13, " inclusive.
At Eufaula, Nov. 8 to 13, " inclusive.
At Sapulpa, Nov. 15 to 20, " inclusive.
At Wetumpka, Nov. 15 to 20, " inclusive.
At Okmulgee, Nov. 22 to 30, " inclusive.

All persons who have not heretofore enrolled before the Dawes Commission should appear and enroll. Parents and guardians can enroll their families and wards.

TAMS BIXBY,
FRANK C. ARMSTRONG,
A. S. McKENNON,
THOS. B. NEEDLES,
Commissioners.

The above illustration is similar in nature to what was found throughout Indian Territory for different tribes as far as postings on bulletin boards, public centers, or wherever they could be read so people would be notified of where and when they needed to be for enrollment with the Dawes Commission.

This is a picture of the Dawes Commission at Camp Jones in Stonewall, Indian Territory on September 8, 1898.

The images below are of two of the original cards given on the microfilm. The cards given in this book have been formatted to fit on one page and still give all the information found on the original cards.

Introduction

This series of Choctaw Enrollment Cards for the Five Civilized Tribes 1898-1914 has been transcribed from National Archive Film M-1186 Rolls 39-46.

The series contains more than 6100 Choctaw enrollment cards. All of the cards list age, sex and degree of blood, the parties' Dawes Roll Numbers, and date of enrollment by the Secretary of Interior for each person. The contents also give the enrollee's parents' names as well as miscellaneous notes pertaining to the enrollee's circumstances, when needed. Most entries indicate whether or not a spouse is an Intermarried White, with the initials I.W.

Enrollment wasn't as simple a process as most would think just by going through these pages. The relationships between the Five Tribes and the Dawes Commission were weak at best. There were political battles going on between the tribes and the U.S. Government as it was, but the struggles didn't stop there. Each tribe had its own political factions pulling it from every direction. On top of everything else, people from every corner of the United States were trying to figure how to get in on the spoils (Money and Land Allotment) by means of political favor. Kent Carter, author of *The Dawes Commission*, describes the continuous effort required to enroll the different tribes and the pressure the Commission incurred from people all over the country who tried to insinuate themselves into the equation:

"In May 1896 the Dawes Commission Returned To Indian Territory for its third visit, establishing its headquarters at Vinita in the Cherokee Nation. It now had to process applications for citizenship in addition to negotiating allotment agreements; these circumstances make the narrative of events more confusing because the commission attempted the two tasks concurrently. The commissioners resumed making their usual speeches to tribal officials and public gatherings to promote negotiations, but now they inevitably had to respond to questions about how the application process for citizenship would work. They also began receiving letters from people all over the United States asking how they could 'get on the rolls' so they could 'get Indian land'."[1]

For the actual process of Choctaw enrollment, "A commission was appointed in each county of the Choctaw Nation under an act of September 18 to make separate rolls of citizens by blood, by intermarriage, and freedmen; it was to deliver them to recently elected Chief Green McCurtain by October 20, but he rejected them even before they were completed because of charges that people were being left off for political reasons. On October 30, the National Council authorized establishment of a five-member

---

[1] *The Dawes Commission* by Kent Carter, page 15, para. 1

ix

commission to revise the rolls within ten days and then directed McCurtain to turn them over to the Dawes Commission on November 11, 1896. The Choctaws hired the law firm of Stuart, Gordon, and Hailey, of South McAlester to represent the tribe at all proceedings held by the Dawes Commission,"[2] another indication that throughout the Commission's efforts there was always controversy between the tribes and the negotiators.

When completed, this multi-volume series will contain thousands of names, all of them accounted for in the indexes carefully prepared by the author. Hopefully this work will help many researchers find their ancestors and satisfy the questions that so many have had about their Native American heritage.

Jeff Bowen
Gallipolis, Ohio
NativeStudy.com

---

[2] *The Dawes Commission* by Kent Carter, page 16, para. 5

Choctaw By Blood Enrollment Cards 1898-1914

RESIDENCE: Kiamitia COUNTY. **Choctaw Nation** **Choctaw Roll** (Not Including Freedmen) CARD NO.
POST OFFICE: Antlers, I.T. FIELD NO. **1801**

Dawes' Roll No.	NAME	Relationship to Person First Named	AGE	SEX	BLOOD	TRIBAL ENROLLMENT		
						Year	County	No.
5110 1 James, Cornelius 44		First Named	41	M	Full	1896	Jacks Fork	7348
5111 2 " Elsie 26		Wife	23	F	"	1893	Cedar	273
5112 3 " Frances 6		Ward	3	"	"	1896	Jacks Fork	7349
4								
5								
6								
7								
8								
9								
10								
11								
12								
13								
14								
15								
16								
17								

ENROLLMENT
OF NOS. 1,2,3 HEREON
APPROVED BY THE SECRETARY
OF INTERIOR JAN 16 1903

TRIBAL ENROLLMENT OF PARENTS

	Name of Father	Year	County	Name of Mother	Year	County
1	James Uakata	Dead	Kiamitia	Pisa-te-ma	Dead	Kiamitia
2	Fa-lan-sa-a	"	Jacks Fork	Lucy	"	Jacks Fork
3	No-wa-tubbee	Dead	Cedar	A-na-na-he	"	Cedar
4						
5						
6	No2 on 1893 Pay roll, Page 25, No 273, Cedar Co as Elsie Willis					
7	See testimony of Cornelius James and other taken Dec 3 as to					
8	identity of No3.					
9						
10						
11						
12						
13						
14						
15						
16						Date of Application for Enrollment. 5/16/99
17						

1

Choctaw By Blood Enrollment Cards 1898-1914

RESIDENCE: Cedar
POST OFFICE: Antlers, I.T.

COUNTY.

Choctaw Nation

Choctaw Roll
(Not Including Freedmen)

CARD NO.
FIELD NO. 1802

Dawes' Roll No.		NAME		Relationship to Person First Named	AGE	SEX	BLOOD	TRIBAL ENROLLMENT		
								Year	County	No.
5113	1	Cole, Turner	47		44	M	Full	1896	Cedar	2436
5114	2	" Elizabeth	45	Wife	42	F	"	1896	"	2437
5115	3	" Eliza A	20	Dau	17	"	"	1896	"	2439
5116	4	" Jensie	18	"	15	"	"	1896	"	2440
5117	5	" Isabelle	15	"	12	"	"	1896	"	2441
5118	6	" Bob	11	Son	8	M	"	1896	"	2442
5119	7	" Charley	7	"	4	"	"	1896	"	2443
5120	8	" James	4	"	1	"	"			
	9									
	10									
	11									
	12									
	13									
	14									
	15	ENROLLMENT OF NOS. 1,2,3,4,5,6,7,8 HEREON								
	16	APPROVED BY THE SECRETARY								
	17	OF INTERIOR JAN 16 1903								

TRIBAL ENROLLMENT OF PARENTS

	Name of Father	Year	County	Name of Mother	Year	County
1	Peter Cole	Dead	Cedar	Molsey Cole	Dead	Jacks Fork
2	Robert Camp	"	Atoka	Betsy Camp	1896	Cedar
3	No 1			No 2		
4	No 1			No 2		
5	No 1			No 2		
6	No 1			No 2		
7	No 1			No 2		
8	No 1			No 2		
9						
10	For child of No 3 see NB (Apr 26'06) Card No 1210					
11						
12	No 3 on 1896 roll as Eliza Ann Cole					
13	No 3 now wife of Grant Noatabbe Choctaw card #1899					
14	No 8 Affidavit of birth to be supplied. Recd May 17/99.					
15						Date of Application for Enrollment.
16						5/16/99
17						

2

Choctaw By Blood Enrollment Cards 1898-1914

RESIDENCE: Cedar	COUNTY.		CARD NO.
POST OFFICE: Antlers, I.T.		Choctaw Nation — Choctaw Roll (Not Including Freedmen)	FIELD NO. 1803

Dawes' Roll No.	NAME		Relationship to Person First Named	AGE	SEX	BLOOD	TRIBAL ENROLLMENT Year	County	No.
5121	1 Cole, Simeon	23	Named	20	M	Full	1896	Cedar	2438
5122	2 " Eliza A	23	Wife	20	F	"	1896	"	9262
5123	3 " Susie	4	Dau	4mo	"	"			
5124	4 Emer, Nellie	5	S "	2	"	"			
	5								
	6								
	7								
	8								
	9								
	10								
	11								
	12								
	13								
	14								
	15	ENROLLMENT OF NOS. 1,2,3,4 HEREON APPROVED BY THE SECRETARY OF INTERIOR JAN 16 1903							
	16								
	17								

TRIBAL ENROLLMENT OF PARENTS

	Name of Father	Year	County	Name of Mother	Year	County
1	Turner Cole	1896	Cedar	Elizabeth Cole	1896	Cedar
2	Goodman McKinzie	1896	"	Nellie McKinzie	Dead	"
3	No 1			No 2		
4	Henry Holly	1896	Non Citz	No 2		
5						
6	No 4 is duplicate of Nellie Locke No 1 on Choctaw card #4896					
7	Enrollment of No4 cancelled under Departmental authority of March 1, 1907 (ITD 5834-1907) DC 12504 1907					
8	No2 on 1896 roll as Lizann McKinzie					
9						
10	Nos 3-4 Affidavits of birth to be supplied. Recd May 17/99					
11	No4 is illegitimate					
12						
13						
14						
15				Date of Application for Enrollment.	5/16/99	
16						
17						

3

Choctaw By Blood Enrollment Cards 1898-1914

RESIDENCE: Cedar   COUNTY. **Choctaw Nation**   **Choctaw Roll**   CARD NO.
POST OFFICE: Kosoma, I.T   (Not Including Freedmen)   FIELD NO. 1804

Dawes' Roll No.	NAME	Relationship to Person First Named	AGE	SEX	BLOOD	TRIBAL ENROLLMENT Year	County	No.
5125	1 Wesley, Thomas 55	Named	52	M	Full	1896	Cedar	13136
5126	2 " Martha 46	Wife	43	F	"	1896	"	13137
5127	3 " Silas 10	Son	7	M	"	1896	"	13138
Dead	4 " Simpson DEAD	Ward	15	"	"	1896	"	5469
	5							
	6							
	7							
	8							
	9							
	10							
	11							
	12							
	13							
	14							
	15	ENROLLMENT						
	16	OF NOS. 1, 2, 3 HEREON APPROVED BY THE SECRETARY						
	17	OF INTERIOR JAN 16 1903						

TRIBAL ENROLLMENT OF PARENTS

	Name of Father	Year	County	Name of Mother	Year	County
1	Anontubbee	Dead	Cedar	Ala-ho-na	Dead	Cedar
2	Fa-lama-tubbee	"	"	Phoebe	"	"
3	No 1			No 2		
4	Ho-te-chubbee	Dead	Cedar	Car-ta-lcah	Dead	Cedar
5						
6						
7						
8	No4 on 1896 roll as Impson Hotechubbe					
9						
10	No4 died Nov 4, 1900; proof of death filed Dec 15, 1902					
11						
12	No. 4 HEREON DISMISSED UNDER					
13	ORDER OF THE COMMISSION TO THE FIVE CIVILIZED TRIBES OF MARCH 31, 1905.					
14						
15				Date of Application for Enrollment.		
16						5/16/99
17	P.O. Antlers, I.T.					

12/10/02

4

Choctaw By Blood Enrollment Cards 1898-1914

RESIDENCE: Cedar   COUNTY. **Choctaw Nation**   **Choctaw Roll** (Not Including Freedmen)   CARD NO.

POST OFFICE: Kosoma I.T.   FIELD NO. 1805

Dawes' Roll No.	NAME	Relationship to Person First Named	AGE	SEX	BLOOD	TRIBAL ENROLLMENT Year	County	No.
5128	1 Frazier, Kinsby ~~DIED PRIOR TO SEPTEMBER 25 1902~~		30	F	Full	1896	Cedar	4098
5129	2 " Sukie 11	Dau	8	"	"	1896	"	4099
	3							
	4							
	5							
	6							
	7							
	8							
	9							
	10							
	11							
	12							
	13							
	14	ENROLLMENT						
	15	OF NOS. 1, 2 HEREON						
	16	APPROVED BY THE SECRETARY OF INTERIOR JAN 16 1903						
	17							

TRIBAL ENROLLMENT OF PARENTS

	Name of Father	Year	County	Name of Mother	Year	County
1	George Homer	Ded	Cedar	Holbatona	Ded	Cedar
2	Peter Frazier	"	"	No. 1		
3						
4						
5						
6	No 1 died in 1901; Enrollment cancelled by Department [illegible]					
7						
8						
9						
10						
11						
12						
13						
14					Date of Application for Enrollment.	
15						
16					5-16-99	
17						

Choctaw By Blood Enrollment Cards 1898-1914

RESIDENCE: Cedar   COUNTY.   **Choctaw Nation**   **Choctaw Roll** (Not Including Freedmen)   CARD No.

POST OFFICE: Kosoma   FIELD No. 1806

Dawes' Roll No.	NAME	Relationship to Person First Named	AGE	SEX	BLOOD	TRIBAL ENROLLMENT		
						Year	County	No.
5130	1 Durant Levi 28	First Named	25	M	Full	1896	Cedar	3368
	2							
	3							
	4							
	5							
	6							
	7							
	8							
	9							
	10							
	11							
	12							
	13							
	14							
	15							
	16							
	17							

ENROLLMENT
OF NOS. 1 HEREON
APPROVED BY THE SECRETARY
OF INTERIOR JAN 16 1903

TRIBAL ENROLLMENT OF PARENTS

	Name of Father	Year	County	Name of Mother	Year	County
1	Edmond Durant	Ded	Cedar	Holbotona	Ded	Cedar
2						
3						
4						
5						
6						
7						
8						
9						
10						
11						
12						
13						
14						
15					Date of Application for Enrollment.	
16					5-16-99	
17						

6

Choctaw By Blood Enrollment Cards 1898-1914

RESIDENCE: Jacks Fork	COUNTY.	**Choctaw Nation**	**Choctaw Roll** (Not Including Freedmen)	CARD NO.
POST OFFICE: Antlers I.T.				FIELD NO. 1807

Dawes' Roll No.	NAME		Relationship to Person	AGE	SEX	BLOOD	TRIBAL ENROLLMENT		
							Year	County	No.
5131	1 Taaffe Maud	20	First Named	17	F	1/16	1896	Tobucksy	12016
5132	2 " Jennie	22	Sis	19	"	1/16	1896	Red River	12332
5133	3 " Joseph	19	Bro	16	M	1/16	1896	" "	12331
5134	4 " May	23	Sis	20	F	1/16	1893	Jacks Fork	P.R.692
14694	5 " Hollis	1	Son	10mo	M	1/16			
	6								
	7								
	8								
	9								
	10								
	11								
	12								
	13								
	14								
	15								
	16								
	17								

ENROLLMENT OF NOS. 1,2,3,4 HEREON APPROVED BY THE SECRETARY OF INTERIOR JAN 16 1903

ENROLLMENT OF NOS. 5 HEREON APPROVED BY THE SECRETARY OF INTERIOR MAY 20 1903

TRIBAL ENROLLMENT OF PARENTS

	Name of Father	Year	County	Name of Mother	Year	County
1	George Taaffe	Ded	Red River	Fredoni Taaffe	Ded	Red River
2	" "	"	" "	" "	"	" "
3	" "	"	" "	" "	"	" "
4	" "	"	" "	" "	"	" "
5	unknown			Nº 1		
6						
7						
8						
9						
10			Nº 1 on 1896 roll as Maud Taffee			
11			Nº 4 " 1893 Pay roll as May Toaffe			
12			Nº5 Born May 28, 1901: proof of birth filed April 13, 1903.			
13						
14						
15						
16						
17						

P.O. Hugo I.T. 11/4/02

7

Choctaw By Blood Enrollment Cards 1898-1914

RESIDENCE: Cedar   COUNTY.   Choctaw Nation   CARD NO.

POST OFFICE: Antlers I.T.   Choctaw Roll (Not Including Freedmen)   FIELD NO. 1808

Dawes' Roll No.	NAME		Relationship to Person First Named	AGE	SEX	BLOOD	TRIBAL ENROLLMENT Year	County	No.
5135	1 Edward Wesley	40	Named	37	M	1/2	1896	Cedar	3722
5136	2 " Cely	34	Wife	31	F	Full	1896	"	3717
5137	3 " Eliza A	12	Dau	9	"	3/4	1896	"	3718
5138	4 " Salena	8	"	5	"	3/4	1896	"	3719
5139	5 " John	4	Son	2/3	M	3/4			
	6								
	7								
	8								
	9								
	10								
	11								
	12								
	13								
	14								
	15								
	16								
	17								

ENROLLMENT
OF NOS. 1,2,3,4,5, HEREON
APPROVED BY THE SECRETARY
OF INTERIOR JAN 16 1903

TRIBAL ENROLLMENT OF PARENTS

	Name of Father	Year	County	Name of Mother	Year	County
1	Tobias Edward	1896	Blue	Rhoda Edward	Ded	Wade
2	Edmond Durant	Ded	Cedar	Arny Durant	"	Cedar
3	No 1			No 2		
4	No 1			No 2		
5	No 1			No 2		
6						
7			No 4 on 1896 roll as Sarena Edward			
8			No 3 " " " " Eliza Ann Edward			
9						
10			For child of No3 see NB (Apr 26'06) Card #1192			
11			" " "Nosland2" " (March 3'05) " #1263			
12						
13						
14						
15						
16				Date of Application for Enrollment	5-16-99	
17						

8

Choctaw By Blood Enrollment Cards 1898-1914

RESIDENCE: Cedar COUNTY. **Choctaw Nation**   **Choctaw Roll** CARD No.
POST OFFICE: Rodney I.T.   (Not Including Freedmen) FIELD No. 1809

Dawes' Roll No.	NAME		55	AGE	SEX	BLOOD	TRIBAL ENROLLMENT		
							Year	County	No.
5140	1 Collin Abel	58		M	Full	1896	Cedar	5432	
	2								
	3								
	4								
	5								
	6								
	7								
	8								
	9								
	10								
	11								
	12								
	13								
	14								
	15								
	16								
	17								

ENROLLMENT
OF NOS. 1 HEREON
APPROVED BY THE SECRETARY
OF INTERIOR JAN 16 1903

TRIBAL ENROLLMENT OF PARENTS

	Name of Father	Year	County	Name of Mother	Year	County
1	James Collin	Ded	Tobucksy	Meashintonah	Ded	Jack Fork
2						
3						
4						
5						
6						
7						
8						
9						
10						
11						
12						
13						
14						
15						
16						
17	P.O. Antlers, I.T.					

Date of Application for Enrollment.
5-16-99

12/2/02

Choctaw By Blood Enrollment Cards 1898-1914

| RESIDENCE: Jacks Fork
POST OFFICE: Antlers I.T. | COUNTY. **Choctaw Nation** | | | | **Choctaw Roll**
(Not Including Freedmen) | | CARD NO.
FIELD NO. 1810 | |

Dawes' Roll No.	NAME	Relationship to Person	AGE	SEX	BLOOD	TRIBAL ENROLLMENT		
						Year	County	No.
5141	1 Peter[sic] John ⁹	First Named	6	M	Full	1896	Kiamatia[sic]	10448
	2							
	3							
	4							
	5							
	6							
	7							
	8							
	9							
	10							
	11							
	12							
	13							
	14							
	15	ENROLLMENT OF NOS. 1 HEREON APPROVED BY THE SECRETARY OF INTERIOR JAN 16 1903						
	16							
	17							

TRIBAL ENROLLMENT OF PARENTS

	Name of Father	Year	County	Name of Mother	Year	County
1	Charlie Peters	De'd	Kiamatia[sic]	Nicey Peters	De'd	Kiamatia[sic]
2						
3						
4						
5						
6						
7						
8						
9						
10						
11						
12						
13						
14						
15				Date of Application for Enrollment.	5-16-99	
16						
17						

10

Choctaw By Blood Enrollment Cards 1898-1914

RESIDENCE: **Jacks Fork** COUNTY. **Choctaw Nation**   **Choctaw Roll** CARD NO.
POST OFFICE: **Antlers** I.T.   *(Not Including Freedmen)* FIELD NO. **1811**

Dawes' Roll No.	NAME	Relationship to Person First Named	AGE	SEX	BLOOD	TRIBAL ENROLLMENT		
						Year	County	RdR.
5142	1 Walker David 21	First Named	18	M	Full	1893	Cedar	41
	2							
	3							
	4							
	5							
	6							
	7							
	8							
	9							
	10							
	11							
	12							
	13							
	14							
	15	ENROLLMENT						
	16	OF NOS. 1 HEREON APPROVED BY THE SECRETARY						
	17	OF INTERIOR JAN 16 1903						

TRIBAL ENROLLMENT OF PARENTS

	Name of Father	Year	County	Name of Mother	Year	County
1	Joe Walker	Ded	Cedar	Liza Walker	Ded	Cedar
2						
3						
4						
5						
6						
7						
8						
9						
10						
11						
12						
13						
14						
15						
16				Date of Application for Enrollment.	5-16-99	
17						

11

Choctaw By Blood Enrollment Cards 1898-1914

RESIDENCE: Jacks Fork   COUNTY. **Choctaw Nation**   **Choctaw Roll** (Not Including Freedmen)   CARD No.

POST OFFICE: Antlers I.T.   FIELD No. **1812**

Dawes' Roll No.	NAME	Relationship to Person First Named	AGE	SEX	BLOOD	TRIBAL ENROLLMENT		P.N.
						Year	County	
5143	1 Cole, Louisa DIED ON SEPTEMBER 25 1902		27	F	Full	1893	Cedar	75
5144	2 " Sampson	Son	5	M	"			
5145	3 Parish John	"	2	"	"			
	4							
	5							
	6							
	7							
	8							
	9							
	10							
	11							
	12							
	13							
	14							
	15							
	16							
	17							

ENROLLMENT OF NOS. 1, 2, 3 HEREON APPROVED BY THE SECRETARY OF INTERIOR JAN 16 1903

TRIBAL ENROLLMENT OF PARENTS

	Name of Father	Year	County	Name of Mother	Year	County
1	Ellis Pickens	Ded	Red River	Ickany Pickens	Ded	Cedar
2	Logan Cole	1896	Cedar	No 1		
3	Helins Parish	1896	Jacks Fork	No 1		
4						
5						
6						
7			No 1 died December 25, 1901; proof [of] death filed Nov. 25, 1902			
8			N°2 lives with Susan Pusley, Choctaw card #3284; 11/20/02			
9			No.3 said to be dead			
10			No.1 died Dec. 25, 1901: Enrollment cancelled by Department [illegible]			
11						
12						
13						
14						Date of Application for Enrollment.
15						
16						5-16-99
17						

Choctaw By Blood Enrollment Cards 1898-1914

RESIDENCE: Jacks Fork	COUNTY.							
POST OFFICE: Kosoma I.T.	**Choctaw Nation**			Choctaw Roll *(Not Including Freedmen)*		CARD NO. FIELD NO. **1813**		

Dawes' Roll No.	NAME	Relationship to Person First Named	AGE	SEX	BLOOD	TRIBAL ENROLLMENT		
						Year	County	No.
5146 ₁ Cooper Columbus ³²		First Named	29	M	Full	1896	Jacks Fork	3007
2								
3								
4								
5								
6								
7								
8								
9								
10								
11								
12								
13								
14								
15								
16								
17								

ENROLLMENT
OF NOS. 1 HEREON
APPROVED BY THE SECRETARY
OF INTERIOR JAN 16 1903

TRIBAL ENROLLMENT OF PARENTS

Name of Father	Year	County	Name of Mother	Year	County
₁ Gilbert Cooer	Ded	Cedar	Kanenuah	Ded	Cedar
2					
3					
4					
5					
6					
7					
8					
9					
10					
11					
12					
13					
14				Date of Application for Enrollment.		
15						
16				5-16-99		
17 P.O. Antlers, I.T.						

12/2/02

13

Choctaw By Blood Enrollment Cards 1898-1914

RESIDENCE: Cedar COUNTY. **Choctaw Nation** **Choctaw Roll** (Not Including Freedmen) CARD No.

POST OFFICE: Kosoma I.T. FIELD No. 1814

Dawes' Roll No.	NAME	Relationship to Person First Named	AGE	SEX	BLOOD	TRIBAL ENROLLMENT		
						Year	County	No.
5147	1 Green Ohoyona 83		80	F	Full	1896	Cedar	9926
	2							
	3							
	4							
	5							
	6							
	7							
	8							
	9							
	10							
	11							
	12							
	13							
	14							
	15							
	16							
	17							

ENROLLMENT
OF NOS. 1 HEREON
APPROVED BY THE SECRETARY
OF INTERIOR JAN 16 1903

TRIBAL ENROLLMENT OF PARENTS

Name of Father	Year	County	Name of Mother	Year	County
1 Red Feather	Ded	Mississippi	Minchihoyo	Ded	Mississippi
2					
3					
4					
5		On 1896 roll as Ohoyona			
6					
7					
8					
9					
10					
11					
12					
13					
14					
15					
16				5-16-99	
17					

14

Choctaw By Blood Enrollment Cards 1898-1914

RESIDENCE: Jacks Fork   COUNTY. **Choctaw Nation**   **Choctaw Roll**   CARD No.
POST OFFICE: Kosoma I.T.   (Not Including Freedmen)   FIELD No.   1815

Dawes' Roll No.	NAME	Relationship to Person First Named	AGE	SEX	BLOOD	TRIBAL ENROLLMENT		
						Year	County	No.
5148	1 Edward Isaac ²⁶	First Named	23	M	Full	1896	Nashoba	3732
	2							
	3							
	4							
	5							
	6							
	7							
	8							
	9							
	10							
	11							
	12							
	13							
	14							
	15	ENROLLMENT OF NOS. 1 HEREON						
	16	APPROVED BY THE SECRETARY OF INTERIOR JAN 16 1903						
	17							

TRIBAL ENROLLMENT OF PARENTS

	Name of Father	Year	County	Name of Mother	Year	County
1	Barnabas Edward	1896	Nashoba	Sallie Edward	1896	Nashoba
2						
3						
4						
5						
6						
7						
8						
9						
10						
11						
12						
13						
14						
15						
16			Date of Application for Enrollment		5-16-99	
17						

15

Choctaw By Blood Enrollment Cards 1898-1914

RESIDENCE: Jacks Fork   COUNTY. **Choctaw Nation**   **Choctaw Roll** CARD NO.
POST OFFICE: Kosoma I.T.   *(Not Including Freedmen)* FIELD NO. 1816

Dawes' Roll No.	NAME		Relationship to Person Named	AGE	SEX	BLOOD	TRIBAL ENROLLMENT		
							Year	County	No.
5149	1 Wilson Brown	51	First Named	48	M	Full	1896	Jacks Fork	14104
5150	2 ~~DIED PRIOR TO SEPTEMBER 25, 1902~~ Minnie	44	Wife	38	F	"	1896	" "	14105
5151	3 " Malena	6	Dau	3	"	"	1896	" "	14107
5152	4 Lewis, Mary	22	S Dau	19	"	1/2	1896	" "	10605
5153	5 Palmer, Katie	20	" "	17	"	1/2	1896	" "	10606
5154	6 " Annie	15	" "	12	"	1/2	1896	" "	10607
5155	7 Lewis, William	2	Son of No 4	6mo	M	3/4			
	8								
	9								
	10								
	11								
	12								
	13								
	14								
	15								
	16								
	17								

ENROLLMENT
OF NOS. 1,2,3,4,5,6,7 HEREON
APPROVED BY THE SECRETARY
OF INTERIOR JAN 16 1903

TRIBAL ENROLLMENT OF PARENTS

	Name of Father	Year	County	Name of Mother	Year	County
1	Ishtivtabi	Ded	Jacks Fork	Sarah	Ded	Jacks Fork
2	Tolabe	"	Cedar	Annie Frazier	"	Kiamatia[sic][sic]
3	No 1			No 2		
4	William Palmer	Ded	Kiamatia	No 2		
5				No 2		
6				No 2		
7	Johnson Lewis	P.R 1893	Jacks Fork 355	No 4		
8						
9	For child of No.4 see NB (Mar 3-1905) #647					
10	For child of No.5 see NB (Apr 26-06) No. 553					
	No.3 on 1896 roll as Line Wilson					
11	No.4 is now the wife of Johnson Lewis on Choctaw Card #1758. Evidence					
12	of marriage filed Aug 20, 1901.					
	No.7 Enrolled Aug 20, 1901					
13	No2 died Oct. 10, 1901; proof of death filed Dec 6, 1902					
14	No.2 died Oct 10, 1901: Enrollment cancelled by Department July 8, 1904					
15						
16						
17	P.O. Antlers, I.T. 12/3/02					

#1 to 6
Date of Application for Enrollment.

5-16-99

16

Choctaw By Blood Enrollment Cards 1898-1914

RESIDENCE: Kiamatia[sic] COUNTY. **Choctaw Nation** Choctaw Roll *(Not Including Freedmen)* CARD No.
POST OFFICE: Antlers I.T. FIELD No. 1817

Dawes' Roll No.	NAME	Relationship to Person	AGE	SEX	BLOOD	Year	County	No.
5156	1 Wright, Jackson 52	First Named	49	M	3/4	1896	Kiamatia[sic]	13768
5157	2 " Victor 10	Son	7	"	3/8	1896	"	13769
I.W. 15	3 Wright, Mary F.	Wife of No 1	50	F	I.W.	1896	Kiamatia[sic]	15183
	4							
	5							
	6							
	7							
	8							
	9							
	10							
	11							
	12							
	13							
	14							
	15							
	16							
	17							

ENROLLMENT OF NOS. 1, 2 HEREON APPROVED BY THE SECRETARY OF INTERIOR JAN 16 1903

ENROLLMENT OF NOS. 3 HEREON APPROVED BY THE SECRETARY OF INTERIOR JUN 13 1903

TRIBAL ENROLLMENT OF PARENTS

	Name of Father	Year	County	Name of Mother	Year	County
1	Ben Wright	Ded	Blue	Sophia LeFlore	Ded	Kiamatia[sic]
2	No 1			Mary F Wright	1896	"
3	Jeff Lewelling	Dead	Non Citz	Hulda Lewelling	Dead	Non Citz
4						
5						
6						
7						
8				Mary F. Wright wife of No 1 on "F" 165 Choctaw Roll		
9				No3 transferred from Choctaw card #D165 March 30, 1903		
10				See decision of March 14, 1903		
11						
12						
13						
14						
15					#1&2	
16				Date of Application for Enrollment	5-16-99	
17						

Choctaw By Blood Enrollment Cards 1898-1914

RESIDENCE: Jacks Fork
POST OFFICE: Antlers, I.T.

COUNTY. **Choctaw Nation**

Choctaw Roll CARD NO.
(Not Including Freedmen) FIELD NO. 1818

Dawes' Roll No.	NAME	Relationship to Person First Named	AGE	SEX	BLOOD	TRIBAL ENROLLMENT		
						Year	County	No.
5158	1 Cole, Morgan 51	Named	48	M	Full	1896	Jacks Fork	2997
5159	2 " Mary J 43	Wife	40	F	"	1896	" "	2998
5160	3 " Forbis 9	Son	6	M	"	1896	" "	3000
5161	4 Home, Edmund DIED PRIOR TO SEPTEMBER 25, 1902	Ward	12	"	"	1896	" "	6114
	5							
	6							
	7							
	8							
	9							
	10							
	11							
	12							
	13							
	14							
	15	ENROLLMENT OF NOS. 1, 2, 3, 4 HEREON APPROVED BY THE SECRETARY						
	16	OF INTERIOR JAN 16 1903						
	17							

TRIBAL ENROLLMENT OF PARENTS

Name of Father	Year	County	Name of Mother	Year	County
1 Peter Cole	Dead	Cedar	Molsey Cole	Dead	Jacks Fork
2 Benj Perry	"		Sally Turner	"	" "
3 No 1			No 2		
4 Charles Home	Dead	Jacks Fork	Agnes Home	Dead	Jacks Fork
5					
6					
7					
8	No 4 Died Nov – 1900; proof of death filed Dec 6, 1902				
9	No.4 died Nov – 1900: Enrollment cancelled by Department July 8, 1904				
10					
11					
12					
13					
14					
15					
16			DATE OF APPLICATION FOR ENROLLMENT.	5/16/99	
17					

Choctaw By Blood Enrollment Cards 1898-1914

RESIDENCE: Jacks Fork   COUNTY. **Choctaw Nation**   **Choctaw Roll** *(Not Including Freedmen)*   CARD NO.

POST OFFICE: Antlers I.T.   FIELD NO. 1819

Dawes' Roll No.	NAME		Relationship to Person	AGE	SEX	BLOOD	TRIBAL ENROLLMENT		
							Year	County	No.
5162	1 Thompson Albert *DIED PRIOR TO SEPTEMBER 25, 1902*		First Named	42	M	Full	1896	Jacks Fork	12502
5163	2 " Melissa	45	Wife	42	F	"	1896	" "	12503
5164	3 " John	15	Son	12	M	"	1896	" "	12504
5165	4 " Ellis	6	"	3	"	"	1896	" "	12506
	5								
	6								
	7								
	8								
	9								
	10								
	11								
	12								
	13								
	14								
	15 ENROLLMENT OF NOS. 1,2,3,4 HEREON								
	16 APPROVED BY THE SECRETARY OF INTERIOR JAN 16 1903								
	17								

TRIBAL ENROLLMENT OF PARENTS

	Name of Father	Year	County	Name of Mother	Year	County
1	William Thompson	Ded	Towson	Aholitima	Ded	Chickasaw N.{sic}
2	Robison Durant	"	Red River		"	Red River
3	No 1			No 2		
4	No 1			No 2		
5						
6						
7						
8	No1 died in 1898; proof of death filed Dec 6, 1902					
9	No 2 wife of No 1 on Choctaw Card #1737					
10	No.1 died - - 1898. Enrollment cancelled by Department July 8, 1904					
11						
12						
13						
14						
15						
16				Date of Application for Enrollment.	5-16-99	
17						

Choctaw By Blood Enrollment Cards 1898-1914

RESIDENCE: Cedar	COUNTY.								

Choctaw Nation — **Choctaw Roll** (Not Including Freedmen)

POST OFFICE: Kosoma I.T. — CARD NO. FIELD NO. 1820

Dawes' Roll No.	NAME	Relationship to Person First Named	AGE	SEX	BLOOD	TRIBAL ENROLLMENT		
						Year	County	No.
5166	1 Emer Stewick ⁵¹	First Named	48	M	Full	1896	Cedar	3709
5167	2 " Charlico ⁴¹	Wife	38	F	"	1896	"	3710
	3							
	4							
	5							
	6							
	7							
	8							
	9							
	10							
	11							
	12							
	13							
	14							
	15							
	16							
	17							

ENROLLMENT OF NOS. 1, 2 HEREON APPROVED BY THE SECRETARY OF INTERIOR JAN 16 1903

TRIBAL ENROLLMENT OF PARENTS

	Name of Father	Year	County	Name of Mother	Year	County
1	Emer	Ded	Cedar	Afamihoma	Ded	Cedar
2	Jim Frazier	"	"	Falama	1896	"
3						
4						
5						
6			No. 1 on 1896 Roll as Stowick Emer			
7						
8						
9						
10						
11						
12						
13						
14						
15					Date of Application for Enrollment.	
16					5-16-99	
17	Antlers I.T. 12/29/02					

20

Choctaw By Blood Enrollment Cards 1898-1914

RESIDENCE: Cedar   COUNTY. **Choctaw Nation**   **Choctaw Roll** (Not Including Freedmen)   CARD NO.

POST OFFICE: Kosoma I.T.   FIELD NO. 1821

Dawes' Roll No.	NAME	Relationship to Person First Named	AGE	SEX	BLOOD	TRIBAL ENROLLMENT Year	County	No.
5168	1 Nelson Ellis H ⁵⁴	First Named	51	M	Full	1896	Cedar	9642
5169	2 " Implin ³⁴	Wife	30	F	"	1893	"	P.R 190
~~5170~~	~~3 DIED PRIOR TO SEPTEMBER 25 1902 Hudson~~	~~Son~~	~~9~~	~~M~~	~~"~~	~~1896~~	~~"~~	~~9643~~
5171	4 " Eslin ⁷	"	4	"	"	1896	"	9644
5172	5 " Solomon ²²	Neph	19	M	"	1896	"	9645
	6							
	7							
	8							
	9							
	10							
	11							
	12							
	13							
	14							
	15							
	16							
	17							

ENROLLMENT
OF NOS. 1,2,3,4,5 HEREON
APPROVED BY THE SECRETARY
OF INTERIOR JAN 16 1903

TRIBAL ENROLLMENT OF PARENTS

	Name of Father	Year	County	Name of Mother	Year	County
1	Jimpson Nelson	Ded	Cedar	Elizabeth Nelson	Ded	Cedar
2	Dixon Feliahkabi	"	"	Eliza	"	"
3	~~No 1~~			~~Tennessee~~	"	"
4	No 1			"	"	"
5	Neeman Nelson	Ded	Cedar	Sallie Nelson	"	"
6						
7						
8		No 2 on 1896 Roll as Implin Felehekatuby also				
9		on 1896 roll Page 100 No 4124 as Emeline Felihkatubbee, Cedar Co				
10						
11		No3 died April – 1902· Proof of death filed Dec 9, 1902				
12		No.3 died April – 1902: Enrollment cancelled by Department July 8, 1904				
13						
14						
15						
16					5-16-99	
17						

Choctaw By Blood Enrollment Cards 1898-1914

RESIDENCE: Kiamatia[sic]   COUNTY. **Choctaw Nation**   **Choctaw Roll** *(Not Including Freedmen)*   CARD No.

POST OFFICE: Nelson I.T.   FIELD No. 1822

Dawes' Roll No.	NAME		Relationship to Person	AGE	SEX	BLOOD	TRIBAL ENROLLMENT		
							Year	County	No.
5173	1 Nelson Isham	40	First Named	37	M	Full	1896	Kiamatia[sic]	9755
5174	2 " Jerusha	30	Wife	27	F	1/4	1896	"	9756
5175	3 Jones Wesley	11	Ward	8	M	Full	1896	Red River	7033
	4								
	5								
	6								
	7								
	8								
	9								
	10								
	11								
	12								
	13								
	14								
	15	ENROLLMENT OF NOS. 1, 2, 3 HEREON APPROVED BY THE SECRETARY OF INTERIOR JAN 16 1903							
	16								
	17								

TRIBAL ENROLLMENT OF PARENTS

	Name of Father	Year	County	Name of Mother	Year	County
1	Thomas Nelson	Ded	Cedar	Bamiah Nelson	Ded	Cedar
2	Ashford			Elizabeth Perkins	1896	Kiamatia[sic]
3	Harmon Jones	Ded	Red River	Nancy Jones	Ded	Red River
4						
5			No 2 on 1896 roll as Jurina Nelson.			
6						
7						
8			Nov 1903 in County & Probate Court Kiamitia			
9	[Back of page]		County Pages 280 and 294, show filing			
10			of Petition and adoption of Wesley Jones			
11			by Isam[sic] Nelson & wife			
12			10-12-1940			
13			JDF			
14						
15						
16			DATE OF APPLICATION FOR ENROLLMENT.	5-16-99		
17						

(over)

22

Choctaw By Blood Enrollment Cards 1898-1914

RESIDENCE: Cedar   COUNTY. **Choctaw Nation**   **Choctaw Roll** CARD No.
POST OFFICE: Rodney, I.T.   *(Not Including Freedmen)* FIELD No. 1823

Dawes' Roll No.	NAME	Relationship to Person	AGE	SEX	BLOOD	TRIBAL ENROLLMENT		
						Year	County	No.
5176	1 Felihkatabbee, Gilbert[47]	First Named	44	M	Full	1896	Cedar	4101
~~5177~~	~~2 Nancy~~ DIED PRIOR TO SEPTEMBER 25, 1902[43]	~~Wife~~	~~40~~	~~F~~	~~"~~	~~1896~~	~~"~~	~~4102~~
5178	3 " Lizzie [20]	Dau	17	"	"	1896	"	4104
5179	4 " Lewie [10]	Son	7	M	"	1896	"	4105
5180	5 " Alexander [6]	"	3	"	"	1896	"	4106
	6							
	7							
	8							
	9							
	10							
	11							
	12							
	13							
	14							
	15	ENROLLMENT						
	16	OF NOS. 1,2,3,4,5 HEREON APPROVED BY THE SECRETARY						
	17	OF INTERIOR JAN 16 1903						

TRIBAL ENROLLMENT OF PARENTS

	Name of Father	Year	County	Name of Mother	Year	County
1	Felihkatabbee	Dead	Cedar	Lucy	Dead	Cedar
2	~~Sam-a-ma~~	"	"	~~Juliana~~	"	"
3	No 1			No 2		
4	No 1			No 2		
5	No 1			No 2		
6						
7						
8	No 2 died Feb 24, 1901; proof of death filed Dec 6, 1902 No 2					
9	died Feb. 24, 1901; Enrollment cancelled by Department July 8, 1904					
10						
11						
12						
13						
14						
15						
16				Date of Application for Enrollment	5-16-99	
17						

Choctaw By Blood Enrollment Cards 1898-1914

RESIDENCE: Cedar   COUNTY. **Choctaw Nation**   **Choctaw Roll** CARD NO.
POST OFFICE: Antlers, I.T.   (Not Including Freedmen)   FIELD NO. 1824

Dawes' Roll No.	NAME	Relationship to Person	AGE	SEX	BLOOD	TRIBAL ENROLLMENT		
						Year	County	No.
5181	1 Homma, Tecumseh ²⁸	First Named	25	M	Full	1896	Cedar	5441
	2							
	3							
	4							
	5							
	6							
	7							
	8							
	9							
	10							
	11							
	12							
	13							
	14							
	15							
	16							
	17							

ENROLLMENT
OF NOS. 1 HEREON
APPROVED BY THE SECRETARY
OF INTERIOR JAN 16 1903

TRIBAL ENROLLMENT OF PARENTS

Name of Father	Year	County	Name of Mother	Year	County
1 Morgan Homma	Dead	Cedar	Sophie Homma	1896	Cedar
2					
3					
4					
5					
6					
7					
8					
9					
10					
11					
12					
13					
14					
15					
16			Date of Application for Enrollment.	5/16/99	
17 P.O. Spencerville, I.T.					

12/10/02

24

Choctaw By Blood Enrollment Cards 1898-1914

RESIDENCE: Cedar COUNTY. **Choctaw Nation** Choctaw Roll CARD No.
POST OFFICE: Antlers, I.T. (Not Including Freedmen) FIELD No. 1825

Dawes' Roll No.	NAME		Relationship to Person	AGE	SEX	BLOOD	TRIBAL ENROLLMENT		
							Year	County	No.
5182	1 Cole, Anderson	34	First Named	31	M	Full	1896	Jacks Fork	2995
5183	2 " Sissie	58	Wife	55	F	"	1896	Cedar	2430
	3								
	4								
	5								
	6								
	7								
	8								
	9								
	10								
	11								
	12								
	13								
	14								
	15								
	16								
	17								

ENROLLMENT
OF NOS. 1, 2 HEREON
APPROVED BY THE SECRETARY
OF INTERIOR JAN 16 1903

TRIBAL ENROLLMENT OF PARENTS

	Name of Father	Year	County	Name of Mother	Year	County
1	Caleb Cole	Dead	Jacks Fork	Elachy Cole	Dead	Jacks Fork
2	Tush-ka-ha-ke	"	Cedar	E-me-she-to-na	"	Cedar
3						
4						
5						
6	No 2 on 1896 roll as Sissie Camp					
7	Nos 1&2 have separated					
8	No 1 is now husband of Molsey Wade, Choctaw card #4199					
9						
10						
11						
12						
13						
14						Date of Application for Enrollment.
15						
16						5-16-99
17						

25

RESIDENCE: Cedar					
POST OFFICE: Kosoma, I.T.	COUNTY. **Choctaw Nation**		**Choctaw Roll** (Not Including Freedmen)	CARD NO. FIELD NO.	1826

Dawes' Roll No.	NAME		Relationship to Person First Named	AGE	SEX	BLOOD	TRIBAL ENROLLMENT		
							Year	County	No.
5184	1 Homma, Paul	32	First Named	29	M	Full	1896	Cedar	5436
5185	2 DIED PRIOR TO SEPTEMBER 25, 1902 Celly		Wife	24	F	"	1896	"	5437
5186	3 " Wilson	10	Son	7	M	"	1896	"	5438
5187	4 " Reuben	8	"	5	"	"	1896	"	5439
5188	5 " Siney	6	Dau	3	F	"	1896	"	5440
5189	6 " Davis	4	Son	5mo	M	"			
	7								
	8								
	9								
	10								
	11								
	12								
	13								
	14								
	15	ENROLLMENT OF NOS. 1,2,3,4,5,6 HEREON APPROVED BY THE SECRETARY							
	16	OF INTERIOR JAN 16 1903							
	17								

TRIBAL ENROLLMENT OF PARENTS

	Name of Father	Year	County	Name of Mother	Year	County
1	Mark Homma	Dead	Cedar	Sophie Homma	1896	Cedar
2	Ellis Campbell	"	"	Kitsey Green	Dead	"
3	No 1			No 2		
4	No 1			No 2		
5	No 1			No 2		
6	No 1			No 2		
7						
8						
9	No2 died Oct 25, 1900; proof of death filed Dec 6, 1902					
10	No1 is now married to Sophia Choate on Choctaw card #806					
11	The notation hereon relative to Nº1 is an error. He was married to Sopha[sic] Choate Choctaw card #1075 Feby 9, 1901. See testimony of Selin Taylor and Reason Hopson					
12	of May 22, 1903					
13	George R Tucker, Orr, I.T. is guardian of Nº5, July 7, 1903.					
14	No.2 died Oct. 25, 1900: Enrollment cancelled by Department July 8, 1904					
15					Date of Application for Enrollment	
16					5/16/99	
17						

Choctaw By Blood Enrollment Cards 1898-1914

RESIDENCE: Jacks Fork   COUNTY. **Choctaw Nation**   **Choctaw Roll**   CARD NO.
POST OFFICE: Antlers I.T.   *(Not Including Freedmen)*   FIELD NO. **1827**

Dawes' Roll No.	NAME	Relationship to Person First Named	AGE	SEX	BLOOD	TRIBAL ENROLLMENT Year	County	No.
5190	1 Frazier Simeon 25		22	M	Full	1896	Jacks Fork	4553
5191	2 DIED PRIOR TO SEPTEMBER 25 1902 Salina	Wife	21	F	"	1896	" "	6123
5192	3 " Jacob 2	Son	5mo	M	"			
	4							
	5							
	6							
	7							
	8							
	9							
	10							
	11							
	12							
	13							
	14							
	15	ENROLLMENT OF NOS. 1, 2, 3 HEREON						
	16	APPROVED BY THE SECRETARY						
	17	OF INTERIOR JAN 16 1903						

TRIBAL ENROLLMENT OF PARENTS

	Name of Father	Year	County	Name of Mother	Year	County
1	Mack Frazier	1896	Jacks Fork	Louisa Frazier	1896	Jacks Fork
2	James Hudson	Ded	" "	Sina Hudson	Ded	" "
3	No.1			No.2		
4						
5						
6			No 2 on 1896 roll as Silma Hudson			
7			No.3 Enrolled December 15, 1900			
8			No2 died April 9, 1902; proof of death filed Dec 6, 1902.			
9			No. 2 died April 9, 1902; Enrollment cancelled by Department July 8, 1904			
10			For child of No.1 see NB (March 3, 1905) #1386			
11						
12						
13						
14					Date of Application for Enrollment.	
15						
16					5-16-99	
17						

RESIDENCE: Jacks Fork   COUNTY. **Choctaw Nation**   **Choctaw Roll**   CARD NO.
POST OFFICE: Stanley I.T.   *(Not Including Freedmen)*   FIELD NO. 1828

Dawes' Roll No.		NAME		Relationship to Person Named	AGE	SEX	BLOOD	TRIBAL ENROLLMENT Year	County	No.
5193	1	Impson William	33	First Named	30	M	Full	1896	Jacks Fork	6325
5194	2	" Liddy	33	Wife	380	F	"	1896	" "	6326
5195	3	" Jincy	11	Dau	8	"	"	1896	" "	6327
5196	4	" Albert	10	Son	7	M	"	1896	" "	6328
5197	5	" Louis	2	Son	3m	M	"			
	6									
	7									
	8									
	9									
	10									
	11									
	12									
	13									
	14									
	15									
	16									
	17									

ENROLLMENT
OF NOS. 1, 2, 3, 4, 5 HEREON
APPROVED BY THE SECRETARY
OF INTERIOR JAN 16 1903

TRIBAL ENROLLMENT OF PARENTS

	Name of Father	Year	County	Name of Mother	Year	County
1	Lewis Impson	Ded	Jacks Fork	Silis Impson	Ded	Jacks Fork
2	Yahinakintebbe	"	" "	Mariah	"	" "
3	No 1			No 2		
4	No 1			No 2		
5	No 1			No 2		
6						
7			No 1 on 1896 roll as Willie Impson			
8			No 5 Enrolled February 4, 1901			
9						
10						
11						
12						
13						
14						
15					#1to4	
16				Date of Application for Enrollment.	5-16-99	
17	P.O. Jumbo, Okla 3/2/08					

28

Choctaw By Blood Enrollment Cards 1898-1914

RESIDENCE: Jacks Fork   COUNTY, **Choctaw Nation**   **Choctaw Roll**   CARD NO.
POST OFFICE: Kosoma I.T.   *(Not Including Freedmen)*   FIELD NO.   1829

Dawes' Roll No.	NAME	Relationship to Person First Named	AGE	SEX	BLOOD	TRIBAL ENROLLMENT Year	County	No.
5198	1 Impson Morris 51	First Named	48	M	Full	1896	Jacks Fork	6329
15785	2 " Susie Burris 1	Dau	5mo	F	1/2			
	3							
	4							
	5							
	6							
	7							
	8							
	9							
	10							
	11							
	12							
	13							
	14							
	15							
	16							
	17							

ENROLLMENT
OF NOS. 2 HEREON
APPROVED BY THE SECRETARY
OF INTERIOR MAR 15 1905

ENROLLMENT
OF NOS. 1 HEREON
APPROVED BY THE SECRETARY
OF INTERIOR JAN 16 1903

TRIBAL ENROLLMENT OF PARENTS

Name of Father	Year	County	Name of Mother	Year	County
1 Josiah Impson	Ded	Jacks Fork		Ded	Jacks Fork
2 No. 1			Lucy Impson		Chick Freed –
3					
4					

N⁰1 is the husband of Lucy Impson & father of
her children on Chickasaw freedman card #1071
       Dec 9, 1902

No.2 was born Aug. 13, 1902
No.2 originally listed for enrollment on Chickasaw Freedman card #1071
Dec. 11, 1902; transferred to this card Jan. 24, 1905. See decision of Jan.
7, 1905
For children of Nos see NB (Apr 26'06) #999

       #1

See Petition No 733   Date of Application for Enrollment. 5-16-99

P.O. Antlers IT 10/29/04

29

Choctaw By Blood Enrollment Cards 1898-1914

POST OFFICE: Antlers, I.T.   (Not including Freedmen) FIELD NO. 1830

Dawes' Roll No.	NAME		Relationship to Person First Named	AGE	SEX	BLOOD	TRIBAL ENROLLMENT Year	County	No.
5199	1 Frazier, Mack	48		45	M	Full	1896	Jacks Fork	4551
5200	2 " Louisa	43	Wife	40	F	"	1896	" "	4552
5201	3 " Sissy	17	Dau	14	"	"	1896	" "	4555
5202	4 " Edmond	15	Son	12	M	"	1896	" "	4556
5203	5 " Sophia	13	Dau	10	F	"	1896	" "	320
5204	6 " Agnes	9	"	6	"	"	1893	" "	321
5205	7 Patterson, James	17	Ward	14	M	"	1896	" "	10584
	8								
	9								
	10								
	11								
	12								
	13								
	14								
	15								
	16								
	17								

ENROLLMENT
OF NOS. 1,2,3,4,5,6,7 HEREON
APPROVED BY THE SECRETARY
OF INTERIOR JAN 16 1903

TRIBAL ENROLLMENT

	Name of Father	Year	County		Name of Mother	Year	County
1	Fisher Frazier	Dead	Jacks Fork	Ho-te...		Dead	Jacks Fork
2	Ho-the-na	"	" " "	Hok-la-...		"	" " "
3	No 1			No 2			
4	No 1			No 2			
5	No 1			No 2			
6	No 1			No 2			
7	Nicholas Patterson	Dead	Jacks Fork	Lucinda Patterson			Tobucky[sic]
8							
9							
10	No 5 on 1893 Pay roll, Page 33, No 320, Jacks Fork County						
11	No 6 " 1893 " " " 33, No 321 " " "						
12							
13							
14							
15					Date of Application for Enrollment.		
16					5-16-99		
17							

No 7 – P.O. Krebs 1/11/04

30

RESIDENCE: Jackson COUNTY. **Choctaw Nation** Choctaw Roll CARD NO.
POST OFFICE: Mayhew, I.T. *(Not Including Freedmen)* FIELD NO. **1831**

Dawes' Roll No.	NAME	Relationship to Person First Named	AGE	SEX	BLOOD	TRIBAL ENROLLMENT		
						Year	County	No.
5206	1 Jones, Simon G DIED PRIOR TO SEPTEMBER 25 26 902		23	M	Full	1896	Jackson	7140
5207	2 " Almeda 23	Wife	20	F	1/2	1896	"	7141
5208	3 " Ida M 6	Dau	3	"	3/4	1896	"	7142
5209	4 " Samantha 4	"	10mo	"	3/4			7143
5210	5 Jackson, Patsy 21	Ward	18	"	Full	1896	Jackson	7144
5211	6 " Sissie 18	"	15	"	"	1896	"	
5212	7 Jones, Wilson 2	Son	9mo	M	3/4			
DP 2/2306	8 Jackson, Dora	Dau of No 6	1	F	1/2			
	9							
	10	Not Dismissed Apr. 19, 1906						
	11							
	12 For child of No 2 see NB (Mar 3-05) #1052							
	13 " " " No 5 " " " " " #1338							
	14							
	15	ENROLLMENT						
	16	OF NOS. 1,2,3,4,5,6,7 HEREON APPROVED BY THE SECRETARY						
	17	OF INTERIOR Jan 16 1903						

TRIBAL ENROLLMENT OF PARENTS

	Name of Father	Year	County	Name of Mother	Year	County
1	Gibson Jones	Dead	Jackson	Liza Bacon[sic]	1896	Jackson
2	Stephen Going	"	Eagle	Samantha Winston	1896	Kiamitia
3	No 1			No 2		
4	No 1			No 2		
5	Calvin Jackson	Dead	Jackson	Isabelle Jackson	Dead	Jackson
6	" "	"	"	" "	"	"
7	No 1			No 2		
8				No 6		
9			No.2 on 1896 roll as Emilia Jones			
10			No 3 " 1896 " " Ida "			
11			Mother of No 2 is a white woman. Evidence of			
12			marriage attached to Card No 1521.			
13			No 7 Enrolled Sept 4, 1901			
14			No 1 died May 1, 1902; proof of death filed Dec 6, 1902			
15			No.1 died May 1, 1902; Enrollment cancelled by Department July 8, 1904		#1 to 6 inc
16			No 8 application made and No8 listed on this card May 2, 1905 under		Date of Application for Enrollment.
17			Act of Congress approved March 3, 1905. Question as to date of birth		5-16-99

P.O. Boswell I.T. 4/5/05

RESIDENCE: Jackson   COUNTY.   **Choctaw Nation**   **Choctaw Roll** CARD NO.

POST OFFICE: Mayhew I.T.   *(Not Including Freedmen)*   FIELD NO. **1832**

Dawes' Roll No.	NAME	Relationship to Person	AGE	SEX	BLOOD	TRIBAL ENROLLMENT		
						Year	County	No.
5213	1 Bacon, Simon 25	First Named	22	M	Full	1896	Jackson	1489
5214	2 DIED PRIOR TO SEPTEMBER 25, 1902 Annie	Wife	19	F	"	1896	"	9410
5215	3 DIED PRIOR TO SEPTEMBER 25, 1902 Alfred	Son	3/4	M	"			
5216	4 Hokubbi Robert 13	Ward	10	"	"	1896	Jackson	6083
	5							
	6							
	7							
	8							
	9							
	10							
	11							
	12							
	13							
	14							
	15	ENROLLMENT OF NOS. 1,2,3,4 HEREON						
	16	APPROVED BY THE SECRETARY OF INTERIOR JAN 16 1903						
	17							

TRIBAL ENROLLMENT OF PARENTS

	Name of Father	Year	County	Name of Mother	Year	County
1	Alfred Bacon	1896	Jackson	Elizabeth Bacon	Ded	Jackson
2	Jackson McCurtain	Ded	Atoka	Sallie McCurtain	"	Atoka
3	No 1			No 2		
4	Impson Hokubbi	Ded	Atoka	Nellie Hokubbi	Ded	Atoka
5						
6						
7						
8				No 2 on 1896 roll as Annie McCurtain		
9				No2 died July 10, 1900; proof of death filed Dec 6, 1902		
10			No3 " Dec 25, 1899; " " " " " " "			
11	No.2 died July 10, 1900: No.3 died Dec. 25, 1899: Enrollment cancelled by Department July 8, 1904					
12						
13						
14						
15				Date of Application for Enrollment	5-16-99	
16						
17						

Choctaw By Blood Enrollment Cards 1898-1914

RESIDENCE: Atoka	COUNTY.	Choctaw Nation	Choctaw Roll (Not Including Freedmen)	CARD No.
POST OFFICE: Limestone, I.T.				FIELD No. 1833

Dawes' Roll No.	NAME		Relationship to Person First Named	AGE	SEX	BLOOD	TRIBAL ENROLLMENT		
							Year	County	No.
I.W. 97	1 Reynolds, E.D.	39		36	M	I.W.	1896	Jacks Fork	14999
5217	2 " Eliza	38	Wife	35	F	Full	1896	" "	11015
	3								
	4								
	5								
	6								
	7								
	8								
	9								
	10								
	11								
	12								
	13								
	14								
	15								
	16								
	17								

ENROLLMENT
OF NOS 2 HEREON
APPROVED BY THE SECRETARY
OF INTERIOR JAN 16 1903

ENROLLMENT
OF NOS. 1 HEREON
APPROVED BY THE SECRETARY
OF INTERIOR JUN 13 1903

	TRIBAL ENROLLMENT OF PARENTS					
	Name of Father	Year	County	Name of Mother	Year	County
1			Non Citz	Harriet Davis	Ded	Atoka
2	George Wesley	Ded	Jackson		"	Jackson
3						
4						
5						
6						
7						
8						
9						
10						
11						
12						
13						
14						
15					Date of Application for Enrollment.
16					5-16-99
17					

RESIDENCE:	Jacks Fork	COUNTY.		Choctaw Roll	CARD NO.	
POST OFFICE:	Kosoma I.T.		**Choctaw Nation**	*(Not Including Freedmen)*	FIELD NO.	1834

Dawes' Roll No.	NAME		Relationship to Person Named	AGE	SEX	BLOOD	TRIBAL ENROLLMENT		
							Year	County	No.
5218	1 Bob Wilson	51	First Named	48	M	Full	1896	Jacks Fork	1945
5219	2 ~~Tennessee~~ DIED PRIOR TO SEPTEMBER 25 1902		~~Wife~~	~~38~~	~~F~~	"	~~1896~~	" "	~~1946~~
5220	3 Moore Ida	21	Dau	18	"	"	1896	" "	1947
5221	4 Bob Bensie	18	"	15	"	"	1896	" "	1948
5222	5 " Tillis	15	Son	12	M	"	1896	" "	1949
5223	6 " Lina	13	Dau	10	F	"	1896	" "	1950
5224	7 Moore Etna	1	Gr Dau	2mo	F	3/4			
	8								
	9								
	10 For child of No3 see NB (Apr 26-06) #369								
	11 " " " No6 " " " #182								
	12								
	13								
	14								
	15 ENROLLMENT								
	16 OF NOS. 1,2,3,4,5,6,7 HEREON APPROVED BY THE SECRETARY								
	17 OF INTERIOR JAN 16 1903								

TRIBAL ENROLLMENT OF PARENTS

	Name of Father	Year	County	Name of Mother	Year	County
1	Kamabe	Ded	Nashoba	Kanchihona	Ded	Nashoba
2	Amos John	"	Jacks Fork	Mully John	"	"
3	No 1			No 2		
4	No 1			No 2		
5	No 1			No 2		
6	No 1			No 2		
7	Christopher Moore		Chickasaw	Nº3		
8						
9						
10						
11	Nº3 is now the wife of Christopher F Moore on Chickasaw card #700. Evidence of marriage filed April 19, 1902 -7-5505					
12	Nº7 Born Feby 28, 1902: enrolled Aril 19, 1902					
13	No2 died July - 1900: proof of death filed Dec 8, 1902					
14	No4 wife of No3 on Chick #648. Evidence of marriage to be supplied.					
15	No.2 died July - 1900: Enrollment cancelled by Department July 8, 1904			#1 to 6		
16				Date of Application for Enrollment.	5-16-99	
17						

Choctaw By Blood Enrollment Cards 1898-1914

RESIDENCE: Jacks Fork	COUNTY.		Choctaw Nation				Choctaw Roll	CARD No.	
POST OFFICE: Kosoma, I.T.							(Not Including Freedmen)	FIELD No. 1835	

Dawes' Roll No.	NAME		Relationship to Person First Named	AGE	SEX	BLOOD	TRIBAL ENROLLMENT		
							Year	County	No.
5225	1 Impson Dennis	34	Named	31	M	Full	1896	Jacks Fork	6332
5226	2 " Elizabeth	12	Dau	9	F	"	1896	" "	6331
	3								
	4								
	5								
	6								
	7								
	8								
	9								
	10								
	11								
	12								
	13								
	14								
	15	ENROLLMENT OF NOS. 1, 2 HEREON APPROVED BY THE SECRETARY OF INTERIOR JAN 16 1903							
	16								
	17								

	TRIBAL ENROLLMENT OF PARENTS						
Name of Father	Year	County	Name of Mother		Year	County	
1 Lewis Impson	Ded	Jacks Fork	Sillis Impson		Ded	Jacks Fork	
2 No 1			Willisy Impson		"	" " "	
3							
4							
5							
6							
7							
8							
9							
10							
11							
12							
13							
14							
15							
16				Date of Application for Enrollment.		5-16-99	
17							

35

RESIDENCE: Jackson COUNTY.
POST OFFICE: Kosoma, I.T

Choctaw Nation

Choctaw Roll
(Not Including Freedmen)

CARD No.
FIELD No. 1836

Dawes' Roll No.	NAME		Relationship to Person	AGE	SEX	BLOOD	TRIBAL ENROLLMENT		
							Year	County	No.
5227	1 Benjamin, Wallace	38	First Named	35	M	Full	1896	Jacks Fork	1928
5228	2 " Winey	46	Wife	43	F	"	1896	" "	1929
	3								
	4								
	5								
	6								
	7								
	8								
	9								
	10								
	11								
	12								
	13								
	14								
	15								
	16								
	17								

ENROLLMENT
OF NOS. 1, 2 HEREON
APPROVED BY THE SECRETARY
OF INTERIOR JAN 16 1903

TRIBAL ENROLLMENT OF PARENTS

	Name of Father	Year	County	Name of Mother	Year	County
1	Yim-ma-bey	Dead	Jacks Fork	Na-na-yo-kee	Dead	Jacks Fork
2	Pitman Loman	"	Atoka	Eliza Bond	1896	" "
3						
4						
5						
6	No 2 on 1896 roll as Willie Benjamin					
7						
8						
9						
10						
11						
12						
13						
14						
15				Date of Application for Enrollment.		
16				5-16-99		
17						

Choctaw By Blood Enrollment Cards 1898-1914

RESIDENCE: Red River COUNTY.
POST OFFICE: Kullituklo, I.T.

Choctaw Nation

Choctaw Roll *(Not Including Freedmen)*   CARD NO.

FIELD NO. 1837

Dawes' Roll No.	NAME	Relationship to Person First Named	AGE	SEX	BLOOD	TRIBAL ENROLLMENT Year	TRIBAL ENROLLMENT County	No.
5229	1 Homer, Aaron H ⁴⁸	First Named	45	M	Full	1896	Sans Bois	5075
5230	2 " Maria ⁴⁹	Wife	46	F	"	1896	" "	5076
	3							
	4							
	5							
	6							
	7							
	8							
	9							
	10							
	11							
	12							
	13							
	14							
	15							
	16							
	17							

ENROLLMENT
OF NOS. 1, 2 HEREON
APPROVED BY THE SECRETARY
OF INTERIOR JAN 16 1903

TRIBAL ENROLLMENT OF PARENTS

	Name of Father	Year	County	Name of Mother	Year	County
1	Simeon Homer	Dead	Blue	Elzira Harkin	Dead	Blue
2	San-le-noah	"	"		"	"
3						
4						
5						
6						
7						
8		No1 on 1896 roll as A. H. Homer				
9						
10						
11						
12						
13						
14						
15						Date of Application for Enrollment.
16						5-16-99
17	P.O. Conser I.T.					

Dec 18/02

37

Choctaw By Blood Enrollment Cards 1898-1914

RESIDENCE: Red River   COUNTY.   Choctaw Nation   Choctaw Roll   CARD NO.
POST OFFICE: Kullituklo, I.T.   (Not Including Freedmen)   FIELD NO. 1838

Dawes' Roll No.	NAME		Relationship to Person First Named	AGE	SEX	BLOOD	TRIBAL ENROLLMENT		
							Year	County	No.
5231	1 Dwight, Edward	44	Named	41	M	Full	1896	Red River	3433
5232	2 " Winnie	40	Wife	37	F	"	1896	" "	3434
5233	3 " Lizzie	12	Dau	9	"	"	1896	" "	3435
5234	4 " Dickson	5	Son	2	M	"			
14695	5 " Bicey	1	Son	5mo	M	"			
	6								
	7								
	8								
	9								
	10								
	11								
	12								
	13								
	14								
	15								
	16								
	17								

ENROLLMENT
OF NOS. 1,2,3,4   HEREON
APPROVED BY THE SECRETARY
OF INTERIOR   JAN 16 1903

ENROLLMENT
OF NOS. 5   HEREON
APPROVED BY THE SECRETARY
OF INTERIOR   MAY 20 1903

TRIBAL ENROLLMENT OF PARENTS

	Name of Father	Year	County	Name of Mother	Year	County
1	William Dwight	Dead	Blue	Jennie Dwight	Dead	Blue
2	Steven Fisher	"	Red River	Sylvia Fisher	1896	
3	No 1			No 2		
4	No 1			No 2		
5	No 1			No 2		
6						
7	No 3 on 1896 roll as Lizzie Dwigh[sic]					
8						
9	No4 Affidavit of birth to be supplied. Recd June 1/99					
10	No5 born July 6, 1902; enrolled Dec. 2, 1902					
11						
12						
13						
14					#1 to 4 inc	
15				Date of Application for Enrollment.		
16				5-16-99		
17						

38

Choctaw By Blood Enrollment Cards 1898-1914

RESIDENCE: **Cedar**   COUNTY. **Choctaw Nation**   Choctaw Roll   CARD No.
POST OFFICE: **Kosoma** I.T.   (Not Including Freedmen)   FIELD No. 1839

Dawes' Roll No.	NAME		Relationship to Person	AGE	SEX	BLOOD	TRIBAL ENROLLMENT		
							Year	County	No.
5235	1 Cole Logan	30	First Named	27	M	Full	1896	Cedar	2431
	2								
	3								
	4								
	5								
	6								
	7								
	8								
	9								
	10								
	11								
	12								
	13								
	14								
	15								
	16								
	17								

ENROLLMENT
OF NOS. 1 HEREON
APPROVED BY THE SECRETARY
OF INTERIOR JAN 16 1903

TRIBAL ENROLLMENT OF PARENTS

	Name of Father	Year	County	Name of Mother	Year	County
1	Nicholas Cole	Ded	Cedar	Susanna Cole	Ded	Cedar
2						
3						
4						
5						
6						
7						
8						
9						
10						
11						
12						
13						
14					Date of Application for Enrollment.	
15						
16					5-16-99	
17	P.O. Antlers I.T.					

RESIDENCE: Red River	COUNTY.							
POST OFFICE: Harris, I.T		**Choctaw Nation**			Choctaw Roll *(Not Including Freedmen)*		CARD No. FIELD No. 1840	

Dawes' Roll No.	NAME	Relationship to Person First Named	AGE	SEX	BLOOD	TRIBAL ENROLLMENT		
						Year	County	No.
15752	1 Harris, John E ⁴⁸	Named	45	M	1/8	1896	Red River	5698
I.W 1499	2 " Mary E ³³	Wife	30	F	I.W	1896	" "	14636
	3							
	4							
	5							
	6							
	7							
	8							
	9							
	10	ENROLLMENT OF NOS. ~~2~~ HEREON APPROVED BY THE SECRETARY OF INTERIOR NOV 27 1905						
	11							
	12							
	13	ENROLLMENT OF NOS. ~~1~~ HEREON APPROVED BY THE SECRETARY OF INTERIOR DEC 15 1904						
	14							
	15							
	16							
	17							

TRIBAL ENROLLMENT OF PARENTS

	Name of Father	Year	County	Name of Mother	Year	County
1	William Harris	Dead	Non Citz	Eliza Harris	Dead	Eagle
2	Benj Knox	"	" "	Frances Knox	"	Non Citz
3						
4			DECISION RENDERED			
5			GRANTED		OCT 5- 1905	
6						
7	No 1 on 1893 Pay Roll, Red River Co, page 29, No 240					
8	No1 on 1896 roll as Jno E Harris					
9	No2 was admitted in 1896 as an intermarried citizen					
10	by Dawes Commission: Choctaw Case #411 No appeal					
11	Was No1 rejected by Dawes Com in 1896, Case No 1378? Yes, and appeal taken					
12	case 205, Central dist. which appeal was dismissed No1 did not apply in 96. Notation that he was in Case #1378 Error					
13						
14						
15					Date of Application for Enrollment.	
16					5-16-99	
17						

Choctaw Nation (Not Including Freedmen)

POST OFFICE: Antlers I.T.   Jackson County   Choctaw Roll   CARD No.

FIELD NO. 1841

	NAME	Relationship to Person First Named	AGE	SEX	BLOOD	TRIBAL ENROLLMENT Year	County	No.
5236	1 Frazier Dixon ^39	First Named	36	M	Full	1896	Jacks Fork	4516
5237	2 " Magdalene ^5	Dau	1	F	"			
	3							
	4							
	5							
	6							
	7							
	8							
	9							
	10							
	11							
	12							
	13							
	14							
	15							
	16							
	17							

ENROLLMENT
OF NOS. 1,2 HEREON
APPROVED BY THE SECRETARY
OF INTERIOR JAN 16 1903

TRIBAL ENROLLMENT OF PARENTS

	Name of Father	Year	County	Name of Mother	Year	County
1	William Frazier	Ded	Jacks Fork	Jennie Frazier	Ded	Jacks Fork
2	No 1			Frances Frazier	"	" "
3						
4						
5						
6	No 1 is now husband of Rhoda Leader, Chickasaw card #1843					
7	For child of No 1 see NB (March 3 1905) #1397					
8						
9						
10						
11						
12						
13						
14						
15						
16				Date of Application for Enrollment.	5-16-99	
17	P.O. Stringtown, I.T.					

12/5/02

41

RESIDENCE: Jacks Fork **COUNTY.** **Choctaw Nation** **Choctaw Roll** (Not Including Freedmen) **CARD NO.**
POST OFFICE: Stringtown, I.T. **FIELD NO.** 1842

Dawes' Roll No.	NAME		Relationship to Person Named	AGE	SEX	BLOOD	TRIBAL ENROLLMENT		
							Year	County	No.
5238	1 Billy, Isaac A	42	First Named	39	M	Full	1896	Jacks Fork	1901
5239	2 " Emily	33	Wife	30	F	"	1896	" "	1902
5240	3 DIED PRIOR TO SEPTEMBER 25, 1902 Eli		Son	17	M	"	1896	" "	1903
5241	4 " Annie	16	Dau	13	F	"	1896	" "	1904
5242	5 " Susan	14	"	11	"	"	1896	" "	1905
5243	6 " William L	10	Son	7	M	"	1896	" "	1906
5244	7 " Anganora[sic]	8	Dau	5	F	"	1896	" "	1907
5245	8 DIED PRIOR TO SEPTEMBER 25, 1902 Isaac A, Jr		Son	4m	M	"			
	9								
	10								
	11 No3 died Aug 24, 1901; proof of								
	12 death filed Dec 12, 1902								
	13 No8 died Nov. 3, 1900; proof of								
	14 death filed Dec 12, 1902								
	15 ENROLLMENT OF NOS. 1,2,3,4,5,6,7,8 HEREON								
	16 APPROVED BY THE SECRETARY								
	17 OF INTERIOR JAN 16 1903								

3/21/07 Daisy

TRIBAL ENROLLMENT OF PARENTS

	Name of Father	Year	County	Name of Mother	Year	County
1	Alexander Billy	Dead	Jacks Fork	Susan Perry	1896	Jacks Fork
2	Joseph Meshiah	"	Towson	Agnes Meshiah	Dead	" "
3	No 1			Liney Billy	"	" "
4	No 1			No 2		
5	No 1			No 2		
6	No 1			No 2		
7	No 1			No 2		
8	No 1			No 2		
9						
10						
11	No.8 died March 13[sic], 1900; Enrollment cancelled by Department May 2, 1906					
12	No6 on 1896 roll as Wm L. Billy					
13	No7 " 1896 " " Enginora "					
14	For child of Nos 1 and 2 see N.B. (Apr 26-06) No 541					
15	No8 enrolled Dec 19/99. Affidavit					Date of Application for Enrollment.
16	irregular and returned for correction Returned corrected and filed Feby. 20, 1900					5/16/99
17	No3 died Aug 24, 1901: Enrollment cancelled by Department July 8, 1904					

For child of Nos 1&2 see NB (Mar 3-1905) Card No 65

Choctaw By Blood Enrollment Cards 1898-1914

RESIDENCE: Jacks Fork   COUNTY.   **Choctaw Nation**   **Choctaw Roll**   CARD NO.
POST OFFICE: Kosoma, I.T.   (Not Including Freedmen)   FIELD NO. 1843

Dawes' Roll No.	NAME	Relationship to Person First Named	AGE	SEX	BLOOD	TRIBAL ENROLLMENT Year	County	No.
I.W. 16	1 Moyer, John F 41	First Named	38	M	I.W.			
5246	2 " Mary J 36	Wife	33	F	1/4	1893	Jacks Fork	530
5247	3 DIED PRIOR TO SEPTEMBER 25, 1902 Clarence L	Son	1½	M	1/8			
5248	4 " Grove S 4	"	3mo	"	1/8			
5249	5 " James C 11	Ward	8	"	3/8	1893	Jacks Fork	531
	6							
	7							
	8							
	9							
	10							
	11							
	12							
	13							
	14							
	15							
	16							
	17							

ENROLLMENT
OF NOS. 2,3,4,5   HEREON
APPROVED BY THE SECRETARY
OF INTERIOR JAN 16 1903

ENROLLMENT
OF NOS. ~~~ 1 ~~~ HEREON
APPROVED BY THE SECRETARY
OF INTERIOR JUN 13 1903

TRIBAL ENROLLMENT OF PARENTS

	Name of Father	Year	County	Name of Mother	Year	County
1	Abraham Moyer	1896	Non Citz	Ruth Moyer	Dead	Non Citz
2	Tom Ellis	Dead	Kiamitia	Adeline Ellis	"	Kiamitia
3	No 1			No 2		
4	No 1			No 2		
5	Campbell	Dead	Non Citz	Louisa Le Flore	Dead	Kiamitia
6						
7	No1 was admitted by Dawes Com. Dec 1896, Case No 357					
8						
9	No2 on 1893 Pay roll Page 59, No 530, Jacks Fork County as Mary Jane Moyer					
10	No5 " 1893 " " " 59 ' 531 " " " " J. C. "					
11	No 3 died Sept – 1901; proof of death filed Dec 6, 1902					
12	No 3 died Sept – 1901; Enrollment cancelled by Department July 8, 1904					
13						
14						
15						
16						
17						

Date of Application for Enrollment.   5/17/99

RESIDENCE:	Jacks Fork
POST OFFICE:	Kosoma, I.T

COUNTY. **Choctaw Nation**

Choctaw Roll *(Not Including Freedmen)*

CARD NO.

FIELD NO. 1844

Dawes' Roll No.	NAME		Relationship to Person Named	AGE	SEX	BLOOD	TRIBAL ENROLLMENT		
							Year	County	No.
5250	1 Platt, Elizabeth F	30	First Named	27	F	1/4	1896	Atoka	10560
5251	2 DIED PRIOR TO SEPTEMBER 25, 1902 Jessie		Dau	5	"	1/8	1896	"	10561
5252	3 DIED PRIOR TO SEPTEMBER 25, 1902 Leo L		Son	2	M	1/8			
5253	4 " Mary E	4	Dau	2mo	F	1/8			
5254	5 " Gracie Jewel	2	Dau	8mo	F	1/8			
5255	6 " James O	1	Son	3wks	M	1/8			
	7								
	8								
	9								
	10								
	11								
	12								
	13								
	14								
	15	ENROLLMENT OF NOS. 1,2,3,4,5,6 HEREON APPROVED BY THE SECRETARY OF INTERIOR JAN 16 1903								
	16								
	17								

TRIBAL ENROLLMENT OF PARENTS

	Name of Father	Year	County	Name of Mother	Year	County
1	Tom Ellis	Dead	Kiamitia	Adeline Ellis	Dead	Kiamitia
2	Frank Plat[sic]	"	Non Citz	No 1		
3	" "	"	" "	No 1		
4	" "	"	" "	No 1		
5	B.F. Platt	"	" "	No 1		
6	" " "	"	" "	No 1		
7		Nos 1 and 2 denied by Dawes Commission in 1896;				
8		Choctaw #1132: no appeal. Error, application was only for husband of No1				
9		No5 Enrolled Aug 13, 1901				
10		Correct name of No.1 is Elizabeth F Platt. See letter of husband filed Aug 21, 1901				
11		N°6 Born Aug. 4, 1902; enrolled Aug 28, 1902				
12		No.2 died July 27, 1898; proof of death filed Dec 12, 1902				
13		No.3 " Aug 6, 1898; " " " " " "				
14	No.2 died July 27, 1898; No.3 died Aug.6, 1898: Enrollment cancelled by Department July 8, 1904					
15		For child of No1 see NB (Apr 26 '06) Card #243				
16		" " " " " " (Mar 3 '05) " #1375.				
17				Date of Application for Enrollment.	5/17/99 1 to 4	

44

RESIDENCE: Red River   COUNTY. **Choctaw Nation**   **Choctaw Roll** CARD NO.
POST OFFICE: Janis, I.T.   *(Not Including Freedmen)*   FIELD NO. **1845**

Dawes' Roll No.		NAME		Relationship to Person First Named	AGE	SEX	BLOOD	TRIBAL ENROLLMENT		
								Year	County	No.
I.W. 17	1	Garland, Ellen	35	First Named	32	F	I.W.	1896	Red River	14571
5256	2	" Thomas	13	Son	10	M	1/16	1896	" "	4807
5257	3	" Leonidas	11	"	8	"	1/16	1896	" "	4808
5258	4	" Margaret	7	Dau	4	F	1/16	1896	" "	4809
5259	5	" Ellen	5	"	1	"	1/16			
	6									
	7									
	8									
	9									
	10									
	11									
	12									
	13									
	14									
	15									
	16									
	17									

ENROLLMENT
OF NOS 2,3,4,5 HEREON
APPROVED BY THE SECRETARY
OF INTERIOR Jan. 16 1903

ENROLLMENT
OF NOS 1 HEREON
APPROVED BY THE SECRETARY
OF INTERIOR Jun 13, 1903

TRIBAL ENROLLMENT OF PARENTS

	Name of Father	Year	County	Name of Mother	Year	County
1	T.D. Payne	Dead	Non Citz	Sarah J Payne	Dead	Non Citz
2	D.C. Garland	1896 "	Red River	No 1		
3	" " "	"	" "	No 1		
4	" " "	"	" "	No 1		
5	" " "	"	" "	No 1		
6						
7						
8	No1 was admitted by Dawes Commission Case 1002					
9						
10	No 5 Affidavit of birth to be supplied. Recd June 1/99					
11						
12						
13						
14					Date of Application for Enrollment.	
15						
16					5/17/99	
17						

Choctaw By Blood Enrollment Cards 1898-1914

RESIDENCE: Jackson   COUNTY.
POST OFFICE: Mayhew, I.T.

Choctaw Nation

Choctaw Roll
(Not Including Freedmen)

CARD NO.
FIELD NO. 1846

Dawes' Roll No.	NAME		Relationship to Person First Named	AGE	SEX	BLOOD	TRIBAL ENROLLMENT		
							Year	County	No.
5260	1 Wade, Alex	26	First Named	23	M	3/4	1896	Jackson	13823
5261	2 " Agnes	23	Wife	20	F	Full	1896	"	13824
5262	3 " Anna	6	Dau	2½	"	7/8	1896	"	13825
5263	4 " Josephine	5	"	1½	"	7/8			
5264	5 " Sissy	4	"	3mo	"	7/8			
5265	6 " Mary	2	Dau	2mo	F	7/8			
	7								
	8								
	9								
	10								
	11								
	12								
	13								
	14								
	15	ENROLLMENT OF NOS. 1,2,3,4,5,6 HEREON							
	16	APPROVED BY THE SECRETARY							
	17	OF INTERIOR JAN 16 1903							

TRIBAL ENROLLMENT OF PARENTS

	Name of Father	Year	County	Name of Mother	Year	County
1	Eastman Wade	Dead	Jackson	Sallie Wade	Dead	Jackson
2	A.S. Bacon	1896	"	Isabelle Bacon	1896	"
3	No 1			No 2		
4	No 1			No 2		
5	No 1			No 2		
6	No.1			No.2		
7						
8						
9			No.6 Enrolled April 3, 1901			
10			Nº5 – Evidence of birth filed Aug 22, 1902.			
11			For child of Nos 1&2 see NB (March 3, 1905) #1393			
12						
13					#1 to 5	
14					Date of Application for Enrollment.	
15						
16					5/17/99	
17						

Choctaw By Blood Enrollment Cards 1898-1914

RESIDENCE: Kiamitia
POST OFFICE: Nelson I.T.

COUNTY. **Choctaw Nation**

Choctaw Roll (Not Including Freedmen)

CARD NO.
FIELD NO. 1847

Dawes' Roll No.	NAME		Relationship to Person First Named	AGE	SEX	BLOOD	TRIBAL ENROLLMENT		
							Year	County	No.
I.W. 98	1 Brown, Charles E	32	First Named	29	M	I.W.	1896	Kiamitia	14318
5266	2 " Mary E	28	Wife	25	F	1/2	1896	"	1448
5267	3 " Lucy	9	Dau	6	"	1/4	1896	"	1449
5268	4 " Emma	7	"	4	"	1/4	1896	"	1450
5269	5 " Charles A	6	Son	3	M	1/4	1896	"	1451
5270	6 " Anna May	3	Dau	3mo	F	1/4			
5271	7 " John Thomas	1	Son	1wk	M	1/4			
	8								
	9								
	10								
	11								
	12								
	13								
	14								
	15								
	16								
	17								

ENROLLMENT OF NOS. 2,3,4,5,6,7 HEREON APPROVED BY THE SECRETARY OF INTERIOR JAN 16 1903

ENROLLMENT OF NOS. 1 HEREON APPROVED BY THE SECRETARY OF INTERIOR JUN 13 1903

TRIBAL ENROLLMENT OF PARENTS

	Name of Father	Year	County	Name of Mother	Year	County
1	E.A. Brown	1896	Non Citz	Emma Brown	1896	Non Citz
2	C.S. Vinson	1896	Atoka	Sophia Vinson	De'd	Jackson
3	No 1			No 2		
4	No 1			No 2		
5	No 1			No 2		
6	No.1			No.2		
7	Nº1			Nº2		
8						
9	No 1 on 1896 roll as Chas. E. Brown					
10	No 5 " 1896 " " Chas A "					
11	No 6 Enrolled June 11, 1900.					
12	Nº7 Born May 26, 1902; enrolled June 3, 1902					
	For child of Nos 1&2 see N.B. (Apr 26, 1906) Card No. 192					
13						
14						#1 to 5 inc
15						Date of Application for Enrollment.
16				Date of application for enrollment		5-17-99
17						

47

Choctaw By Blood Enrollment Cards 1898-1914

RESIDENCE: Jacks Fork COUNTY. **Choctaw Nation** Choctaw Roll (Not Including Freedmen) CARD No. FIELD No. 1848

POST OFFICE: Antlers, I.T.

Dawes' Roll No.	NAME		Relationship to Person First Named	AGE	SEX	BLOOD	TRIBAL ENROLLMENT		
							Year	County	No.
5272	1 Patterson, James	27		24	M	Full	1893	Jacks Fork	628
	2								
	3								
	4								
	5								
	6								
	7								
	8								
	9								
	10								
	11								
	12								
	13								
	14								
	15								
	16								
	17								

ENROLLMENT OF NOS. 1 HEREON APPROVED BY THE SECRETARY OF INTERIOR JAN 16 1903

TRIBAL ENROLLMENT OF PARENTS

	Name of Father	Year	County	Name of Mother	Year	County
1	Austin William	1896	Atoka		Dead	Atoka
2						
3						
4						
5						
6	On 1893 Pay roll Page 70, No 628, Jacks Fork Co as John Patterson					
7						
8	In penitentiary					
9						
10						
11						
12						
13						
14						
15						
16				Date of Application for Enrollment.	5/17/99	
17						

Choctaw By Blood Enrollment Cards 1898-1914

RESIDENCE: Kiamitia   COUNTY. **Choctaw Nation**   **Choctaw Roll**   CARD NO.
POST OFFICE: Antlers, I.T.   *(Not Including Freedmen)*   FIELD NO. **1849**

Dawes' Roll No.	NAME	Relationship to Person First Named	AGE	SEX	BLOOD	TRIBAL ENROLLMENT Year	County	No.
5273	1 Baker, Jackson 37		34	M	1/4	1896	Tobucksy	908
DEAD	2 " ~~Mollie~~ DEAD	~~Wife~~	~~26~~	~~F~~	~~I.W.~~			
I.W. 816	3 " Augusta ㉘	Wife	38	F	I.W.			
	4							
	5							
	6							
	7							
	8							
	9							
	10							
	11							
	12							
	13							
	14							
	15							
	16							
	17							

ENROLLMENT
OF NOS. 3 HEREON
APPROVED BY THE SECRETARY
OF INTERIOR May 21 1904

ENROLLMENT
OF NOS. 1 HEREON
APPROVED BY THE SECRETARY
OF INTERIOR Jan 16 1903

TRIBAL ENROLLMENT OF PARENTS

	Name of Father	Year	County	Name of Mother	Year	County
1	Alex Baker	Dead	Non Citz	Sophia Baker	Dead	Skullyville
2	~~Bill Jackson~~	"	" "		"	~~Non Citz~~
3	Watt Morrow	"	" "	Silona Morrow	"	" " "
4						
5	For child of Nos 1&3 see NB (Mar 3, 1905) card #678					
6	~~For child of Nos 1&3 see NB (Apr 26-06) Card #765~~					
7	No2 died May 27, 1901; proof of death filed Dec 2, 1902					
8						
9	No3 transferred from Choctaw card D941 April 16, 1904. See decision of March 15, 1904					
10						
11						
12						
13	No. 2 hereon dismissed under order					
14	of the Commission to the Five Civilized					
15	Tribes of March 31, 1905.					
16				Date of Application for Enrollment.	5/17/99	
17	P.O. Valliant, I.T.					

11/20/02

49

Choctaw By Blood Enrollment Cards 1898-1914

RESIDENCE: Jacks Fork COUNTY. **Choctaw Nation**
POST OFFICE: Antlers, I.T.

Choctaw Roll
(Not Including Freedmen)

CARD No. FIELD No. 1850

Dawes' Roll No.	NAME	Relationship to Person First Named	AGE	SEX	BLOOD	TRIBAL ENROLLMENT		
						Year	County	No.
5274	1 Christie, Amanda 28		25	F	Full	1896	Jackson	2806
5275	2 " Louvina 10	Dau	7	"	"	1896	"	2807
5276	3 Jefferson, Wallace 4	Son	1	M	"			
	4							
	5							
	6							
	7							
	8							
	9							
	10							
	11							
	12							
	13							
	14							
	15	ENROLLMENT OF NOS. 1,2,3 HEREON						
	16	APPROVED BY THE SECRETARY OF INTERIOR JAN 16 1903						
	17							

TRIBAL ENROLLMENT OF PARENTS

	Name of Father	Year	County	Name of Mother	Year	County
1	Len Drew	Dead	Jackson	Elsie Drew	Dead	Jackson
2	Adam Christie	1896	"	No 1		
3	Chas. Jefferson	1896	Jacks Fork	No 1		
4						
5						
6		No2 on 1896 roll as Leona Christie				
7						
8		No3 Affidavit of birth to be supplied				
9		No.3 is the ward of R.F. Tutt, Choctaw card D651				
10		11/21/02				
11						
12						
13						
14						
15					Date of Application for Enrollment.	
16					5/17/99	
17	P.O. Bennington, I.T. 2/18/07	P.O. Mayhew				

Choctaw By Blood Enrollment Cards 1898-1914

RESIDENCE: Jacks Fork   COUNTY. **Choctaw Nation**   **Choctaw Roll**   CARD NO.

POST OFFICE: Antlers, I.T.   *(Not Including Freedmen)*   FIELD NO. 1851

Dawes' Roll No.	NAME		Relationship to Person	AGE	SEX	BLOOD	TRIBAL ENROLLMENT		
							Year	County	No.
5277	1 Jefferson, Charles	29	First Named	26	M	Full	1896	Jackson	7093
	2								
	3								
	4								
	5								
	6								
	7								
	8								
	9								
	10								
	11								
	12								
	13								
	14								
	15								
	16								
	17								

ENROLLMENT
OF NOS. 1 HEREON
APPROVED BY THE SECRETARY
OF INTERIOR JAN 16 1903

TRIBAL ENROLLMENT OF PARENTS

	Name of Father	Year	County	Name of Mother	Year	County
1	Wallace Jefferson	1896	Jacks Fork	Siney Jefferson	Dead	Jacks Fork
2						
3						
4						
5			Also on 1896 roll Page 175, No 7123			
6						
7						
8						
9						
10						
11						
12						
13						
14						
15						
16				Date of Application for Enrollment.	5/17/99	
17						

Choctaw By Blood Enrollment Cards 1898-1914

RESIDENCE: Jacks Fork COUNTY. **Choctaw Nation** Choctaw Roll CARD NO.
POST OFFICE: Antlers, I.T. *(Not Including Freedmen)* FIELD NO. **1852**

Dawes' Roll No.	NAME	Relationship to Person First Named	AGE	SEX	BLOOD	TRIBAL ENROLLMENT Year	County	No.
5278	1 Wright, Sophia DIED SEPTEMBER 23 1902		29	F	Full	1896	Jacks Fork	14123
5279	2 " Ransis 12	Dau	9	F	"	1896	" "	14124
	3							
	4							
	5							
	6							
	7							
	8							
	9							
	10							
	11							
	12							
	13							
	14							
	15							
	16							
	17							

ENROLLMENT OF NOS. 1, 2 HEREON APPROVED BY THE SECRETARY OF INTERIOR JAN 16 1903

TRIBAL ENROLLMENT OF PARENTS

	Name of Father	Year	County	Name of Mother	Year	County
1	Dixon Billy	Dead	Jacks Fork	Siney Jefferson	Dead	Jacks Fork
2	Noel Wright	"	" "	No 1		
3						
4						
5						
6			No 2 on 1896 roll as Rinsey Wright			
7		No.1 died Oct. 28, 1900: Enrollment cancelled by Department July 8, 1904				
8						
9						
10						
11						
12						
13						
14						
15						
16				Date of Application for Enrollment.	5/17/99	
17						

52

Choctaw By Blood Enrollment Cards 1898-1914

RESIDENCE: Jacks Fork   COUNTY.   **Choctaw Nation**   **Choctaw Roll**   CARD NO.
POST OFFICE: Antlers, I.T.   (Not Including Freedmen)   FIELD NO.   **1853**

Dawes' Roll No.	NAME		Relationship to Person First Named	AGE	SEX	BLOOD	TRIBAL ENROLLMENT		
							Year	County	No.
5280	1 Carn, Jackson	23		20	M	Full	1893	Kiamitia	1
DEAD	2 " Eliza A		Wife	23	F	"	1896	"	13778
5281	3 " Rufus	5	Son	1	M	"			
	4								
	5								
	6								
	7								
	8								
	9								
	10								
	11	No.2 hereon dismissed under order of							
	12	the Commission to the Five Civilized Tribes of March 31, 1905.							
	13								
	14								
	15	ENROLLMENT OF NOS. 1, 3 HEREON							
	16	APPROVED BY THE SECRETARY							
	17	OF INTERIOR Jan 16 1903							

TRIBAL ENROLLMENT OF PARENTS

	Name of Father	Year	County	Name of Mother	Year	County
1	Wilmon Carn	Dead	Bok Tuklo	Lucy Carn	Dead	Bok Tuklo
2	Geo. Washington	"	Cedar	Melissa Washington	"	Cedar
3	No 1			No 2		
4						
5	No1 on 1893 Pay roll Page 114, No.1 Kiamitia Co (List in back of book)					
6	No1 " 1896 " " 70 " 2966 Atoka Co, as Jack Carns					
7	No2 on 1896 roll as Eliza Washington					
8						
9	No1 is the father of Mary Ann Carnes No3 on Choctaw card #4022					
10						
11	No2 died August 4, 1900: proof of death filed Nov. 25, 1902					
12	Nº1 was married to Levina Robinson, Choctaw card #4022 March 11, 1901					
13						
14						
15					Date of Application for Enrollment.	
16					5/17/99	
17						

RESIDENCE: Jacks Fork
POST OFFICE: Antlers, I.T.

COUNTY. **Choctaw Nation**

Choctaw Roll (Not Including Freedmen)

CARD NO.
FIELD NO. 1854

Dawes' Roll No.	NAME	Relationship to Person First Named	AGE	SEX	BLOOD	TRIBAL ENROLLMENT Year	County	No.
5282	1 Homma, Lillie DIED PRIOR TO SEPTEMBER 25, 1902		33	F	Full	1896	Jacks Fork	6135
5283	2 Fisher, Kirk DIED PRIOR TO SEPTEMBER 25, 1902	Son	9	M	"	1896	" "	4557
5284	3 McFarland, Willie 7	"	4	"	"	1896	" "	9474
	4							
	5							
	6							
	7							
	8							
	9							
	10							
	11							
	12							
	13							
	14							
	15							
	16							
	17							

ENROLLMENT
OF NOS. 1, 2, 3 HEREON
APPROVED BY THE SECRETARY
OF INTERIOR JAN 16 1903

TRIBAL ENROLLMENT OF PARENTS

Name of Father	Year	County	Name of Mother	Year	County
1 Chubby Homma	Dead	Jacks Fork	En-la-he-ma	Dead	Jacks Fork
2 Wilson Fisher	1896	Red River	No 1		
3 Tillow McFarland	1896	Nashoba	No 1		
4					
5					
6		No2 on 1896 roll as Kaik Fisher			
7					
8		No1 died February 15, 1901; proof of death filed November 25, 1902			
9		No2 died January 15, 1901; proof of death filed November 25, 1902			
10	No 1 died Feb 15, 1901. No 2 died Jan 15, 1901. Enrollment cancelled by Department July 8, 1904				
11					
12					
13					
14					
15					
16					
17					

Date of Application for Enrollment.

5/17/99

54

Choctaw By Blood Enrollment Cards 1898-1914

RESIDENCE: Cedar COUNTY. **Choctaw Nation** **Choctaw Roll** CARD No.
POST OFFICE: Kosoma, I.T. (Not Including Freedmen) FIELD No. 1855

Dawes' Roll No.		NAME		Relationship to Person	AGE	SEX	BLOOD	TRIBAL ENROLLMENT		
								Year	County	No.
5285	1	Jefferson, Gilbert	47	First Named	44	M	Full	1896	Cedar	6743
5286	2	" Bessie	50	Wife	47	F	"	1896	"	6744
	3									
	4									
	5									
	6									
	7									
	8									
	9									
	10									
	11									
	12									
	13									
	14									
	15									
	16									
	17									

ENROLLMENT
OF NOS. 1,2 HEREON
APPROVED BY THE SECRETARY
OF INTERIOR JAN 16 1903

TRIBAL ENROLLMENT OF PARENTS

	Name of Father	Year	County	Name of Mother	Year	County
1	Wallace Jefferson	1896	Jacks Fork	Ka-ne-a-e-ma	Dead	Cedar
2	Alex Green	Dead	Cedar	Hoyona Green	1896	"
3						
4						
5						
6						
7						
8						
9						
10						
11						
12						
13						
14						
15						
16				Date of Application for Enrollment.	5/18/99	
17						

55

Choctaw By Blood Enrollment Cards 1898-1914

RESIDENCE: Red River COUNTY. **Choctaw Nation** **Choctaw Roll** CARD NO.
POST OFFICE: Shawneetown, I.T. (Not Including Freedmen) FIELD NO. 1856

Dawes' Roll No.	NAME	Relationship to Person First Named	AGE	SEX	BLOOD	TRIBAL ENROLLMENT Year	County	No.
I.W. 1456	1 Swink, William 25	First Named	31	M	I.W.	1896	Jacks Fork	15070
15854	2 " Inez 6	Dau	2	F	1/4			
	3							
	4							
	5	ENROLLMENT						
	6	OF NOS. ~~2~~ HEREON APPROVED BY THE SECRETARY						
	7	OF INTERIOR JUN 12 1905						
	8							
	9	ENROLLMENT						
	10	OF NOS. ~~1~~ HEREON APPROVED BY THE SECRETARY						
	11	OF INTERIOR JUN 12 1905						
	12							
	13							
	14							
	15							
	16							
	17							

TRIBAL ENROLLMENT OF PARENTS

	Name of Father	Year	County	Name of Mother	Year	County
1	Wilburn Swink	1896	Non Citz	Mary Swink	Dead	Non Citz
2	No 1			Nannie Swink	1896	Jacks Fork
3						
4	No1 was admitted by Dawes Commission Case No 931					
5						
6	Wife of No1, Nannie Swink, on Card F 168 Transferred to #5823					
7						
8	No2 Affidavit of birth to be supplied. Recd May 24/99					
9	Additional proof of birth filed February 17, 1905					
10	No1 is husband of Nannie Swink, Choctaw card #5823, roll No15706					
11	For child of No.1 see NB (Mar 3'05) #435					
12						
13						
14						
15						
16			Date of Application for Enrollment.	5/18/99		
17	P.O. Valiant I.T. 12/3/02					

RESIDENCE:	Jacks Fork								CARD No.	
POST OFFICE: Antlers, I.T		COUNTY. **Choctaw Nation**				**Choctaw Roll** (Not Including Freedmen)			FIELD No. 1857	

Dawes' Roll No.	NAME		Relationship to Person	AGE	SEX	BLOOD	TRIBAL ENROLLMENT		
							Year	County	No.
5287	1 Wesley, Simeon	32	First Named	29	M	Full	1896	Jacks Fork	14133
5288	2 " Mary	23	Wife	20	F	"	1896	" "	4555
5289	3 " Isaac	3	Son	4mo	M	"			
5290	4 " Clarame	1	Dau	1mo	F	"			
	5								
	6								
	7								
	8								
	9								
	10								
	11								
	12								
	13								
	14								
	15	ENROLLMENT OF NOS. 1,2,3,4 HEREON							
	16	APPROVED BY THE SECRETARY							
	17	OF INTERIOR JAN 16 1903							

TRIBAL ENROLLMENT OF PARENTS

	Name of Father	Year	County	Name of Mother	Year	County
1	Thompson Wesley	Dead	Jacks Fork	Ellen Wesley	1896	Choctaw residing in Chick Natn
2	Mack Frazier	1896	" "	Louisa Frazier	1896	Jacks Fork
3	No 1			No 2		
4	№1			№2		
5						
6						
7			No2 on 1896 roll as Mary Frazier			
8			№4 Born March 18, 1902: enrolled April 24, 1902			
9			For child of Nos 1&2 see NB (Apr 26-06) Card #589			
10						
11						
12						
13						
14						
15				No3[sic] enrolled Dec 19/99		
16				Date of Application for Enrollment.	5/17/99	
17					1 to 3	

57

Choctaw By Blood Enrollment Cards 1898-1914

RESIDENCE: Jacks Fork COUNTY. **Choctaw Nation** **Choctaw Roll** (Not Including Freedmen) CARD NO.

POST OFFICE: Antlers, I.T. FIELD NO. 1858

Dawes' Roll No.	NAME	Relationship to Person First Named	AGE	SEX	BLOOD	TRIBAL ENROLLMENT Year	TRIBAL ENROLLMENT County	TRIBAL ENROLLMENT No.
1	McCulic, Annie T	Named	27	F	1/8	1896	Jacks Fork	9472
2	" Vivian M	Dau	6	"	1/16	1896	" "	9473
3								
4								
5								
6								
7	Void							
8								
9								
10								
11								
12								
13								
14								
15								
16								
17								

CANCELLED

TRIBAL ENROLLMENT OF PARENTS

	Name of Father	Year	County	Name of Mother	Year	County
1	George Taaffe	Dead	Non Citz	Fredonia Taaffe	Dead	Red River
2	Robt P McCulic	"	" "	No 1		
3						
4						
5						
6		Transferred to Card #4761				
7						
8						
9						
10						
11						
12						
13						
14						
15						
16				Date of Application for Enrollment.	5/18/99	
17						

Choctaw By Blood Enrollment Cards 1898-1914

RESIDENCE:	Kiamitia		COUNTY.	**Choctaw Nation**				**Choctaw Roll**		CARD NO.	
POST OFFICE:	Goodland, I.T.							*(Not Including Freedmen)*		FIELD NO.	1859

Dawes' Roll No.	NAME		Relationship to Person First Named	AGE	SEX	BLOOD	TRIBAL ENROLLMENT		
							Year	County	No.
I.W. 897	1 Parsons, John M	(57)	First Named	53	M	I.W.	1896	Kiamitia	14938
	2								
	3								
	4								
	5	ENROLLMENT							
	6	OF NOS. 1 HEREON APPROVED BY THE SECRETARY							
	7	OF INTERIOR AUG 3 1904							
	8								
	9								
	10								
	11								
	12								
	13								
	14								
	15								
	16								
	17								

TRIBAL ENROLLMENT OF PARENTS

	Name of Father	Year	County	Name of Mother	Year	County
1	John Parsons	Dead	Non Citz	Mary Parsons	1896	Non Citz
2						
3						
4						
5	No1 father of children on Choctaw Card #1611					
6	Husband of Eliza Parson[sic] who died in 91. Father of Mary Parsons on final Roll #4563					
7						
8						
9						
10						
11						
12						
13						
14						
15						
16				Date of Application for Enrollment.	5/18/99	
17	Hugo I.T. 12/2/02					

Choctaw By Blood Enrollment Cards 1898-1914

RESIDENCE: Red River COUNTY.					

Choctaw Nation

RESIDENCE: Red River   COUNTY.
POST OFFICE: Goodwater, I.T.

Choctaw Roll *(Not Including Freedmen)*

CARD NO.
FIELD NO. 1860

Dawes' Roll No.	NAME	Relationship to Person First Named	AGE	SEX	BLOOD	TRIBAL ENROLLMENT		
						Year	County	No.
5291	1 Battiest, Lewis G ³³	First Named	30	M	Full	1896	Red River	1379
DEAD.	2 " Effie DEAD.	Wife	24	F	I.W.	1896	" "	14316
5292	3 " Lewis G, Jr ⁷	Son	4	M	1/2	1896	" "	1380
5293	4 " Doyle ⁴	"	6mo	"	1/2			
5294	5 " Henry Lloyd ²	"	6wks	"	1/2			
	6							
	7							
	8							
	9 No. 2 HEREON DISMISSED UNDER							
	10 ORDER OF THE COMMISSION TO THE FIVE CIVILIZED TRIBES OF MARCH 31, 1905.							
	11							
	12							
	13							
	14							
	15 ENRO OF NOS.1,3,4, REON							
	16 APPROVED BY TARY							
	17 OF INTERIOR 1903							

TRIBAL ENROLLMENT OF PARENTS

	Name of Father	Year	County	Name of Mother	Year	County
1	Gibson Battiest	1896	Sugar Loaf	Winnie Battiest	Dead	Sugar Loaf
2	J.W. Ashworth	1896	Non Citz	Sarah M Ashworth	1896	Non Citz
3	No 1			No 2		
4	No 1			No 2		
5	No 1			No 2		
6						
7	No 1 on 1896 roll as Louis G Battieste					
8	No2 " 1896 " " Effie "					
9	No3 " 1896 " " Louis G " Jr.					
10	No.5 Enrolled January 8, 1901.					
11	No2 Died March 8, 1901; proof of death filed December 1, 1902					
12						
13	For child of No1 see NB (Mar 3-1905) Card #234					
14	" " " " " " (Apr 26-06) " #235					
15						#1 to 4
16						Date of Application for Enrollment. 5/18/99
17						

Choctaw By Blood Enrollment Cards 1898-1914

RESIDENCE: Kiamitia   COUNTY. **Choctaw Nation**   Choctaw Roll   CARD NO.

POST OFFICE: Nelson, I.T.   (Not Including Freedmen)   FIELD NO. **1861**

Dawes' Roll No.	NAME	Relationship to Person First Named	AGE	SEX	BLOOD I.W.	TRIBAL ENROLLMENT Year	County	No.
I.W. 1669	1 Riley, Dora 33		30	F	N4			
	2 " Florence L. 3	Dau	1 1/2	F	1/8	Born Dec 22-97		
	3							
	4	ENROLLMENT OF NOS. 1 HEREON APPROVED BY THE SECRETARY OF INTERIOR Mar 4 1907						
	5							
	6 cant locate							
	7							
	8 Refused Feb 27 1907							
	9							
	10 Record forwarded Department							
	11 Feb 27 1907							
	12							
	Mch 4/07 Secretary affirmed decision of Feb. 27/07 denying							
	Nos 1&2 as citizens by blood but reversed same							
	as enrollment of No1 as citizen by intermarriage							
	15 and directed that she be enrolled as such citizen.							
	16							
	17							

TRIBAL ENROLLMENT OF PARENTS

Name of Father	Year	County	Name of Mother	Year	County
1 Isaac Hampton	Dead	Red River	Isabelle Hampton	1896	Red River
2 J.R. Riley		non citizen	No 1		
3					
4					
5		Admitted by Dawes Com Case No 412 as Dora Hampton			
6		No.2 Enrolled July 16, 1902			
7					
8		3/16/03 Dora Riley admitted by Com in 1896 as intermarried			
9		citizen child apparently white and not			
10		entitled to enrollment T.P.			
11		Status requested 8/3/04			
12					
13					
14					
15				Date of Application for Enrollment.	
16				5/18/99	
17 Antlers, I.T. 12/17/02			Notice of Departmental action		

Feby. 1903 P.O. Clarksville Texas —   mailed parties herein Apr 11 1907

Choctaw By Blood Enrollment Cards 1898-1914

RESIDENCE:	Jackson	COUNTY.	
POST OFFICE:	Mayhew, I.T.		

Choctaw Nation

Choctaw Roll (Not Including Freedmen)

CARD NO.

FIELD NO. 1862

Dawes' Roll No.	NAME	Relationship to Person First Named	AGE	SEX	BLOOD	TRIBAL ENROLLMENT		
						Year	County	No.
5295	1 Carns, Solomon 21		18	M	Full	1896	Jackson	2788
	2							
	3							
	4							
	5							
	6							
	7							
	8							
	9							
	10							
	11							
	12							
	13							
	14							
	15	ENROLLMENT OF NOS. 1 HEREON						
	16	APPROVED BY THE SECRETARY OF INTERIOR JAN 16 1903						
	17							

TRIBAL ENROLLMENT OF PARENTS

	Name of Father	Year	County	Name of Mother	Year	County
1	Ben Carns	Dead	Jackson	Sarah Carns	1896	Jackson
2						
3						
4						
5	For child of No.1 see NB (Apr. 26, 1906) Card No.6.					
6						
7						
8						
9						
10						
11						
12						
13						
14				Date of Application for Enrollment.		
15						
16				5/18/99		
17						

| RESIDENCE: | Jacks Fork | COUNTY. | **Choctaw Nation** | Choctaw Roll | CARD No. |
| POST OFFICE: | Antlers, I.T. | | | (Not Including Freedmen) | FIELD No. **1863** |

Dawes' Roll No.	NAME	Relationship to Person First Named	AGE	SEX	BLOOD	TRIBAL ENROLLMENT Year	County	No.
	1 Bennett, Ella	Named	23	F	1/8		D	
	2 " Lela	Dau	4	"	1/16		F	
DP	3 " Bettie Rosetty	"	2 wks	"	1/16		Dis	
	4 Martin, Ida	Sister	15	"	1/8		F	
	5 " Maud	"	13	"	1/8		F	
DP	6 Bennett, Charles N.	Nep	1 mo	M	1/16		Dis	
DP	7 " Lena	Dau	2 wks	F	1/16		Dis	
	8 No.2 denied by C.C.C.C. as Lealer Ann or Lela Ann Bennett							
	9 Nos 1 to 7 incl in C.C.C.C. Case #114							
	10 Nos 3, 6 and 7 Dismissed by CCCC Case #114 M Sept 19'04							
	11 the Court having no jurisdiction							
	12 Judgement[sic] of U.S. Court Admitting Nos 1,2,4 and 5 vacated and set aside by							
	13 Decree of Choctaw Chickasaw Citizenship Court Decʳ 17'02							
	14 No.5 denied by C.C.C.C. as Maud Bennett							
	15 (nee Maud Martin) or Maud Martin.							
	16 #3-6-7 – Dismissed							
	17 Nov 12 1904							

TRIBAL ENROLLMENT OF PARENTS

	Name of Father	Year	County	Name of Mother	Year	County
1	James Martin	1896	Non-Citz	Mary Martin	Dead	Non-Citz
2	Wᵐ Bennett	1896	" "	No 1		
3	" "	1896	" "	No 1		
4	James Martin	1896	" "	Mary Martin	Dead	Non-Citz
5	" "	1896	" "	" "	"	" "
6	Monroe Bennett		" "	No. 5		
7	Wᵐ Bennett		" "	No. 1		
8	Nos 1,2,4 and 5 Denied citizenship by the Choctaw and Chickasaw citizenship court #114 M Sept 19 '04					
9	Nos 1,2,4 and 5 denied by Dawes Com in 96 Case #869					
10	No 1-2-4-5 were admitted by U.S. Court Southern District August 24, 1897 Case No 49. C.C.C.C.114 5/16/03					
11	Husband of No 1 and father of Nos 2-3 on Card No D172					
	Evidence of marriage to William Bennett on Card No D172					
12	No.5 is now married to Monroe Bennett, a non-citizen Oct. 15, 1901					
13	No.6 born Sept. 14, 1901 and enrolled Oct. 15, 1901					
14	Marriage license and certificate of M.F. Bennett and No.5 filed Nov. 8, 1901					
15	No.7 Born March 10, 1902: enrolled March 25, 1902.				Date of Application for Enrollment.
16	For child of No1 see (Act Apr 26 '06) NB #1048				5/19/99
17						

Choctaw By Blood Enrollment Cards 1898-1914

RESIDENCE: Wade   COUNTY. **Choctaw Nation** **Choctaw Roll** CARD NO.
POST OFFICE: Tushkahomma[sic], I.T. *(Not Including Freedmen)* FIELD NO. 1864

Dawes' Roll No.		NAME		Relationship to Person	AGE	SEX	BLOOD	TRIBAL ENROLLMENT		
								Year	County	No.
5296	1	Thompson, Gilbert W	52	First Named	49	M	1/2	1896	Wade	12043
5297	2	" Isabel	48	Wife	45	F	Full	1896	"	12044
5298	3	" Ellis S	32	Son	29	M	3/4	1896	"	12047
5299	4	" Harris J	21	"	18	"	3/4	1896	"	12045
5300	5	" Susie E	13	Dau	10	F	3/4	1896	"	12046
	6									
	7									
	8									
	9									
	10									
	11									
	12									
	13									
	14									
	15	ENROLLMENT OF NOS. 1,2,3,4,5 HEREON APPROVED BY THE SECRETARY OF INTERIOR JAN 16 1903								
	16									
	17									

TRIBAL ENROLLMENT OF PARENTS

	Name of Father	Year	County	Name of Mother	Year	County
1	Garret Thompson	Dead	Creek Roll	Melinda Thompson	Dead	Wade
2	Dixon Anderson	"	Wade	Annie Anderson	"	"
3	No 1			No 2		
4	No 1			No 2		
5	No 1			No 2		
6						
7			No1 on 1896 roll as Gilbert Thompson			
8			No3 " 1896 " " Ellis "			
9			No4 " 1896 " " Harris "			
10			No5 " 1896 " " Susie "			
			For child of No4 see NB (Apr 26-06) Card #410			
11						
12						
13						
14						
15						
16			Date of Application for Enrollment.	5/22/99		
17						

64

RESIDENCE: Jacks Fork   COUNTY. **Choctaw Nation**   Choctaw Roll   CARD No.
POST OFFICE: Tushkahomma[sic], I.T.   *(Not Including Freedmen)*   FIELD No. 1865

Dawes' Roll No.	NAME		Relationship to Person First Named	AGE	SEX	BLOOD	TRIBAL ENROLLMENT		
							Year	County	No.
5301	1 Anderson, Watson	56	First Named	53	M	Full	1896	Jacks Fork	472
5302	2 " Lucinda	41	Wife	38	F	"	1896	" "	473
5303	3 " Reason	25	Son	22	M	"	1896	" "	479
5304	4 " Hattie	19	Dau	16	F	"	1896	" "	474
5305	5 " Lonzo W	16	Son	13	M	"	1896	" "	475
5306	6 " Minerva	13	Dau	10	F	"	1896	" "	476
5307	7 " James H	10	Son	7	M	"	1896	" "	477
5308	8 " Emily	7	Dau	4	F	"	1896	" "	478
5309	9 " Barnabas	5	Son	2	M	"			
~~5310~~	10 DIED PRIOR TO SEPTEMBER 25, 1902 ~~Pontius~~		~~Son~~	~~3mo~~	M	"			
	11								
	12 ENROLLMENT OF NOS. 1,2,3,4,5,6,7,8,9,10 HEREON APPROVED BY THE SECRETARY								
	13 OF INTERIOR JAN 16 1903								
	14 No10 died May 19, 1901; proof of								
	15 death filed Dec 17. 1902								
	16 No10 died May 19, 1901: Enrollment cancelled by								
	17 Department July 8, 1904								

TRIBAL ENROLLMENT OF PARENTS

	Name of Father	Year	County	Name of Mother	Year	County
1	Jos. Anderson	Dead	Jacks Fork	Julia A. Anderson	Dead	Jacks Fork
2	Edward Wall	1896	" "	Melina Wall	"	Cedar
3	No1			No2		
4	No1			No2		
5	No1			No2		
6	No1			No2		
7	No1			No2		
8	No1			No2		
9	No1			No2		
10	~~No.1~~			~~No.2~~		
11	No5 on 1896 roll as S W Anderson		"			
12	No7 " 1896 " " J.H.		"	For child of Nos 1&2 see NB (Mar 3,1905) #858		
13	No.10 Enrolled November 17th 1900		"	" No 3 " " " " #860		
	No3 is now the husband of Artimissa White on			" " " " (April26,1906) #397		
14	Choctaw Card #2177 February 13, 1901.					
15	No3 is now husband of Emeline Taylor on Choctaw card #4872 12/8/02					
16	For children of No4 see NB (Apr 26-06) Card #331				Date of Application for Enrollment.	5/22/99
17	" child " " 3 " " " " #397					

Choctaw By Blood Enrollment Cards 1898-1914

RESIDENCE: Wade   COUNTY: **Choctaw Nation**   Choctaw Roll   CARD NO.

POST OFFICE: Tushkahomma[sic], I.T.   FIELD NO.

Dawes' Roll No.	NAME	Relationship to Person Named	AGE	SEX	BLOOD	TRIBAL ENROLLMENT Year	TRIBAL ENROLLMENT County	TRIBAL ENROLLMENT No.
5311	1 Benton, Emerson ³⁸	First Named	35	M	Full	1896	Wade	977
5312	2 " Nellie ²⁶	Wife	23	F	"	1896	Nashoba	5536
5313	3 " Clara Mabel ²	Dau	7mo	F	"			
	4							
	5							
	6							
	7							
	8							
	9							
	10							
	11							
	12							
	13							
	14							
	15							
	16							
	17							

ENROLLMENT
OF NOS. 1, 2, 3 HEREON
APPROVED BY THE SECRETARY
OF INTERIOR JAN 16 1903

TRIBAL ENROLLMENT OF PARENTS

	Name of Father	Year	County	Name of Mother	Year	County
1	John Benton	Dead	Wade	Min-tehima	Dead	Wade
2	James Holmes	Dead	Nashoba	Susan Holmes	Dead	Nashoba
3	No.1			No.2		
4						
5						
6			No2 On 1896 roll as Nellie Holmes			
7			No.3 Enrolled May 17, 1901.			
8			For child of Nos 1&2 see NB (Apr 26-06) Card #350			
9						
10						
11						
12						
13						
14						
15					#1&2	
16				Date of Application for Enrollment	5/22/99	
17						

Choctaw By Blood Enrollment Cards 1898-1914

RESIDENCE: Jack's Fork	COUNTY.	**Choctaw Nation**	Choctaw Roll	CARD NO.
POST OFFICE: Stringtown I.T.			(Not Including Freedmen)	FIELD NO. **1867**

Dawes' Roll No.	NAME	Relationship to Person First Named	AGE	SEX	BLOOD	TRIBAL ENROLLMENT		
						Year	County	No.
5314	1 Frazier Simon 47		44	M	Full	1896	Jacks Fork	4511
5315	2 " Sissy 19	Dau	16	F	"	1896	" "	4512
5316	3 " John 16	Son	13	M	"	1896	" "	4513
5317	4 " Melvina 13	Dau	10	F	"	1896	" "	4514
	5							
	6							
	7							
	8							
	9							
	10							
	11							
	12							
	13							
	14 P.O. 11/17/05 Owl							
	15 ENROLLMENT OF NOS. 1,2,3,4 HEREON							
	16 APPROVED BY THE SECRETARY OF INTERIOR Jan 16, 1903							
	17							

TRIBAL ENROLLMENT OF PARENTS

	Name of Father	Year	County	Name of Mother	Year	County
1	John Frazier	Dead	Atoka	Emishtona Frazier	Dead	Atoka
2	No 1			Liney Frazier	Dead	Jacks Fork
3	No 1			Anna Frazier	Dead	" "
4	No 1			" "	"	" "
5						
6						
7						
8						
9			See note on Card D 173			
10						
11						
12						
13						
14						
15						
16			Date of Application for Enrollment	5/22/99		
17						

P.O. No4 Blanco I.T. 6/13/05

Choctaw By Blood Enrollment Cards 1898-1914

RESIDENCE: Jacks Fork COUNTY.
POST OFFICE: Tushkahomma[sic], I.T.

Choctaw Nation

Choctaw Roll
(Not Including Freedmen)

CARD NO.
FIELD NO. 1868

Dawes' Roll No.	NAME	Relationship to Person First Named	AGE	SEX	BLOOD	TRIBAL ENROLLMENT		
						Year	County	No.
5318	1 Anderson, Calvin ⁵³		50	M	Full	1896	Jacks Fork	480
5319	2 " Zona ¹⁶	Dau	13	F	"	1896	" "	482
5320	3 " Jackson ¹²	Son	9	M	"	1896	" "	483
	4							
	5							
	6							
	7							
	8							
	9							
	10							
	11							
	12							
	13							
	14							
	15							
	16							
	17							

ENROLLMENT
OF NOS. 1,2,3 HEREON
APPROVED BY THE SECRETARY
OF INTERIOR JAN 16 1903

TRIBAL ENROLLMENT OF PARENTS

	Name of Father	Year	County	Name of Mother	Year	County
1	Joe Anderson	Dead	Jacks Fork	Julia Ann Anderson	Dead	Jacks Fork
2	Calvin Anderson		" "	Selina Anderson	Dead	" "
3	" "		" "	" "	" "	" "
4						
5						
6	No3 On 1896 roll as Jacob Anderson					
7						
8						
9						
10						
11						
12						
13						
14					Date of Application for Enrollment.	5/22/99
15						
16						
17						

Choctaw By Blood Enrollment Cards 1898-1914

RESIDENCE: Cedar   COUNTY.   **Choctaw Nation**   **Choctaw Roll**   CARD No.
POST OFFICE: Kosoma I.T.   *(Not Including Freedmen)*   FIELD No. **1869**

Dawes' Roll No.	NAME	Relationship to Person First Named	AGE	SEX	BLOOD	TRIBAL ENROLLMENT Year	County	No.
5321	1 Eyachabbe William ~~DIED PRIOR TO SEPTEMBER 25, 1902~~		38	M	Full	1896	Cedar	3711
5322	2 " Emily 48	Wife	45	F	"	1896	"	3712
5323	3 " Lizzie 18	Dau	15	F	"	1896	"	3714
5324	4 " Colbert 12	Son	9	M	"	1896	"	3715
5325	5 Einer, Mary ~~DIED PRIOR TO SEPTEMBER 25, 1902~~	S Dau	13	F	"	1896	"	3716
15760	6 Morris, Agnes 1	Dau of Nº 5	3	F	"			
	7							
	8							
	9	ENROLLMENT						
	10	OF NOS. ~~ 6 ~~ HEREON APPROVED BY THE SECRETARY						
	11	OF INTERIOR Dec 5, 1904						
	12							
	13							
	14							
	15	ENROLLMENT OF NOS. 1,2,3,4,5 HEREON						
	16	APPROVED BY THE SECRETARY OF INTERIOR Jan 16. 1903						
	17							

TRIBAL ENROLLMENT OF PARENTS

	Name of Father	Year	County	Name of Mother	Year	County
1	Eyachabbe	Dead	Cedar	Temechi	Dead	Cedar
2	McKenzie	"	"	Julia McKenzie	"	"
3	No 1			Ginsey Eyachabbe	"	"
4	No 1			No 2		
5	Stuick Einer	1896	Cedar	Emily Eyachabbe		
6	Unknown			Nº5		
7						
8	No1 On 1896 roll as Wᵐ Eyachabbe					
9	No5 Daughter of Emily, above					

10 No.1 died Dec 26, 1900: No.5 died May 7, 1902: Enrollment cancelled by Department July 8, 1904
11 No6 Born Jany 3, 1902 Application for enrollment made at Antlers Ind Ter Dec 4, 1902. Proof
of birth filed Nov. 16, 1904. Nº6 was adopted by Simeon and Emily Morris, Nov 6, 1902. See
12 ~~copy of adoption papers filed herein.~~
13
14
15   #1 to 5
16   Date of Application for Enrollment.
17   5/22/99

RESIDENCE: Nashoba   COUNTY. **Choctaw Nation**   **Choctaw Roll**   CARD NO.
POST OFFICE: Tushkahomma[sic] I.T.   *(Not Including Freedmen)*   FIELD NO. 1870

Dawes' Roll No.	NAME	Relationship to Person First Named	AGE	SEX	BLOOD	TRIBAL ENROLLMENT		
						Year	County	No.
5326	1 Battice Byington ³⁴	First Named	31	M	Full	1896	Wade	1029
5327	2 " Lizzie ⁶³	Wife	60	F	"	1896	"	1030
	3							
	4							
	5							
	6							
	7							
	8							
	9							
	10							
	11							
	12							
	13							
	14							
	15							
	16							
	17							

ENROLLMENT
OF NOS. 1,2 HEREON
APPROVED BY THE SECRETARY
OF INTERIOR JAN 16 1903

TRIBAL ENROLLMENT OF PARENTS

	Name of Father	Year	County	Name of Mother	Year	County
1	Fallonson Battice	1896	Jacks Fork	Lista Battice	Dead	Nashoba
2		Dead			Dead	
3						
4						
5						
6						
7						
8						
9						
10						
11						
12						
13						
14						
15						
16				Date of Application for Enrollment.	5/22/99	
17	P.O. Dexter I.T					

12/2/02

RESIDENCE: Nashoba	COUNTY.	**Choctaw Nation**	**Choctaw Roll**	CARD NO.
POST OFFICE: Albion I.T.			*(Not Including Freedmen)*	FIELD NO. 1871

Dawes' Roll No.	NAME	Relationship to Person First Named	AGE	SEX	BLOOD	TRIBAL ENROLLMENT		
						Year	County	No.
5328	1 Johnson James *DIED PRIOR TO SEPTEMBER 25, 1902*	First Named	28	M	Full	1896	Nashoba	6890
5329	2 Belinda *DIED PRIOR TO SEPTEMBER 25, 1902*	Wife	22	F	"	1896	"	6891
5330	3 " Abner 10	Son	7	M	"	1896	"	6892
5331	4 Ada *DIED PRIOR TO SEPTEMBER 25, 1902*	Dau	1	F	"			
	5							
	6							
	7							
	8							
	9							
	10							
	11							
	12							
	13							
	14							
	15	ENROLLMENT						
	16	OF NOS. 1,2,3,4 HEREON APPROVED BY THE SECRETARY						
	17	OF INTERIOR JAN 16 1903						

TRIBAL ENROLLMENT OF PARENTS

	Name of Father	Year	County	Name of Mother	Year	County
1	Peter Johnson	1896	Nashoba	Wilsey Johnson	Dead	Nashoba
2	Amos Bohannan	1896	Wade	Listia Bohannan	"	"
3	No 1			No 2		
4	No 1			No 2		
5						
6	No.1 died Spring of 1901: Enrollment cancelled by Department August 5, 1904					
7	No1 died in Spring of 1902; proof of death filed Dec 16, 1902					
8	No4 " May 15, 1902; " " " " Dec 16, 1902					
9	No2 " Aug 1901; " " " " Dec 30, 1902					
10	No3 is now living with Byington Battice, Choctaw card #1870					
11	No.2 died Aug - 1901: No 4 died May 15, 1902: Enrollment cancelled by Department					
12	July 8, 1904					
13					Date of Application for Enrollment.	
14					5/22/99	
15						
16						
17						

No3 Nashoba Okla

Choctaw By Blood Enrollment Cards 1898-1914

RESIDENCE: Nashoba COUNTY. **Choctaw Nation** **Choctaw Roll** (Not Including Freedmen) CARD NO.

POST OFFICE: Talihani[sic] I.T. FIELD NO. 1872

Dawes' Roll No.	NAME		Relationship to Person First Named	AGE	SEX	BLOOD	TRIBAL ENROLLMENT		
							Year	County	No.
5332	1 White, Arten	23	First Named	20	M	Full	1896	Nashoba	13297
5333	2 " Nettie	22	Wife	19	F	"	1896	"	5552
5334	3 " Ancey	1	Dau	1	F	"			
	4								
	5								
	6								
	7								
	8								
	9								
	10								
	11								
	12								
	13								
	14								
	15								
	16								
	17								

ENROLLMENT
OF NOS. 1,2,3 HEREON
APPROVED BY THE SECRETARY
OF INTERIOR JAN 16 1903

TRIBAL ENROLLMENT OF PARENTS

	Name of Father	Year	County	Name of Mother	Year	County
1	Barton White	Dead	Nashoba	Lucy White	1896	Nashoba
2	Yahokatabe	Dead	Wade	Sukey Bohanan	Dead	Wade
3	Nº1			Nº2		
4						
5						
6			No 2 On roll 1896 as Hettie Harrison			
7			Nº3 Born Aug. 15, 1901; enrolled Sept. 4, 1902.			
8						
9						
10						
11						
12						
13						
14						
15					Date of Application for Enrollment.	
16					5/22/99	
17						

72

Choctaw By Blood Enrollment Cards 1898-1914

RESIDENCE: Nashoba COUNTY. **Choctaw Nation**   Choctaw Roll   CARD No.
POST OFFICE: Tushkahomma[sic] I.T.   (Not Including Freedmen)   FIELD No. 1873

Dawes' Roll No.		NAME		Relationship to Person	AGE	SEX	BLOOD	TRIBAL ENROLLMENT		
								Year	County	No.
5335	1	Wilkin, John	43	First Named	40	M	Full	1896	Nashoba	13285
DEAD	2	" Hantone DEAD		Wife	40	F	"	1896	"	13286
5336	3	" Levi	17	Son	14	M	"	1896	"	13287
5337	4	" Laymon	16	Son	13	M	"	1896	"	13288
5338	5	" John	7	Son	4	M	"	1896	"	13289
	6									
	7									
	8									
	9									
	10									
	11									
	12									
	13									
	14									
	15									
	16									
	17									

No. 2 HEREON DISMISSED UNDER ORDER OF THE COMMISSION TO THE FIVE CIVILIZED TRIBES OF MARCH 31, 1905.

ENROLLMENT
OF NOS. 1,3,4,5 HEREON
APPROVED BY THE SECRETARY
OF INTERIOR JAN 16 1903

TRIBAL ENROLLMENT OF PARENTS

	Name of Father	Year	County	Name of Mother	Year	County
1	James Hoke	Dead	Nashoba	Mollie Hoke	Dead	Cedar
2	Alexander Green	"	Cedar	Hoyona	1896	"
3	No 1			No 2		
4	No 1			No 2		
5	No 1			No 2		
6						
7	No.5 "Died prior to September 25, 1902: not entitled to land or money."					
8	(See Indian Office letter of June 20, 1910, D.C. #845-1910)					
9						
10	No2 on 1896 roll as Hantona Wilkin					
11	No2 died June 28, 1899: Proof of death filed Feby 13th 1902					
12	No.1 is now the husband of Lillie Push on Choctaw card #2025: Feby 13, 1902					
13	No5 died Jany 5, 1902; proof of death filed Dec 12, 1902					
13	Nº3 is now husband of Leon Frazier on Choctaw card #2047 Dec 9/02					
14	For child of No.3 see NB (March 3,1905) #793					
15						
16					Date of Application for Enrollment.	
17					5/22/99	

Choctaw By Blood Enrollment Cards 1898-1914

RESIDENCE: Cedar   COUNTY. **Choctaw Nation**   **Choctaw Roll** CARD NO.
POST OFFICE: Tushkahomma[sic], I.T.   *(Not Including Freedmen)* FIELD NO. 1874

Dawes' Roll No.	NAME	Relationship to Person First Named	AGE	SEX	BLOOD	TRIBAL ENROLLMENT		
						Year	County	No.
5339	1 Bacon, Sora ³⁶	First Named	33	F	Full	1896	Cedar	1059
	2							
	3							
	4							
	5							
	6							
	7							
	8							
	9							
	10							
	11							
	12							
	13							
	14							
	15							
	16							
	17							

ENROLLMENT
OF NOS. 1
APPROVED BY THE SECRETARY HEREON
OF INTERIOR JAN 16 1903

TRIBAL ENROLLMENT OF PARENTS

	Name of Father	Year	County	Name of Mother	Year	County
1	Joseph Morris	Dead	Cedar	Liney Morris	Dead	Cedar
2						
3						
4						
5			On 1896 roll as Sarah Bacon			
6						
7						
8						
9						
10						
11						
12						
13						
14					Date of Application for Enrollment.	
15						
16					5/22/99	
17						

74

Choctaw By Blood Enrollment Cards 1898-1914

RESIDENCE:	Jacks Fork	COUNTY.	**Choctaw Nation**	Choctaw Roll	CARD No.	
POST OFFICE:	Hartshorne, I.T.			(Not Including Freedmen)	FIELD No.	1875

Dawes' Roll No.	NAME		Relationship to Person First Named	AGE	SEX	BLOOD	TRIBAL ENROLLMENT		
							Year	County	No.
DEAD.	1 Clay, Louisa		Named	30	F	Full	1896	Jacks Fork	2981
5340	2 " Andrew	20	Son	17	M	"	1896	" "	2982
5341	3 " Gibson	18	"	15	"	"	1896	" "	2983
5342	4 " Jincey	16	Dau	13	F	"	1896	" "	2984
5343	5 " Sallie	14	"	11	"	"	1896	" "	2985
5344	6 " Lizzie	10	"	7	"	"	1896	" "	2986
5345	7 " Kizzie	3	"	6	"	"	1896	" "	2987
	8								
	9								
	10								

No. 1 HEREON DISMISSED UNDER ORDER OF THE COMMISSION TO THE FIVE CIVILIZED TRIBES OF MARCH 31, 1905.

ENROLLMENT
OF NOS. 2,3,4,5,6,7 HEREON
APPROVED BY THE SECRETARY
OF INTERIOR JAN 16 1903

TRIBAL ENROLLMENT OF PARENTS

	Name of Father	Year	County	Name of Mother	Year	County
1	Billy William	Dead	Jacks Fork	Sillen William	Dead	Jacks Fork
2	William Clay	"	" " "	No 1		
3	" "	"	" " "	No 1		
4	" "	"	" " "	No 1		
5	" "	"	" " "	No 1		
6	" "	"	" " "	No 1		
7	" "	"	" " "	No 1		
8						
9						
10						
11			For child of No 4 see NB (Apr 26-06) No 805			
12			No1 on 1896 roll as Lyda Clay			
13			No2 " 1896 " " Anderson "			
14			No1 died Feb 25, 1901; proof of death filed Dec 12, 1902			
15			No2 now husband of Louisa Anderson on Choctaw card #5415 12/1/02			
16				Date of Application for Enrollment.	5/22/99	
17	P.O. Ti, I.T.		For child of No4 see NB (Mar 3-1905) Card No 58			

12/9/02   "   "   " No2 "   "   "   "   "   " 868

Choctaw By Blood Enrollment Cards 1898-1914

RESIDENCE:	Wade	COUNTY.
POST OFFICE:	Talihina, I.T.	

Choctaw Nation

Choctaw Roll (Not Including Freedmen)

CARD NO. FIELD NO. **1876**

Dawes' Roll No.	NAME	Relationship to Person First Named	AGE	SEX	BLOOD	TRIBAL ENROLLMENT		
						Year	County	No.
Void	1 Mauldin, Edwin A		42	M	I.W.			
5346	2 Mauldin, Josephine 21	Wife	18	F	3/8	1896	Wade	989
5347	3 " Joseph Q 4	Son	7mo	M	3/16			
5348	4 " Alberta P 2	Dau	4mo	F	3/16			
5349	5 " Gertrude 1	Dau	5mo	F	3/16			
I.W. 1104	6 " Edwin A 44	Husband of No.2	44	M	I.W.			
	7							
	8	ENROLLMENT						
	9	OF NOS. ~~~ 6 ~~~ HEREON APPROVED BY THE SECRETARY						
	10	OF INTERIOR NOV 16 1904						
	11							
	12							
	13							
	14							
	15	ENROLLMENT OF NOS. 2,3,4,5 HEREON						
	16	APPROVED BY THE SECRETARY OF INTERIOR JAN 16 1903						
	17							

TRIBAL ENROLLMENT OF PARENTS

	Name of Father	Year	County	Name of Mother	Year	County
1	Ransom Mauldin	Dead	Non-Citz	Eliz. Mauldin	Dead	Non Citz
2	David Burney	1896	Wade	Bettie Burney	1896	Wade
3	No 1			No 2		
4	Edwin Mauldin		intermarried	No.2		
5	" "		"	Nº2		
6	Ransom Mauldin	dead	non-citizen	Eliz. Mauldin	dead	non-citizen
7	No.2 is the wife of Edwin A Mauldin on Choctaw card #D 625					
8						
9						
10	No2 on 1896 roll as Josephine Burney					
11	No.6 transferred from Choctaw card #D-625 Oct. 31, 1904 See decision of Oct 15, 1904					
12	No3 Affidavit of birth to be supplied. Recd May 30/99					
13	Sept 12/99: No1: See his testimony as to re-marriage					
14	Name of No.1 stricken from this card and placed on Choctaw card #D.625. March 20th, 1901.					
15	No.4 Enrolled March 20th, 1901					#1 to 3 inc
16					Date of Application for Enrollment.	5/22/99
17	P.O. Albian, I.T.	Nº5 Born April 29, 1902; enrolled Sept. 24, 1902				

9/24/02

For child of Nos 2&6 see NB (Mar 3-'05) Card #109

76

Choctaw By Blood Enrollment Cards 1898-1914

R........shoba								Choctaw R......		
POST OFFICE: Tushkahomma[sic], I.T.							(Not Including Freedmen)	FIELD NO.	1877	

Dawes' No.	NAME		Relationship to Person First Named	AGE	SEX	BLOOD	TRIBAL ENROLLMENT		
							Year	County	No.
0	1 LeFlore, Watson	33		30	M	Full	1896	Nashoba	7984
51	2 " Elizabeth	30	Wife	27	F	"	1896	"	7985
52	3 " Davis	16	Son	13	M	"	1896	"	7986
53	4 " Wesley	10	"	7	"	"	1896	"	7987
54	5 " Silwee	6	Dau	3	F	"	1896	"	7988
55	6 Willis DIED PRIOR TO SEPTEMBER 25, 1902		Son	9mo	M	"			
	7								
	8								
	9								
	10								
	11								
	12								
	13								
	14								
	15	ENROLLMENT OF NOS. 1,2,3,4,5,6 HEREON APPROVED BY THE SECRETARY OF INTERIOR JAN 16 1903							
	16								
	17								

TRIBAL ENROLLMENT OF PARENTS

	Name of Father	Year	County	Name of Mother	Year	County
1	Thomas LeFlore	Dead	Nashoba	Phoebe Wall	1896	Nashoba
2	Po-tubbee	"	Gaines	Si-o-key	Dead	"
3	No1			No2		
4	No1			No2		
5	No1			No2		
6	№ 1			№ 2		
7						
8			No5 on 1896 roll as Silwy LeFlore			
9			№6 Born July 23, 1901: enrolled May 10, 1902			
10			No.6 Died June 17, 1902: Proof of death filed Dec 23, 1902			
11		No.6 died June 17, 1902: Enrollment cancelled by Department July 8, 1904				
12						
13						
14						#1 to 5
15					Date of Application for Enrollment.	
16					5/22/99	
17						

RESIDENCE: Nashoba COUNTY. **Choctaw Nation** **Choctaw Roll** CARD NO.
POST OFFICE: Tushkahomma[sic] I.T. _(Not Including Freedmen)_ FIELD NO. 1878

Dawes' Roll No.	NAME	Relationship to Person First Named	AGE	SEX	BLOOD	TRIBAL ENROLLMENT		
						Year	County	No.
5356	1 Garland, Simon 48	First Named	45	M	Full	1896	Cedar	4721
5357	2 " Lucy 53	Wife	50	F	"	1896	"	4722
5358	3 " Minnie 14	Dau	11	"	"	1896	"	4723
	4							
	5							
	6							
	7							
	8							
	9							
	10							
	11							
	12							
	13							
	14							
	15	ENROLLMENT OF NOS. 1,2,3 HEREON						
	16	APPROVED BY THE SECRETARY OF INTERIOR JAN 16 1903						
	17							

TRIBAL ENROLLMENT OF PARENTS

	Name of Father	Year	County	Name of Mother	Year	County
1	Bar-na-tub-bi	Ded	Red River	Ho-tima	Ded	Wade
2	Silas Pain	"	Towson		"	Towson
3	No 1			Martha Underwood	1896	Jacks Fork
4						
5						
6						
7						
8						
9						
10						
11						
12						
13						
14						
15						Date of Application for Enrollment
16						5-22-99
17						

Choctaw By Blood Enrollment Cards 1898-1914

RESIDENCE: Jacks Fork   COUNTY. **Choctaw Nation**   **Choctaw Roll**   CARD No.
POST OFFICE: Lyceum I.T.   *(Not Including Freedmen)*   FIELD No. 1879

Dawes' Roll No.	NAME		Relationship to Person First Named	AGE	SEX	BLOOD	TRIBAL ENROLLMENT		
							Year	County	No.
5359	1 Bond David	31	First Named	28	M	Full	1896	Jacks Fork	1886
5360	2 " Silvey	41	Wife	38	F	"	1896	" "	1887
	3								
	4								
	5								
	6								
	7								
	8								
	9								
	10								
	11								
	12								
	13								
	14								
	15								
	16								
	17								

ENROLLMENT
OF NOS. 1,2 HEREON
APPROVED BY THE SECRETARY
OF INTERIOR JAN 16 1903

TRIBAL ENROLLMENT OF PARENTS

	Name of Father	Year	County	Name of Mother	Year	County
1	Jesse Bond	1896	Jacks Fork	Lucy Ann Bond	1896	Atoka
2	John Frazier	Ded	Atoka	Tony Frazier	Ded	"
3						
4						
5						
6						
7						
8						
9						
10						
11						
12						
13						
14						
15				Date of Application for Enrollment.		
16				5-22-99		
17						

79

Choctaw By Blood Enrollment Cards 1898-1914

Dawes' Roll No.	NAME		Relationship to Person First Named	AGE	SEX	BLOOD	TRIBAL ENROLLMENT		
							Year	County	No.
5361	1 Bryant, Raymond	44	First Named	41	M	Full	1896	Wade	1023
DEAD.	2 " Emily DEAD.		Wife	21	F	"	1896	"	3327
5362	3 " Jesse	20	Son	17	M	"	1896	"	1025
5363	4 " Jimmie	15	"	12	"	"	1896	"	1026
5364	5 " Laura	11	Dau	8	F	"	1896	"	1027
5365	6 " Ora	8	"	5	"	"	1896	"	1028
5366	7 " Bertha	4	"	mon2	"	"			
5367	8 " Dave	1	Son	16mo	M	"			
	9								
	10	No. 2 HEREON DISMISSED UNDER							
	11	ORDER OF THE COMMISSION TO THE FIVE CIVILIZED TRIBES OF MARCH 31, 1905							
	12								
	13								
	14								
	15	ENROLLMENT OF NOS. 1,3,4,5,6,7 and 8 HEREON APPROVED BY THE SECRETARY							
	16	OF INTERIOR JAN 16 1903							
	17								

TRIBAL ENROLLMENT OF PARENTS

	Name of Father	Year	County	Name of Mother	Year	County
1	Nathan Bryant	Ded	Wade	Lucy Ann Bryant	Ded	Wade
2	Daniel Dancy	1896	"	Nancy Dancy	"	"
3	No 1			Becky Bryant	"	Sans Bois
4	No 1			Mary Bryant	"	Wade
5	No 1			" "		
6	No 1			" "		
7	No 1			No 2		
8	No 1			No 2		
9						
10			No 2 on 1896 roll as Emily Daney			
11			No 3 " " " " Jessie Bryant			
12			No 2 Died Jany 31, 1901, proof of death filed May 8, 1902			
13			No 8 Born Jany 26, 1901; enrolled June 14, 1902 For child of No.1 see NB (March 3, 1905) #768			
14					#1 to 7 inc	
15					Date of Application for Enrollment.	
16					5-22-99	
17	P.O. Talihina Okla. 7/2/07					

80

Choctaw By Blood Enrollment Cards 1898-1914

| RESIDENCE: Wade | COUNTY. | | | | |
| POST OFFICE: Kiamatia[sic] I.T. | | | | | |

Choctaw Nation

Choctaw Roll *(Not Including Freedmen)*

CARD NO. FIELD NO. 1881

Dawes' Roll No.	NAME	Relationship to Person First Named	AGE	SEX	BLOOD	TRIBAL ENROLLMENT Year	County	No.
5368	1 Anderson Lavisa 24	First Named	21	F	Full	1896	Wade	173
	2							
	3							
	4							
	5							
	6							
	7							
	8							
	9							
	10							
	11							
	12							
	13							
	14							
	15							
	16							
	17							

ENROLLMENT
OF NOS. 1 HEREON
APPROVED BY THE SECRETARY
OF INTERIOR JAN 16 1903

TRIBAL ENROLLMENT OF PARENTS

Name of Father	Year	County	Name of Mother	Year	County
1 Andle Anderson	1896	Tobucksy	Elizabeth Anderson	De'd	Jacks Fork
2					
3					
4					
5					
6					
7					
8					
9					
10					
11					
12					
13					
14					
15				Date of Application for Enrollment.	
16				5-22-99	
17 P.O. Sulphur, Okla 12/1/11					

Choctaw By Blood Enrollment Cards 1898-1914

RESIDENCE: Cedar   COUNTY. **Choctaw Nation** 1882 **Choctaw Roll**
POST OFFICE: Kosoma I.T.   *(Not Including Freedmen)*

Dawes' Roll No.	NAME		Relationship to Person	AGE	SEX	BLOOD	TRIBAL ENROLLMENT		
							Year	County	No.
5369	1 Ben Henry	28	First Named	25	M	Full	1896	Nashoba	1222
5370	2 " Sillis	24		21	F	"	1896	Cedar	2433
	3								
	4								
	5								
	6								
	7								
	8								
	9								
	10								
	11								
	12								
	13								
	14								
	15	ENROLLMENT OF NOS. 1,2 HEREON APPROVED BY THE SECRETARY OF INTERIOR JAN 16 1903							
	16								
	17								

TRIBAL ENROLLMENT OF PARENTS

	Name of Father	Year	County	Name of Mother	Year	County
1	Wallis Ben	1896	Nashoba	Hak-lo-ta-ma	Ded	Nashoba
2	Abel Collins	1896	Cedar	Rhoda Collins	"	Cedar
3						
4						
5						
6			No 2 on 1896 roll as Sillis Collin			
7			N°2 is now wife of McCasson Anderson Choctaw card #1789			
8						
9						
10						
11						
12						
13						
14					Date of Application for Enrollment.	
15						
16					5-22-99	
17						

Choctaw By Blood Enrollment Cards 1898-1914

Dawes' Roll No.	NAME		Relationship to Person	AGE	SEX	BLOOD	TRIBAL ENROLLMENT		
							Year	County	No.
5371	1 Carnes, Selina	57	First Named	54	F	Full	1896	Jacks Fork	3018
5372	2 Anderson, Jackman	22	Son	19	M	"	1896	" "	471
5373	3 Carnes, Sophia	17	Dau	14	F	"	1896	" "	3019
5374	4 " Adeline	14	"	11	"	"	1896	" "	3030
5375	5 " Harriet	12	"	9	"	"	1896	" "	3021
5376	6 " Dora	10	"	7	"	"	1896	" "	256
	7								
	8								
	9								
	10								
	11								
	12								
	13								
	14								
	15	ENROLLMENT OF NOS. 1,2,3,4,5,6 HEREON							
	16	APPROVED BY THE SECRETARY							
	17	OF INTERIOR Jan 16 1903							

TRIBAL ENROLLMENT OF PARENTS

	Name of Father	Year	County	Name of Mother	Year	County
1	Joseph Anderson	Dead	Jacks Fork	Julia A. Anderson	Dead	Jacks Fork
2	Steve Anderson	"	" "	No 1		
3	Louis Carnes	"	" "	No 1		
4	" "	"	" "	No 1		
5	" "	"	" "	No 1		
6	" "	"	" "	No 1		
7						
8						
9						
10	For child of No 3 see NB (Mar 3, 1905) card #853					
11	For child of No 3 see NB (Apr 26-06) Card #717					
12	No6 on 1893 Pay roll as Dora Carn Page 26, No 256, Jacks Fork Co					
13	Nº2 is now the husband of Ida Impson on Chickasaw card #1082 May 13, 1902.					
14						
15					Date of Application for Enrollment.	
16					5/22/99	
17						

P.O. Dexter I.T. 4/11/05

Choctaw By Blood Enrollment Cards 1898-1914

RESIDENCE: Jacks Fork   COUNTY.   **Choctaw Nation**   **Choctaw Roll**   CARD No.
POST OFFICE: Tushkahomma[sic], I.T   (Not Including Freedmen)   FIELD No. 1884

Dawes' Roll No.	NAME	Relationship to Person First Named	AGE	SEX	BLOOD	TRIBAL ENROLLMENT		
						Year	County	No.
5377	1 Anderson, Josephine 24		21	F	Full	1896	Jacks Fork	470
5378	2 " Nora 4	Dau	4mo	"	"			
	3							
	4							
	5							
	6							
	7							
	8							
	9							
	10							
	11							
	12							
	13							
	14							
	15	ENROLLMENT OF NOS. 1,2 HEREON						
	16	APPROVED BY THE SECRETARY OF INTERIOR JAN 16 1903						
	17							

TRIBAL ENROLLMENT OF PARENTS

	Name of Father	Year	County	Name of Mother	Year	County
1	Steve Anderson	Dead	Jacks Fork	Selina Carnes	1896	Jacks Fork
2	Jimmie Anderson	1896		No 1		
3						
4						
5						
6						
7						
8						
9						
10						
11						
12						
13						
14						
15						
16				Date of Application for Enrollment.	5/22/99	
17						

84

Choctaw By Blood Enrollment Cards 1898-1914

| RESIDENCE: Jacks Fork | COUNTY. | **Choctaw Nation** | Choctaw Roll | CARD NO. |
| POST OFFICE: Tighe, I.T. | | | (Not Including Freedmen) | FIELD NO. 1885 |

Dawes' Roll No.	NAME		Relationship to Person	AGE	SEX	BLOOD	TRIBAL ENROLLMENT		
							Year	County	No.
5379	1 Read, Lizzie	48	First Named	45	F	1/4	1896	Jacks Fork	11010
5380	2 James, Katie	25	Dau	22	"	3/8	1896	" "	11697
5381	3 Burris, Isham	10	G. Son	7	M	7/16	1896	" "	1899
5382	4 " Caroline	9	G. Dau	6	F	7/16	1896	" "	1900
5383	5 Spring, Willie	6	G. Son	3	M	7/16	1896	" "	11698
5384	6 James, Emma	1	G. Dau	11mo	F	3/16			
14696	7 Carney Ida	3	Dau of No 2	3	F	7/16			
	8								
	9								
	10								
	11								
	12								
	13								
	14								
	15	ENROLLMENT OF NOS. 1,2,3,4,5,6 HEREON APPROVED BY THE SECRETARY OF INTERIOR JAN 16 1903					ENROLLMENT OF NOS. 7 HEREON APPROVED BY THE SECRETARY OF INTERIOR MAY 20 1903		
	16								
	17								

TRIBAL ENROLLMENT OF PARENTS

	Name of Father	Year	County	Name of Mother	Year	County
1	Louis Green	Dead	Non Citz	Nellie Green	Dead	Gaines
2	Hardy Henderson	"	Tobucksy	No1		
3	Turner Burris	1896	Jacks Fork	No2		
4	" "	1896	" "	No2		
5	Solomon Spring	1896	Wade	No2		
6	Jacob James	1896	Chickasaw	No2		
7	Allen Carney			No2		
8						
9						
10						
11	No 2 on 1896 roll as Kitty Spring					
12	No 3 " 1896 " " Ismon Burris					
13						
14	N°2 is now the wife of Jacob James. Evidence of marriage requested Oct. 7 1902.				#1 to 5 inc	
15					Date of Application for Enrollment.	
16	N°6 Born Nov. 1, 1901, enrolled Oct. 7, 1902. N°7 born October 1899; enrolled December 15, 1902.				5/22/99	
17						

85

Choctaw By Blood Enrollment Cards 1898-1914

RESIDENCE: Nashoba COUNTY. **Choctaw Nation** **Choctaw Roll** CARD NO.
POST OFFICE: Tushkahomma[sic], I.T (Not Including Freedmen) FIELD NO. 1886

Dawes' Roll No.	NAME	Relationship to Person	AGE	SEX	BLOOD	TRIBAL ENROLLMENT		
						Year	County	No.
5385	1 Anderson, Hickman 34	First Named	31	M	Full	1896	Wade	174
	2							
	3							
	4							
	5							
	6							
	7							
	8							
	9							
	10							
	11							
	12							
	13							
	14							
	15							
	16							
	17							

ENROLLMENT
OF NOS. 1 HEREON
APPROVED BY THE SECRETARY
OF INTERIOR JAN 16 1903

TRIBAL ENROLLMENT OF PARENTS

	Name of Father	Year	County	Name of Mother	Year	County
1	Joe Anderson	Dead	Jacks Fork	Lisen Paxton	Dead	Wade
2						
3						
4						
5						
6						
7						
8						
9						
10						
11						
12						
13						
14						
15				Date of Application for Enrollment.		
16				5/22/99		
17						

Choctaw By Blood Enrollment Cards 1898-1914

RESIDENCE: Jacks Fork   COUNTY. **Choctaw Nation**   Choctaw Roll   CARD No.

POST OFFICE: Stringtown, I.T   (Not Including Freedmen)   FIELD No. 1887

Dawes' Roll No.	NAME	Relationship to Person	AGE	SEX	BLOOD	TRIBAL ENROLLMENT		
						Year	County	No.
5386	1 Billy, Isom 26	First Named	23	M	1/2	1896	Jacks Fork	1888
	2							
	3							
	4							
	5							
	6							
	7							
	8							
	9							
	10							
	11							
	12							
	13							
	14							
	15	ENROLLMENT OF NOS. 1 HEREON APPROVED BY THE SECRETARY OF INTERIOR JAN 16 1903						
	16							
	17							

TRIBAL ENROLLMENT OF PARENTS

Name of Father	Year	County	Name of Mother	Year	County
1 Charlie Billy	Dead	Chick Roll	Silway Bond	1896	Jacks Fork
2					
3					
4					
5		N°1 is now the husband of Melvina Peter on Choctaw card #1919 May 7 1902			
6					
7					
8					
9					
10					
11					
12					
13					
14					
15					
16			Date of Application for Enrollment.	5/22/99	
17					

Choctaw By Blood Enrollment Cards 1898-1914

RESIDENCE: Nashoba   COUNTY. **Choctaw Nation**   Choctaw Roll   CARD NO.

POST OFFICE: Tushkahomma[sic], I.T   *(Not Including Freedmen)*   FIELD NO. 1888

Dawes' Roll No.	NAME		Relationship to Person	AGE	SEX	BLOOD	TRIBAL ENROLLMENT		
							Year	County	No.
5387	1 Wall, Abel	55	First Named	52	M	Full	1896	Nashoba	13295
5388	2 " Phoebe	57	Wife	54	F	"	1896	"	13296
5389	3 Jackson, Grace	13	Ward	10	"	"	1896	"	6893
5390	4 Ben, Sibbie	7	"	4	"	"	1896	"	1248
	5								
	6								
	7								
	8								
	9								
	10								
	11								
	12								
	13								
	14								
	15								
	16								
	17								

ENROLLMENT
OF NOS. 1,2,3,4 HEREON
APPROVED BY THE SECRETARY
OF INTERIOR JAN 16 1903

TRIBAL ENROLLMENT OF PARENTS

	Name of Father	Year	County	Name of Mother	Year	County
1	Thomas Wall	Dead	Wade	Sema Wall	Dead	Wade
2	"	"		Yim-mie	"	Nashoba
3	Jackson	"	Nashoba	Silma Jackson	"	"
4	Cephus Ben	"	"	Lucy Cephus	"	"
5						
6						
7	No 1 on 1896 roll as Abel Waull					
8	No 2 " 1896 " " Phoebe "					
9						
10						
11						
12						
13						
14						
15					Date of Application for Enrollment.	
16					5/22/99	
17						

Choctaw By Blood Enrollment Cards 1898-1914

RESIDENCE: Cedar COUNTY. **Choctaw Nation**

Choctaw Roll CARD NO.

POST OFFICE: Tushkahomma[sic], I.T. (Not Including Freedmen) FIELD NO. 1889

Dawes' Roll No.	NAME	Relationship to Person	AGE	SEX	BLOOD	TRIBAL ENROLLMENT		
						Year	County	No.
5391	1 Battiest, Silway 69	First Named	66	F	Full	1896	Cedar	1050
	2							
	3							
	4							
	5							
	6							
	7							
	8							
	9							
	10							
	11							
	12							
	13							
	14							
	15							
	16							
	17							

ENROLLMENT
OF NOS. 1 HEREON
APPROVED BY THE SECRETARY
OF INTERIOR JAN 16 1903

TRIBAL ENROLLMENT OF PARENTS

Name of Father	Year	County	Name of Mother	Year	County
1 Simon Posh	Dead	Wade	E-me-la-huna	Dead	Nashoba
2					
3					
4					
5					
6					
7					
8					
9					
10					
11					
12					
13					
14					
15					
16					
17					

On 1896 roll as Silphia Battiest
No 1 is wife of Stayman Bohanon Choctaw card #2062. Evidence
of marriage filed Jany 20, 1903

Date of Application for Enrollment. 5/22/99

RESIDENCE: Jacks Fork   COUNTY.
POST OFFICE: Lyceum, I.T.

Choctaw Nation

Choctaw Roll
(Not Including Freedmen)

CARD NO.
FIELD NO. 1890

Dawes' Roll No.	NAME	Relationship to Person First Named	AGE	SEX	BLOOD	TRIBAL ENROLLMENT Year	County	No.
5392	1 Anderson, Lucy A ⁶⁰	First Named	57	F	Full	1896	Jacks Fork	521
5393	2 DIED PRIOR TO SEPTEMBER 25, 2002 " Jane	Dau	17	"	"	1896	" "	524
5394	3 " Elum ¹⁸	Son	15	M	"	1896	" "	525
	4							
	5							
	6							
	7							
	8							
	9							
	10							
	11							
	12							
	13							
	14							
	15	ENROLLMENT						
	16	OF NOS. 1,2,3 HEREON APPROVED BY THE SECRETARY						
	17	OF INTERIOR JAN 16 1903						

TRIBAL ENROLLMENT OF PARENTS

	Name of Father	Year	County	Name of Mother	Year	County
1	Tush-ka	Dead	Nashoba	Na-na-yo-ke	Dead	Jacks Fork
2	Graham Anderson	"	Jacks Fork	No 1		
3	" "	"	" "	No 1		
4						
5						
6						
7			No1 on 1896 roll as Lucy Anderson			
8			No2 " 1896 " Jincy "			
9			No.2 died Feby 1, 1901, Proof of death filed Dec 30, 1902			
			No.2 died Feb 1, 1901: Enrollment cancelled by Department July 8, 1904 a			
10						
11						
12						
13						
14						
15						
16				Date of Application for Enrollment.	5/22/99	
17	Tuskohoma[sic], I.T.					

12/11/02

Choctaw By Blood Enrollment Cards 1898-1914

RESIDENCE: COUNTY. **Choctaw Nation**   Choctaw Roll   CARD NO.
POST OFFICE: *(Not Including Freedmen)*   FIELD NO. 1891

Dawes' Roll No.	NAME	Relationship to Person	AGE	SEX	BLOOD	TRIBAL ENROLLMENT		
						Year	County	No.
5395	1 Choate, Alexsie[sic] 43	First Named	40	M	Full	1896	Nashoba	2543
5396	2 " Elesie 33	Wife	30	F	"	1896	"	2544
5397	3 Isabel DIED PRIOR TO SEPTEMBER 25, 1902	Dau	1	"	"			
	4							
	5							
	6							
	7							
	8							
	9							
	10							
	11							
	12							
	13							
	14							
	15	ENROLLMENT OF NOS. 1,2,3 HEREON APPROVED BY THE SECRETARY OF INTERIOR JAN 16 1903						
	16							
	17							

TRIBAL ENROLLMENT OF PARENTS

	Name of Father	Year	County	Name of Mother	Year	County
1	Lyman Choate	1896	Cedar	Betsy Choate	Ded	Nashoba
2	Billy Frazier	Ded	Nashoba	Atoklantima	1896	"
3	No 1			No 2		
4						
5						
6						
7						
8			No 2 on 1896 roll as Losie Choate			
9						
10			No3 died Sept. - 1900: Proof of death filed Dec 15, 1902			
11			No.3 died Sept - 1900: Enrollment cancelled by Department July 8, 1904			
12						
13						
14						
15						
16				Date of Application for Enrollment.	5-22-99	
17						

Choctaw By Blood Enrollment Cards 1898-1914

RESIDENCE: Cedar
POST OFFICE: Kosoma, I.T.
COUNTY.
Choctaw Nation
Choctaw Roll (Not Including Freedmen)
CARD NO.
FIELD NO. 1892

Dawes' Roll No.	NAME	Relationship to Person First Named	AGE	SEX	BLOOD	TRIBAL ENROLLMENT		
						Year	County	No.
5398	1 McKinzie, Goodman 45	First Named	42	M	Full	1896	Cedar	9260
5399	2 " Biney 25	Wife	22	F	"	1896	"	9638
5400	3 DIED PRIOR TO SEPTEMBER 25, 1902 Hebert	Son	16	M	"	1896	"	9263
5401	4 DIED PRIOR TO SEPTEMBER 25, 1902 Keener	"	6mo	"	"			
5402	5 Battiest, Silas 10	S. Son	7	"	"	1896	Cedar	1051
5403	6 McKinzie, May Lina 2	Dau	3mo	F	"			
	7							
	8							
	9							
	10							
	11							
	12							
	13							
	14							
	15	ENROLLMENT OF NOS. 1,2,3,4,5,6 HEREON						
	16	APPROVED BY THE SECRETARY OF INTERIOR JAN 16 1903						
	17							

TRIBAL ENROLLMENT OF PARENTS

	Name of Father	Year	County	Name of Mother	Year	County
1	McKinzie	Dead	Cedar	Judie McKinzie	Dead	Cedar
2	Louis Noahtubbee	"	"	Sillen Noahtubbee	1896	"
3	No 1			Nellie McKinzie	Dead	"
4	No 1			No 2		
5	Campson Battiest	Dead	Cedar	No 2		
6	No 1			No 2		
7						
8						
9						
10			No2 on 1896 roll as Bainey Noatabbe			
11						
12	No.3 died March10,1901: No4 died Jan10,1900: Enrollment cancelled by Department July 8, 1904					
13			No.6 Enrolled July 14, 1900			
14	No 3 died March 10, 1901: proof of death filed Dec 12, 1901 No 4 " June 10, 1900: " " " " " "					
15				#1 to 5 inc		
16				Date of Application for Enrollment.	5/22/99	
17	P.O. Antlers, I.T.		For child of Nos 1&2 see NB (Mar 3-1905) Card #111			

12/8/02

92

Choctaw By Blood Enrollment Cards 1898-1914

Dawes Roll No.	NAME	Relationship to Person First Named	AGE	SEX	BLOOD	TRIBAL ENROLLMENT Year	County	No.
5404	McCurtain Jane F ⁵⁹		56	F	7/8	1896	Wade	9231
5405	" Eliza A ³³	Dau	30	F	7/8	1896	"	9232
5406	" Lucinda F ²⁶	Dau	23	F	7/8	1896		9234
5407	" Ida N ²⁴	Dau	21	F	7/8	1896		9235
5408	" Lizzie D ¹⁸	Dau	15	F	7/8	1896		9236
5409	Hampton Josephine R¹²	G. Dau	9	F	3/4	1896	Blue	5904
5410	McCurtain, Cleopatra A²	G. Dau	1mo	F	7/16			
15038	McCoy, Claud E	Son of No.5	1	M	7/16			

ENROLLMENT
OF NOS. ~~~ 8 ~~~ HEREON
APPROVED BY THE SECRETARY
OF INTERIOR NOV 24 1905

For child of No 4 see NB (Apr 26-06) Card #327

ENROLLMENT
OF NOS. 1,2,3,4,5,6,7 HEREON
APPROVED BY THE SECRETARY
OF INTERIOR JAN 16 1903

TRIBAL ENROLLMENT OF PARENTS

	Name of Father	Year	County	Name of Mother	Year	County
1	Louis Austin	Dead	Gaines	Mollie Austin	Dead	Gaines
2	Jackson F McCurtain	"	Wade	No 1	1896	Wade
3	" " "		"	" "	1896	"
4	" " "		"	" "	1896	"
5	" " "		"	" "	1896	"
6	Simeon Hampton	Dead	Gaines	Comelia B Hampton	1896	Blue
7	Unknown		Illegitimate	No.5		
8	Robert McCoy		Creek	No 5		
9						
10			No2 On 1896 roll as Eliza T. McCurtain			
11			No3 " " " " Lou McCurtain			
12			No4 " " " " Ida "			
			No5 " " " " Lizzie S. "			
13			No.7 Enrolled Oct. 1st, 1900			
14			No8 was born February 21, 1902: application received and No8 listed			
15			on this card April 10, 1905 under Act of Congress approved March 3, 1905.			
16			For child of No.4 see NB (Mar 3 '05) #553			
17			Date of Application for Enrollment.	5/22/99		

Choctaw By Blood Enrollment Cards 1898-1914

RESIDENCE: Cedar COUNTY. **Choctaw Nation** **Choctaw Roll** CARD NO.

POST OFFICE: Tushkahomma[sic] I.T. (Not Including Freedmen) FIELD NO. 1894

Dawes' Roll No.	NAME		Relationship to Person	AGE	SEX	BLOOD	TRIBAL ENROLLMENT		
							Year	County	No.
5411	1 Morris Simeon	49	First Named	46	M	Full	1896	Cedar	8588
5412	2 " Polly	41	Wife	38	F	"	1896	"	8589
5413	3 Battiest, Frances	19	Dau	16	F	"	1896	"	8590
5414	4 Morris, Minnie	11	Dau	8	F	"	1896	"	8591
5415	5 " Sidney	8	Son	5	M	"	1896	"	8592
5416	6 DIED PRIOR TO SEPTEMBER 25, 6902 Johnson		Son	3	M	"	1896	"	8593
5417	7 " Rowdy	4	Son	3mo	M	"			
5418	8 Battiest, Milton	1	Son of No3	5mo	M	"			
	9								
	10								
	11								
	12								
	13								
	14								
	15								
	16								
	17								

ENROLLMENT
OF NOS. 1,2,3,4,5,6,7,8 HEREON
APPROVED BY THE SECRETARY
OF INTERIOR JAN 16 1903

TRIBAL ENROLLMENT OF PARENTS

	Name of Father	Year	County	Name of Mother	Year	County
1	Thomas Morris	Dead	Cedar	Sukey Morris	Dead	Cedar
2	Eastman Peter	"	Kiamatia[sic]	Lizzie Peter	"	Kiamatia[sic]
3	No 1			No 2		
4	" "			" "		
5	" "			" "		
6	" "			" "		
7	" "			" "		
8	Stephen Battiest		on Choctaw card 1997	No 3		
9						
10						
11	For child of No.3 see NB (March 3, 1905) #1227					
12	No3 now the wife of Stephen Battiest on Choctaw Card #1997. Evidence of marriage filed July 19 1902					
12	No8 Born Feb 5 1902. Enrolled July 19th 1902					
13	No6 Died December 26 1899. Proof of death filed Dec 22nd, 1902					
14	Nos1 and 2 have been divorced					
15	N°2 is now wife of Thompson Eyachubbe Choctaw card #1970				#1 to 7	
	N°1 is now husband of Emily Eyachubbe Choctaw card #1869				Date of Application for Enrollment.	
16	No.6 died Dec 26, 1899: Enrollment cancelled by Department Sept 16, 1904					
17	P.O. Antlers I.T. 12/13/02				5/22/99	

Choctaw By Blood Enrollment Cards 1898-1914

RESIDENCE: Jacks Fork COUNTY. **Choctaw Nation** **Choctaw Roll** CARD NO.
POST OFFICE: Stringtown I.T. *(Not Including Freedmen)* FIELD NO. **1895**

Dawes' Roll No.	NAME	Relationship to Person First Named	AGE	SEX	BLOOD	TRIBAL ENROLLMENT Year	County	No.
5419	1 Watson Julius J 33	First Named	30	M	Full	1896	Jacks Fork	14084
	2							
	3							
	4							
	5							
	6							
	7							
	8							
	9							
	10							
	11							
	12							
	13							
	14							
	15							
	16							
	17							

ENROLLMENT
OF NOS. 1 HEREON
APPROVED BY THE SECRETARY
OF INTERIOR JAN 16 1903

TRIBAL ENROLLMENT OF PARENTS

	Name of Father	Year	County	Name of Mother	Year	County
1	Jonas Watson	Dead	Nashoba	Mahantuna	Dead	Nashoba
2						
3						
4						
5						
6			No 1 is husband of No 1 on Chickasaw			
7			roll card #1045 and father of child thereon			
8			For child of No.1 see NB (Mar 3 '05) #414			
9						
10						
11						
12						
13						
14					Date of Application for Enrollment.	
15						
16					July 16/99	
17						

Choctaw By Blood Enrollment Cards 1898-1914

RESIDENCE: Cedar COUNTY. **Choctaw Nation** **Choctaw Roll** CARD No.
POST OFFICE: Tushkahomma[sic] I.T. *(Not Including Freedmen)* FIELD No. 1896

Dawes' Roll No.	NAME	Relationship to Person	AGE	SEX	BLOOD	TRIBAL ENROLLMENT		
						Year	County	No.
5420	1 Hampton Cornelius 56	First Named	53	M	Full	1896	Cedar	5432
5421	2 " Mary 56	Wife	53	F	"	1896	"	5433
	3							
	4							
	5							
	6							
	7							
	8							
	9							
	10							
	11							
	12							
	13							
	14							
	15	ENROLLMENT OF NOS. 1, 2 HEREON APPROVED BY THE SECRETARY OF INTERIOR JAN 16 1903						
	16							
	17							

TRIBAL ENROLLMENT OF PARENTS

Name of Father	Year	County	Name of Mother	Year	County
1 Felemontabe	Dead	Nashoba	Lizzie	Dead	Nashoba
2 Wm Bishop	Dead	Wade		"	Wade
3					
4					
5					
6					
7					
8					
9					
10					
11					
12					
13					
14			Date of Application for Enrollment.		
15					
16			Date of Application for Enrollment.	5/22/99	
17					

Choctaw By Blood Enrollment Cards 1898-1914

RESIDENCE: Jacks Fork   COUNTY.   **Choctaw Nation**   **Choctaw Roll**   CARD NO.
POST OFFICE: Tushkahomma[sic] I.T.   *(Not Including Freedmen)*   FIELD NO.   1897

Dawes' Roll No.	NAME		Relationship to Person First Named	AGE	SEX	BLOOD	TRIBAL ENROLLMENT		
							Year	County	No.
5422	1 Allen, David	54	First Named	51	M	Full	1896	Jacks Fork	517
5423	2 " Lydia	DIED PRIOR TO SEPTEMBER 25 1902	Wife	46	F	"	1896	" "	518
5424	3 " Rufus	23	Son	20	M	"	1896	" "	519
5425	4 " Isom	21	Son	18	M	"	1896	" "	520
5426	5 " John	9	G. Neph	6	M	"	1896	" "	739
	6								
	7								
	8								
	9								
	10								
	11								
	12								
	13								
	14								
	15	ENROLLMENT OF NOS. 1,2,3,4,5 HEREON							
	16	APPROVED BY THE SECRETARY OF INTERIOR JAN 16 1903							
	17								

TRIBAL ENROLLMENT OF PARENTS

	Name of Father	Year	County	Name of Mother	Year	County
1	Chaffatekabe	Dead	Nashoba	Sally	Dead	Nashoba
2	Willis	"	Jack's Fork		"	Jacks Fork
3	No 1			Anna Frazier	"	Nashoba
4	No 1			" "	"	Nashoba
5	Albert John	Dead	Jacks Fork	Sally Allen	"	Jacks Fork
6						
7						
8						
9						
10						
11		No5 On 1893 roll as John Ward P 83, No 739 Jacks Fork Co				
12						
13		No5 on 1896 roll, Jacks Fork Co, Page 48, No 1984 as John Battiest No3 is now husband of Adaline Benton on Choctaw card #5485				
14		Evidence of marriage filed December 15, 1902				
15	No2 died Dec 17, 1898; proof of death filed Dec 17, 1902				Date of Application for Enrollment.	
16	No.2 died Dec 17 1898 Enrollment cancelled by Department July 8, 1904				5-22-99	
17						

Choctaw By Blood Enrollment Cards 1898-1914

RESIDENCE: Wade   COUNTY. **Choctaw Nation**   **Choctaw Roll**   CARD NO.
POST OFFICE: Tushkahomma[sic] I.T.   (Not Including Freedmen)   FIELD NO. 1898

Dawes' Roll No.	NAME	Relationship to Person First Named	AGE	SEX	BLOOD	TRIBAL ENROLLMENT		
						Year	County	No.
5427	1 Spring, Solomon 25		22	M	3/4	1896	Wade	11328
5428	2 ~~Zena~~ DIED PRIOR TO SEPTEMBER 25, 1902	~~Son~~	~~7mo~~	~~M~~	~~3/8~~			
	3							
	4							
	5							
	6							
	7							
	8							
	9							
	10							
	11							
	12							
	13							
	14							
	15	ENROLLMENT OF NOS. 1,2 HEREON APPROVED BY THE SECRETARY OF INTERIOR JAN 16 1903						
	16							
	17							

TRIBAL ENROLLMENT OF PARENTS

	Name of Father	Year	County	Name of Mother	Year	County
1	Edward Spring	Ded	Wade	Sinie Spring	1896	Wade
2	~~No 1~~			~~Ida Spring~~		~~Skullyville~~
3						
4						
5						
6						
7						
8						
9						
10	No1 is husband of Ida Spring on Choctaw card #5630					
11	For wife see Doubtful Choctaw No 175					
12	No2 Enrolled Sept 25, 1901					
13	~~No2 died January 26, 1902; proof of death filed Dec 12, 1902~~					
	No.2 died Jan 26, 1902: Enrollment cancelled by Department July 8, 1904					
14						Date of Application for Enrollment.
15						
16						5-22-99
17						

Choctaw By Blood Enrollment Cards 1898-1914

POST OFFICE: Tushkahomma[sic], I.T.   *(Not Including Freedmen)*   FIELD NO. 1899

Dawes' Roll No.	NAME	Relationship to Person First Named	AGE	SEX	BLOOD	TRIBAL ENROLLMENT		
						Year	County	No.
5429	1 Noatabbe, Cilin *DIED PRIOR TO SEPTEMBER 25, 1902*	First Named	59	F	Full	1896	Cedar	9634
5430	2 " Grant ¹⁹	Son	16	M	"	1896	"	9635
5431	3 " Antlin ¹⁶	Dau	13	F	"	1896	"	9636
5432	4 " Felix ¹⁴	Son	11	M	"	1896	"	9637
	5							
	6							
	7							
	8							
	9							
	10							
	11							
	12							
	13							
	14							
	15	ENROLLMENT OF NOS. 1,2,3,4 HEREON						
	16	APPROVED BY THE SECRETARY						
	17	OF INTERIOR Jan 16 1903						

TRIBAL ENROLLMENT OF PARENTS

Name of Father	Year	County	Name of Mother	Year	County
1 An-ta-tubbee	Dead	Cedar	Sincy	Dead	Cedar
2 Louis Noatabbee	"	"	No 1		
3 " "	"	"	No 1		
4 " "	"	"	No 1		
5					
6					
7					
8					
9		No2 on 1896 roll as Grand Noatabbe			
10		No3 " 1896 " " England "			
11		No1 died January 18, 1899; proof of death filed Dec 12, 1902			
12		N°2 is now husband of Eliza A. Cole, Choctaw card #1802.			
13		No.1 died Jan. 18, 1899; Enrollment cancelled by Department July 8, 1904			
		For child of No.3 see NB (March 3, 1905) #1454			
14					
15					Date of Application for Enrollment.
16					5/22/99
17					

Choctaw By Blood Enrollment Cards 1898-1914

RESIDENCE:	Jacks Fork	COUNTY.								

Choctaw Nation — **Choctaw Roll** (Not Including Freedmen)

RESIDENCE: Jacks Fork
POST OFFICE: Stringtown, I.T.
COUNTY. Choctaw Nation
Choctaw Roll (Not Including Freedmen)
CARD NO.
FIELD NO. 1900

Dawes' Roll No.	NAME		Relationship to Person First Named	AGE	SEX	BLOOD	TRIBAL ENROLLMENT		
							Year	County	No.
5433	1 Bond, Jesse	68	First Named	65	M	Full	1896	Jacks Fork	1872
	2								
	3								
	4								
	5								
	6								
	7								
	8								
	9								
	10								
	11								
	12								
	13								
	14								
	15								
	16								
	17								

ENROLLMENT
OF NOS. 1 HEREON
APPROVED BY THE SECRETARY
OF INTERIOR JAN 16 1903

TRIBAL ENROLLMENT OF PARENTS

	Name of Father	Year	County	Name of Mother	Year	County
1	Na-ka-steah	Dead	in Mississippi	Ish-te-ma-ya	Dead	Gaines
2						
3						
4						
5			No 1 is husband of No 1 on Chickasaw roll card			
6			#648 and father of children thereon.			
7						
8						
9						
10						
11						
12						
13						
14						
15						
16				Date of Application for Enrollment.	5/22/99	
17						

Choctaw By Blood Enrollment Cards 1898-1914

RESIDENCE: Atoka   COUNTY. **Choctaw Nation**   **Choctaw Roll** *(Not Including Freedmen)*   CARD NO.

POST OFFICE: Guertie I.T.   FIELD NO. **1901**

Dawes' Roll No.	NAME		Relationship to Person First Named	AGE	SEX	BLOOD	TRIBAL ENROLLMENT		
							Year	County	No.
5434	1 Anderson, Charles	31	Named	28	M	1/2	1893	Kiamatia[sic]	P.R. 25
I.W. 898	2 " Lue	(31)	Wife	26	F	I.W.	1896	Jacks Fork	14268
5435	3 " Eva	9	Dau	6	"	1/4	1893	Kiamatia[sic]	P.R. 26
5436	4 " Lillie	6	"	3	"	1/4			
	5								
No 2	6 Evid. req. Oct 29-03								
	7								
	8								
	9 ENROLLMENT OF NOS. 2 HEREON								
	10 APPROVED BY THE SECRETARY OF INTERIOR Aug 3 1904								
	11								
	12								
	13								
	14 ENROLLMENT OF NOS. 1,3,4 HEREON								
	15 APPROVED BY THE SECRETARY OF INTERIOR Jan 16 1903								
	16								
	17								

TRIBAL ENROLLMENT OF PARENTS

	Name of Father	Year	County	Name of Mother	Year	County
1	Rogers Anderson	1896	Kiamatia[sic]	Lucinda Wade	1896	Tobucksy
2	Joe Satterfield		Non Citz	Eliza Jane Satterfield		Non Citz
3	No 1			No 2		
4	No 1			No 2		
5						
6						
7						
8	For child of Nos 1&2 see NB (March 3 1905) #1342					
9				No 2 on 1896 roll as Lula Anderson		
10				No 1 on 1893 Pay Roll #25 page 115		
11				Kiamatia[sic] Co, as Chas. Anderson.		
12				No one attended Mrs Anderson		
13				at birth of Lillie Anderson		
14	P.O. Farris I.T. 4/20/05			except sister and she lives		
15				in Arkansas.		Date of Application for Enrollment.
16						
17	P.O. Caloway[sic] I.T. 1/20/02	12/23-03 P O Red Oak I T				5-22-99

101

RESIDENCE: Jacks Fork		COUNTY.	**Choctaw Nation**				Choctaw Roll		CARD NO.	
POST OFFICE: Tushkahomma[sic] I.T.							(Not Including Freedmen)		FIELD NO.	**1902**

Dawes' Roll No.	NAME	Relationship to Person First Named	AGE	SEX	BLOOD	TRIBAL ENROLLMENT		
						Year	County	No.
14896	1 Anderson Bradley	First Named	22	M	Full	1893	Kiamitia	27
I.W. 1401	2 " Ada	Wife	19	F	I.W.			
	3							
	4							
	5 CITIZENSHIP CERTIFICATE							
	6 ISSUED FOR NO 1 AUG 15 1903							
	7							
	8							
	9							
TIFICATE	10							
OR NO 2 1907	11 ENROLLMENT							
	12 OF NOS. ~~2~~ HEREON APPROVED BY THE SECRETARY							
	13 OF INTERIOR JUN 12 1905							
	14							
	15 ENROLLMENT OF NOS. One HEREON							
	16 APPROVED BY THE SECRETARY OF INTERIOR MAY 21 1903							
	17							

TRIBAL ENROLLMENT OF PARENTS

	Name of Father	Year	County	Name of Mother	Year	County
1	Jesse Baker	Dead	Jacks Fork	Lucinda Squire	1896	Tobucksy
2	J.W. Davis		non citizen	Mary F. Davis		non citizen
3						
4						
5	No2 originally listed for enrollment on Choctaw card #D-687 Nov. 16, 1901;					
6	transferred to this card May 15, 1905: See decision of April 22, 1905					
7						
8	On 1893 Pay roll Kiamitia Co Page 115, No 27					
9						
10	Correct name of No1 is Bradley Anderson See testimony taken					
11	this day in Choctaw case D #687					
12	No 1 is the husband of Ada Anderson on Choctaw Card D#687					
13	P.O. Address. Pontotoc I.T. Sept 13, 1902					
14	Mother of No 1 on Choc 5766					
15						
16					5/22/99	
17						

Choctaw By Blood Enrollment Cards 1898-1914

RESIDENCE: Wade COUNTY. **Choctaw Nation** Choctaw Roll CARD NO.
POST OFFICE: Tushkahomma[sic], I.T. (Not Including Freedmen) FIELD NO. **1903**

Dawes Roll No.		NAME		Relationship to Person First Named	AGE	SEX	BLOOD	TRIBAL ENROLLMENT		
								Year	County	No.
5437	1	Spring, Siney	53	First Named	50	F	3/4	1896	Wade	11326
5438	2	" Winnie	42	Dau	39	"	5/8	1896	"	11329
5439	3	" Nancy	22	"	19	"	5/8	1896	"	11330
5440	4	" Rebecca	15	Dau	12	F	5/8	1896	"	11331
(illegible)	5	Bryant, Bert	1	Gr Son	5mo	M	3/4			
	6									
	7									
	8									
	9									
	10									
	11									
	12									
	13									
	14									
	15	ENROLLMENT OF NOS. 1,2,3,4 HEREON APPROVED BY THE SECRETARY OF INTERIOR JAN 15 1903			ENROLLMENT OF NOS. 5 HEREON APPROVED BY THE SECRETARY OF INTERIOR MAY 20 1903						
	16									
	17									

TRIBAL ENROLLMENT OF PARENTS

	Name of Father	Year	County	Name of Mother	Year	County
1	Reuben Anderson	Dead	Jacks Fork	Ho-tu-na	Dead	Wade
2	Eward[sic] Spring	"	Wade	No 1		
3	" "	"	"	No 1		
4	" "	"	"	No 1		
5	William Bryant	1896	"	Nº3		
6						
7			Nº 3 was wife of No.1 on Choctaw card #1942			
8			who is now dead.			
9			Nº5 Born July 11, 1902 enrolled Dec. 24 1902.			
10						
11						
12						
13						
14						
15					#1 to 4 inc	
16				Date of Application for Enrollment:	5/22/99	
17						

Choctaw By Blood Enrollment Cards 1898-1914

RESIDENCE: Jacks Fork COUNTY. **Choctaw Nation** **Choctaw Roll** (*Not Including Freedmen*) CARD NO.
POST OFFICE: Tushkahomma[sic], I.T. FIELD NO. 1904

Dawes' Roll No.		NAME	Relationship to Person	AGE	SEX	BLOOD	TRIBAL ENROLLMENT		
							Year	County	No.
Wanted	1 a.w.	Henderson, George W[37]	First Named	33	M	I.W.			
DEAD.	2	" Hattie DEAD.	Wife	20	F	1/4	1896	Jacks Fork	6096
DEAD.	3	" Nancy E DEAD.	Dau	9mo	"	1/8			
	4								
	5								
	6	No. 2 and 3 HEREON DISMISSED UNDER ORDER OF THE COMMISSION TO THE FIVE							
	7	CIVILIZED TRIBES OF MARCH 31, 1905.							
	8								
	9								
	10								
	11								
	12								
	13								
	14	Judgement[sic] of U.S. Court admitting No.1 vacated and set aside by Decree of Choctaw							
	15	Chickasaw Citizenship Court Dec[r] 17 '02							
	16	No.1 in C.C.C.C. case # 112 3/16/03							
	17								

TRIBAL ENROLLMENT OF PARENTS

	Name of Father	Year	County	Name of Mother	Year	County
1	B.P. Henderson	1896	Non Citz	Nancy Henderson	1896	Non Citz
2	J.C. Hewitt	1896	" "	Edna Hewitt	1896	Jacks Fork
3	No 1			No 2		
4						
5	No2 on 1896 roll as Hattie Hewitt					
6						
7	No3 Affidavit of birth to be supplied					
8	See testimony of No.1 as to death of Nos 2 and 3					
9	No1 admitted as a citizen by blood; (Dec. 11 1900) by U.S. Court, Central district, Ind. Ter., Jany, 18th, 1898,					
10	Court case #44, Nancy Henderson vs. Choctaw Nation					
11						
12						
13						
14					Date of Application for Enrollment.	
15						
16					5/22/99	
17	P O Stringtown IT					

104

Choctaw By Blood Enrollment Cards 1898-1914

RESIDENCE: Jacks Fork   COUNTY. **Choctaw Nation**   **Choctaw Roll** CARD No.
POST OFFICE: Stringtown, I.T.   *(Not Including Freedmen)* FIELD No. 1905

Dawes' Roll No.	NAME	Relationship to Person First Named	AGE	SEX	BLOOD	TRIBAL ENROLLMENT		
						Year	County	No.
5441	1 Bond, Lizzie 38	First Named	35	F	Full	1896	Jacks Fork	2974
	2							
	3							
	4							
	5							
	6							
	7							
	8							
	9							
	10							
	11							
	12							
	13							
	14							
	15							
	16							
	17							

ENROLLMENT
OF NOS. 1 HEREON
APPROVED BY THE SECRETARY
OF INTERIOR JAN 16 1903

TRIBAL ENROLLMENT OF PARENTS

Name of Father	Year	County	Name of Mother	Year	County
1 Aleck Billy	Ded	Jacks Fork	Susan Perry	1896	Jacks Fork
2					
3					
4		On 1896 roll as Lizzie Carnes.			
5					
6					
7					
8					
9					
10					
11					
12					
13					
14				Date of Application for Enrollment.	
15					
16				5/22/99	
17					

Choctaw By Blood Enrollment Cards 1898-1914

RESIDENCE: Jacks Fork	COUNTY.							
POST OFFICE: Stringtown, I.T.	**Choctaw Nation**							

CARD NO.
FIELD NO. 1906

Choctaw Roll (Not Including Freedmen)

Dawes' Roll No.	NAME	Relationship to Person First Named	AGE	SEX	BLOOD	TRIBAL ENROLLMENT		
						Year	County	No.
5442	1 Folsom, Eliza DIED PRIOR TO SEPTEMBER 25, 1902		80	F	Full	1896	Jacks Fork	6124
	2							
	3							
	4							
	5							
	6							
	7							
	8							
	9							
	10							
	11							
	12							
	13							
	14							
	15							
	16							
	17							

ENROLLMENT
OF NOS. 1 HEREON
APPROVED BY THE SECRETARY
OF INTERIOR JAN 16 1903

TRIBAL ENROLLMENT OF PARENTS

	Name of Father	Year	County	Name of Mother	Year	County
1	A-nok-fi-le-hana	Dead	Red River	Yi-me-hu-na	Dead	in Mississippi
2						
3						
4						
5	No.1 died October 21, 1900; proof of death filed Nov 25, 1902					
6	No.1 died Oct 21, 1900	Enrollment cancelled by Department July 8, 1904				
7						
8						
9						
10						
11						
12						
13						
14						
15					Date of Application for Enrollment.	
16					5/22/99	
17						

106

Choctaw By Blood Enrollment Cards 1898-1914

RESIDENCE: Jacks Fork	COUNTY.							CARD NO.	
POST OFFICE: Tushkahomma[sic], I.T.	**Choctaw Nation**					Choctaw Roll (Not Including Freedmen)		FIELD NO. 1907	

Dawes' Roll No.	NAME	Relationship to Person First Named	AGE	SEX	BLOOD	TRIBAL ENROLLMENT		
						Year	County	No.
5443	1 Bohanan, Nicholas 24		21	M	Full	1896	Jacks Fork	1966
5444	2 ~~DIED PRIOR TO SEPTEMBER 25 1902~~ ~~Lillie~~	~~Wife~~	~~19~~	~~F~~	~~"~~	~~1896~~	~~" "~~	~~506~~
5445	3 ~~DIED PRIOR TO SEPTEMBER 25, 1902~~ ~~Ritchard~~	~~Son~~	~~1 1/2 mo~~	~~M~~	~~"~~			
	4							
	5							
	6							
	7							
	8							
	9							
	10							
	11							
	12							
	13							
	14							
	15	ENROLLMENT OF NOS. 1,2,3 HEREON APPROVED BY THE SECRETARY OF INTERIOR JAN 16 1903						
	16							
	17							

TRIBAL ENROLLMENT OF PARENTS

	Name of Father	Year	County	Name of Mother	Year	County
1	Ellis Bohanan	1896	Jacks Fork	Patsey Bohanan	Dead	Wade
2	~~Burney Anderson~~	~~Dead~~	~~" "~~	~~Susan Anderson~~	~~1896~~	~~Jacks Fork~~
3	No 1			No 2		
4						
5						
6			No2 on 1896 roll as Lillie Anderson			
7						
8			No2 died April 10, 1901; proof of death filed Dec 12, 1902			
9			No3 " April 12, 1901; " " " " " " "			
10	No.2 died April 10, 1901; No.3 died April 12, 1901; Enrollment cancelled by Department July 8, 1904					
11						
12						
13						
14						
15					Date of Application for Enrollment.	
16			No3 enrolled 6/5/1900		5/22/99	
17						

Choctaw By Blood Enrollment Cards 1898-1914

RESIDENCE: Jacks Fork	COUNTY. **Choctaw Nation**	**Choctaw Roll** *(Not Including Freedmen)*	CARD No.
POST OFFICE: Stringtown, I.T.			FIELD No. 1908

Dawes' Roll No.	NAME	Relationship to Person	AGE	SEX	BLOOD	TRIBAL ENROLLMENT		
						Year	County	No.
5446	1 Frazier, Jackson 23	First Named	20	M	Full	1896	Jacks Fork	4506
	2							
	3							
	4							
	5							
	6							
	7							
	8							
	9							
	10							
	11							
	12							
	13							
	14							
	15							
	16							
	17							

ENROLLMENT
OF NOS. 1 HEREON
APPROVED BY THE SECRETARY
OF INTERIOR JAN 16 1903

TRIBAL ENROLLMENT OF PARENTS

	Name of Father	Year	County	Name of Mother	Year	County
1	David Frazier	Dead	Jacks Fork	Liley Frazier	Dead	Jacks Fork
2						
3						
4						
5	Nº1 is now the husband of Sarah Johnson on Choctaw card #1783, Oct. 15, 1902.					
6						
7						
8						
9						
10						
11						
12						
13						
14					Date of Application for Enrollment.	
15						
16					5/22/99	
17						

108

Choctaw By Blood Enrollment Cards 1898-1914

	RESIDENCE: Wade COUNTY.								
	POST OFFICE: Tushkahomma[sic] I.T.	**Choctaw Nation**			**Choctaw Roll** (Not Including Freedmen)	CARD NO. FIELD NO. **1909**			

Dawes' Roll No.	NAME	Relationship to Person First Named	AGE	SEX	BLOOD	TRIBAL ENROLLMENT		
						Year	County	No.
5447	1 Williams Betsy 65	Named	57	F	Full	1896	Wade	13118
5448	2 Yolah, Joshua 25	Son	22	M	"	1896	"	14226
	3							
	4							
	5							
CERTIFICATE 2 15 1903	6							
	7							
	8							
	9	ENROLLMENT						
	10	OF NOS. 1 and 2 HEREON APPROVED BY THE SECRETARY						
	11	OF INTERIOR Jan 16 1903						
	12							
	13							
	14							
ERTIFICATE 1904	15							
	16							
	17							

TRIBAL ENROLLMENT OF PARENTS

Name of Father	Year	County	Name of Mother	Year	County
1 Ok-lash-ta	Dead	Wade	O-che-hu-na	Dead	Wade
2 Jesse Yolah	"	Jacks Fork	No 1		
3					
4					
5					
6					
7					
8					
9					
10					
11					
12					
13					
14					
15					
16				5/22/99	
17					

Choctaw By Blood Enrollment Cards 1898-1914

RESIDENCE: Jacks Fork
POST OFFICE: Stringtown, I.T

COUNTY. **Choctaw Nation**

Choctaw Roll
(Not Including Freedmen)

CARD NO.

FIELD NO. 1910

Dawes' Roll No.	NAME		Relationship to Person First Named	AGE	SEX	BLOOD	TRIBAL ENROLLMENT		
							Year	County	No.
5449	1 Calvin, Ellen	39	First Named	36	F	Full	1896	Jacks Fork	3041
5450	2 Graham, David	19	Son	16	M	"	1896	" "	3042
5451	3 Calvin, Nelson	DIED PRIOR TO SEPTEMBER 25, 1902	"	12	"	"	1896	" "	3043
5452	4 " Betsy	12	Dau	9	F	"	1896	" "	3044
5453	5 " Edmond	6	Son	3	M	"	1896	" "	3045
	6								
	7								
	8								
	9								
	10								
	11								
	12								
	13								
	14								
	15								
	16								
	17								

ENROLLMENT
OF NOS. 1,2,3,4,5 HEREON
APPROVED BY THE SECRETARY
OF INTERIOR JAN 16 1903

TRIBAL ENROLLMENT OF PARENTS

	Name of Father	Year	County	Name of Mother	Year	County
1	Mitchell Cavin[sic]	Dead	Jacks Fork	Betsey Cavin[sic]	Dead	Jacks Fork
2	Charles Graham	"	" " "	No 1		
3	Joshia[sic] Calvin	"	" " "	No 1		
4	"	"	" " "	No 1		
5	"	"	" " "	No 1		
6						
7						
8			No2 on 1896 roll as Louie Cobb			
9			No3 died Nov, 1901; proof of death filed Dec 12, 1902			
10			No.3 died Nov - 1901; Enrollment cancelled by Department July 8, 1904			
11						
12						
13						
14						
15				Date of Application for Enrollment.		
16				5/22/99		
17						

Choctaw By Blood Enrollment Cards 1898-1914

RESIDENCE: Jackson	COUNTY.						
POST OFFICE: Bennington I.T.	Choctaw Nation	Choctaw Roll (Not Including Freedmen)		CARD NO. FIELD NO. **1911**			

Dawes' Roll No.	NAME	Relationship to Person	AGE	SEX	BLOOD	TRIBAL ENROLLMENT		
						Year	County	No.
5454	1 Jones Rodgers 24	First Named	21	M	Full	1896	Jackson	7095
	2							
	3							
	4							
	5							
	6							
	7							
	8							
	9							
	10							
	11							
	12							
	13							
	14							
	15							
	16							
	17							

ENROLLMENT
OF NOS. 1 HEREON
APPROVED BY THE SECRETARY
OF INTERIOR Jan 16 1903

TRIBAL ENROLLMENT OF PARENTS

	Name of Father	Year	County	Name of Mother	Year	County
1	Billie Jones	1896	Jackson	Isabel Going	Dead	Jackson
2						
3						
4						
5						
6			On 1896 roll as Rogers Jones.			
7						
8						
9						
10						
11						
12						
13						
14						
15					Date of Application for Enrollment.	
16					5/22/99	
17						

RESIDENCE: Jacks Fork	COUNTY:	**Choctaw Nation**			Choctaw Roll	CARD NO.		
OFFICE: Stringtown, I.T					(Not Including Freedmen)	FIELD NO.		1912

Dawes' Roll No.	NAME	Relationship to Person First Named	AGE	SEX	BLOOD	TRIBAL ENROLLMENT		
						Year	County	No.
455 ₁	Perry, Israel M ⁵³	Named	50	M	Full	1896	Jacks Fork	10589
456 ₂	" Susan ⁶⁹	Wife	66	F	"	1896	" "	10590
457 ₃	Billy, John F ¹³	Ward	10	M	"	1896	" "	1885
₄								
₅								
₆								
₇								
₈								
₉								
₁₀								
₁₁								
₁₂								
₁₃								
₁₄								
₁₅	ENROLLMENT OF NOS. 1,2,3 HEREON APPROVED BY THE SECRETARY OF INTERIOR JAN 16 1903							
₁₆								
₁₇								

TRIBAL ENROLLMENT OF PARENTS

	Name of Father	Year	County	Name of Mother	Year	County
₁	Moses Perry	Dead	Atoka	Betsey Perry	Dead	Jacks Fork
₂	Ca-ne-mon-tubbee	"	Jacks Fork		"	Bok Tuklo
₃	Jeff Billy	Dead	Jacks Fork	Cillen Billy	Dead	Jacks Fork
₄						
₅						
₆						
₇			No 1 on 1896 roll as I.W. Perry			
₈						
₉						
₁₀						
₁₁						
₁₂						
₁₃						
₁₄						
₁₅						
₁₆				DATE OF APPLICATION FOR ENROLLMENT.	5/22/99	
₁₇						

112

Choctaw By Blood Enrollment Cards 1898-1914

RESIDENCE: Cedar COUNTY.
POST OFFICE: Tushkahomma[sic], I.T. **Choctaw Nation**

Choctaw Roll (Not Including Freedmen)

CARD NO.
FIELD NO. 1913

Dawes' Roll No.		NAME		Relationship to Person	AGE	SEX	BLOOD	TRIBAL ENROLLMENT		
								Year	County	No.
5458	1	Edward, Allington	47	First Named	44	M	Full	1896	Cedar	3721
5459	2	" Sissie	42	Wife	39	F	"	1893	Jacks Fork	533
	3									
	4									
	5									
	6									
	7									
	8									
	9									
	10									
	11									
	12									
	13									
	14									
	15	ENROLLMENT OF NOS. 1,2 HEREON								
	16	APPROVED BY THE SECRETARY OF INTERIOR JAN 16 1903								
	17									

TRIBAL ENROLLMENT OF PARENTS

	Name of Father	Year	County	Name of Mother	Year	County
1	Tobias Edward	1896	Jackson	Rhoda Edward	Dead	Wade
2	William Ward	Dead	Cedar	Nellie Ward	"	Cedar
3						
4						
5						
6						
7	No2 on 1893 Pay roll as Sissie Misher, Page 60, No 533, Jacks Fork Co					
8	also on 1896 roll Page 223, No 8886 as Narcissa Misha					
9						
10						
11						
12						
13						
14						
15						
16				Date of Application for Enrollment.	5/22/99	
17	P.O. Nashoba, Okla 2/6/08					

113

RESIDENCE: Jacks Fork COUNTY. **Choctaw Nation** **Choctaw Roll** *(Not Including Freedmen)* CARD NO.

POST OFFICE: Tushkahomma[sic], I.T. FIELD NO. 1914

Dawes' Roll No.	NAME	Relationship to Person	AGE	SEX	BLOOD	TRIBAL ENROLLMENT		
						Year	County	No.
5460	1 Cravette, Amy 39	First Named	36	F	Full	1896	Jacks Fork	1893
	2							
	3							
	4							
	5							
	6							
	7							
	8							
	9							
	10							
	11							
	12							
	13							
	14							
	15							
	16							
	17							

ENROLLMENT
OF NOS. 1 HEREON
APPROVED BY THE SECRETARY
OF INTERIOR JAN 16 1903

TRIBAL ENROLLMENT OF PARENTS

	Name of Father	Year	County	Name of Mother	Year	County
1	Silas Cravette	Dead	Jackson	Ellen Cravette	Dead	Jackson
2						
3						
4						
5						
6	On 1896 roll as Sinie Billy					
7	Nº1 now wife of George W. Bell Choctaw card #2145 Dec/02					
8						
9						
10						
11						
12						
13						
14						
15						
16			Date of Application for Enrollment.	5/22/99		
17						

Choctaw By Blood Enrollment Cards 1898-1914

RESIDENCE: Jacks Fork COUNTY. **Choctaw Nation**   **Choctaw Roll** (Not Including Freedmen)   CARD NO.
POST OFFICE: Tushkahomma[sic], I.T.   FIELD NO. **1915**

Dawes' Roll No.		NAME		Relationship to Person First Named	AGE	SEX	BLOOD	TRIBAL ENROLLMENT		
								Year	County	No.
5461	1	Bohanan, Simpson	26	First Named	23	M	1/2	1896	Jacks Fork	1957
5462	2	" Sinie	23	Wife	20	F	Full	1896	" "	523
5463	3	" John	4	Son	6mo	M	3/4			
	4									
	5									
	6									
	7									
	8									
	9									
	10									
	11									
	12									
	13									
	14									
	15									
	16									
	17									

ENROLLMENT
OF NOS. 1,2,3 HEREON
APPROVED BY THE SECRETARY
OF INTERIOR Jan 16, 1903

TRIBAL ENROLLMENT OF PARENTS

	Name of Father	Year	County	Name of Mother	Year	County
1	Ellis Bohanan	1896	Jacks Fork	Patsey Bohanan	Dead	Wade
2	Dixon Anderson	Dead	" "	Louisana[sic] Anderson	1896	Jacks Fork
3	No 1			No 2		
4						
5						
6	No 1 on 1896 roll as Sim Bohanan					
7	No2 " 1896 " " Sinie Anderson					
8	For child of Nos 1&2 see N.B. (Apr. 26, 1896) Card No. 195					
	" " " " " " " (Mar 3rd 1905) " " 66					
9						
10						
11						
12						
13						
14						
15				Date of Application for Enrollment.		
16				5/22/99		
17						

Choctaw By Blood Enrollment Cards 1898-1914

RESIDENCE: Jacks Fork   COUNTY. **Choctaw Nation**   **Choctaw Roll**   CARD NO.
POST OFFICE: Tushkahomma[sic], I.T.   (Not Including Freedmen)   FIELD NO. 1916

Dawes' Roll No.	NAME		Relationship to Person First Named	AGE	SEX	BLOOD	TRIBAL ENROLLMENT		
							Year	County	No.
5464	1 Calvin, Sissie	36	First Named	23	F	Full	1896	Jacks Fork	7338
5465	2 John, Robert	16	Son	13	M	"	1896	" "	7344
5466	3 " Emerson	13	"	10	"	"	1896	" "	7339
5467	4 " Mary	7	Dau	4	F	"	1896	" "	7341
	5								
	6								
ZENSHIP CERTIFICATE	7								
ED FOR NO 8	1-2-3-4 JUL 7 1903								
	9								
	10	ENROLLMENT							
	11	OF NOS. 1 2 3 and 4 HEREON APPROVED BY THE SECRETARY							
	12	OF INTERIOR JAN 16 1903							
	13								
	14								
	15								
	16								
	17								

TRIBAL ENROLLMENT OF PARENTS

	Name of Father	Year	County	Name of Mother	Year	County
1	Joe Anderson	Dead	Jacks Fork	Julie A Anderson	Dead	Jacks Fork
2	Colbert John	"	" "	No 1		
3	" "	"	" "	No 1		
4	" "	"	" "	No 1		
5						
6						
7			No 1 on 1896 roll as Siston John			
8						
9						
10						
11						
12						
13						
14						
15						
16						5/22/99
17						

Choctaw By Blood Enrollment Cards 1898-1914

RESIDENCE:	Wade	COUNTY.						CARD No.	
POST OFFICE:	Tushkahomma[sic], I.T.	**Choctaw Nation**			**Choctaw Roll** *(Not Including Freedmen)*			FIELD No.	**1917**

Dawes' Roll No.	NAME	Relationship to Person First Named	AGE	SEX	BLOOD	TRIBAL ENROLLMENT		
						Year	County	No.
I.W. 99	1 Isherwood, William H	Named	39	M	I.W	1896	Wade	14677
5468	2 " Josephine R 27	Wife	25	F	1/2	1896	"	6256
5469	3 " Lillie I 7	Dau	4	"	1/4	1896	"	6257
5470	4 " Edgar R 5	Son	2	M	1/4	DIED PRIOR TO SEPTEMBER 25, 1902		
5471	5 " Pearl I 1	Dau	3wks	F	1/4			
	6							
	7							
	8							
	9							
	10	ENROLLMENT OF NOS. 2 3 4 and 5 HEREON APPROVED BY THE SECRETARY OF INTERIOR JAN 16 1903						
	11							
	12							
	13							
	14	ENROLLMENT OF NOS. 1 HEREON APPROVED BY THE SECRETARY OF INTERIOR JUN 13 1903						
	15							
	16							
	17							

TRIBAL ENROLLMENT OF PARENTS

	Name of Father	Year	County	Name of Mother	Year	County
1	Robert J Isherwood		Non Citz	Isabella A. Isherwood		Non Citz
2	G.W. Thompson	1896	Wade	Isabell Thompson	1896	Wade
3	No 1			No 2		
4	No 1			No 2		
5	No 1			No 2		
6						
7	No 4 Died Jan 24, 1900: Enrollment cancelled by Department September 16, 1904					
8						
9						
10			No1 on 1896 roll as Wm Isherwood			
11			No2 " " " " Josephine Isherwood			
12			No3 " " " " Lillie "			
			No5 Enrolled June 3, 1901			
13			The full correct name of No 2 is Josephine Roena Isherwood. See			
14			letter of W.H. Isherwood filed June 11, 1901.			
15	No 4 died January 24, 1900; proof of death filed Dec 12, 1902					
16						5-22-99
17						

117

Choctaw By Blood Enrollment Cards 1898-1914

RESIDENCE: Jacks Fork		COUNTY. **Choctaw Nation**				**Choctaw Roll**	CARD NO.	
POST OFFICE: Kosoma I.T.						(Not Including Freedmen)	FIELD NO.	**1918**

Dawes' Roll No.	NAME	Relationship to Person	AGE	SEX	BLOOD	TRIBAL ENROLLMENT		
						Year	County	No.
5472	1 Battiest Franseway 66	First Named	63	M	Full	1896	Jacks Fork	1971
	2							
	3							
	4							
	5							
	6							
	7							

HIP CERTIFICATE
N° 1
JL 23 1903

8
9

10
ENROLLMENT
11 OF NOS. 1 HEREON
APPROVED BY THE SECRETARY
12 OF INTERIOR JAN 16 1903
13

14
15
16
17

TRIBAL ENROLLMENT OF PARENTS

	Name of Father	Year	County	Name of Mother	Year	County
1	Onatabe	Ded	Bok Tuklo	Nayoke	Ded	Jacks Fork
2						
3						
4						
5						
6	No 1 is now husband of Liney Elachetubbe Choctaw card #1574					
7						
8						
9						
10						
11						
12						
13						
14						
15						
16						5-22-99
17						

118

Choctaw By Blood Enrollment Cards 1898-1914

RESIDENCE: Jacks Fork   COUNTY. **Choctaw Nation**   **Choctaw Roll** CARD NO.
POST OFFICE: Tushkahomma[sic], I.T.   *(Not Including Freedmen)*   FIELD NO. **1919**

Dawes' Roll No.	NAME		Relationship to Person First Named	AGE	SEX	BLOOD	TRIBAL ENROLLMENT		
							Year	County	No.
5473	1 Billy Melvina	37	Named	34	F	Full	1896	Jacks Fork	10609
5474	2 Peter Osborn	15	Son	12	M	3/4	1896	" "	10610
5475	3 " Jacob	12	"	9	"	3/4	1896	" "	10611
5476	4 " Caroline	9	Dau	6	F	3/4	1896	" "	10612
5477	5 " Billy	6	Son	3	M	3/4	1896	" "	10613
5478	6 " James	5	"	1	"	3/4			
5479	7 Billy Helen	1	Dau	4mo	F	5/8			
	8								
	9								
	10	ENROLLMENT							
TIFICATE 7	11	OF NOS. 1 2 3 4 5 6 and 7 HEREON APPROVED BY THE SECRETARY							
	12	OF INTERIOR JAN 16 1903							
	13								
2-3-4-5-6	14								
	15								
	16								
	17								

TRIBAL ENROLLMENT OF PARENTS

	Name of Father	Year	County	Name of Mother	Year	County
1	Gimpson[sic] Carns	Ded	Jacks Fork	Micey Carns	Ded	Jacks Fork
2	Aaron Peter	"	" "	No 1		
3	" "	"	" "	No 1		
4	" "	"	" "	No 1		
5	" "	"	" "	No 1		
6	" "	"	" "	No 1		
7	Isom Billy	1896	Jacks Fork	No 1		
8						
9						
10	No 1 is now the wife of Isom Billy on Choctaw card #1887: Evidence					
11	of marriage requested May 7, 1902					
12	No 7 Born Jany 19, 1902; enrolled May 7, 1902					
13						
14						
15						
16					5-22-99	
17						

119

Choctaw By Blood Enrollment Cards 1898-1914

RESIDENCE: Wade COUNTY.
POST OFFICE: Tushkahomma[sic] I.T. **Choctaw Nation**

Choctaw Roll (Not Including Freedmen)

CARD NO.

FIELD NO. 1920

Dawes' Roll No.	NAME	Relationship to Person	AGE	SEX	BLOOD	TRIBAL ENROLLMENT		
						Year	County	No.
5480	1 Whartner Sophia ²¹	First Named	18	F	Full	1893	Wade	P.R. 338
	2							
	3							
	4	Died prior to September 25, 1902; not entitled to land or money						
	5	(See Indian Office letter Aug 25-1910 D.C. #1204-1910)						
	6							
	7							
	8							
	9							
	10							
	11							
	12							
	13							
	14							
	15	ENROLLMENT OF NOS. 1 HEREON APPROVED BY THE SECRETARY OF INTERIOR JAN 16 1903						
	16							
	17							

TRIBAL ENROLLMENT OF PARENTS

	Name of Father	Year	County	Name of Mother	Year	County
1	Delen Whartner	Ded	Wade	Eliza Whartner	Ded	Wade
2						
3						
4						
5						
6		Died June 24 1900 Investigating				
7						
8						
9						
10						
11						
12						
13						
14					Date of Application for Enrollment.	
15					5-22-99	
16						
17						

Choctaw By Blood Enrollment Cards 1898-1914

RESIDENCE: Jacks Fork COUNTY. **Choctaw Nation** Choctaw Roll CARD No.

POST OFFICE: Tushkahomma[sic] I.T. *(Not Including Freedmen)* FIELD No. 1921

Dawes' Roll No.	NAME	Relationship to Person First Named	AGE	SEX	BLOOD	TRIBAL ENROLLMENT		
						Year	County	No.
5481	1 M°Gee Ellen DIED PRIOR TO SEPTEMBER 25 24 902	First Named	21	F	Full	1896	Jacks Fork	6131
	2							
	3							
	4							
	5							
	6							
	7							
	8							
	9							
	10							
	11							
	12							
	13							
	14							
	15							
	16							
	17							

ENROLLMENT
OF NOS. 1 HEREON
APPROVED BY THE SECRETARY
OF INTERIOR JAN 16 1903

TRIBAL ENROLLMENT OF PARENTS

	Name of Father	Year	County	Name of Mother	Year	County
1	James Peter	Ded	Jacks Fork	Mary Peter	Ded	Atoka
2						
3						
4						
5			On 1896 roll as Ellen Horne			
6			Husband on Chickasaw rolls No 1433 in Choctaw Nation			
7			No 1 died Dec 4, 1898; proof of death filed Dec 15, 1902			
8			No.1 died Dec. 4, 1898 Enrollment cancelled by Department July 8, 1904			
9						
10						
11						
12						
13						
14						Date of Application for Enrollment.
15						
16						5-22-99
17						

121

Choctaw By Blood Enrollment Cards 1898-1914

RESIDENCE: Jacks Fork COUNTY. **Choctaw Nation** **Choctaw Roll** CARD NO.
POST OFFICE: Tushkahomma[sic] I.T. (Not Including Freedmen) FIELD NO. **1922**

Dawes' Roll No.	NAME	Relationship to Person	AGE	SEX	BLOOD	TRIBAL ENROLLMENT		
						Year	County	No.
5482	1 Impson, Ellis ³²	First Named	29	M	Full	1893	Jacks Fork	431
	2							
	3							
	4							
	5							
	6							
	7							
	8							
	9							
	10							
	11							
	12							
	13							
	14							
	15	ENROLLMENT OF NOS. 1 HEREON						
	16	APPROVED BY THE SECRETARY OF INTERIOR Jan 16 1903						
	17							

TRIBAL ENROLLMENT OF PARENTS

	Name of Father	Year	County	Name of Mother	Year	County
1	Morris Impson	1896	Jacks Fork	Selina Impson	Dead	Jacks Fork
2						
3						
4						
5						
6						
7	On 1893 Pay Roll Page 47 No 431 Jacks Fork Co					
8						
9						
10						
11						
12						
13						
14						
15						
16				Date of Application for Enrollment.	5/22/99	
17						

Choctaw By Blood Enrollment Cards 1898-1914

RESIDENCE: **Wade**　COUNTY. **Choctaw Nation**　**Choctaw Roll** *(Not Including Freedmen)*　CARD NO.

POST OFFICE: **Lyceum, I.T.**　FIELD NO. **1923**

Dawes' Roll No.	NAME	Relationship to Person First Named	AGE	SEX	BLOOD	TRIBAL ENROLLMENT Year	County	No.
5483	1 Hudson, Peter J 41		38	M	Full	1896	Wade	5407
5484	2　"　Amanda J 28	Wife	25	F	1/2	1896	"	5408
5485	3　"　Helen 9	Dau	6	"	3/4	1896	"	5409
5486	4　"　Preston 7	Son	4	M	3/4	1896	"	5410
5487	5　"　Irene 5	Dau	2	F	3/4			
5488	6　"　Nathan Hale 2	Son	2mo	M	3/4			
	7							
	8							
	9							
	10							
	11							
	12							
	13							
	14							
	15	ENROLLMENT OF NOS. 1,2,3,4,5,6 HEREON APPROVED BY THE SECRETARY OF INTERIOR Jan 16 1903						
	16							
	17							

TRIBAL ENROLLMENT OF PARENTS

	Name of Father	Year	County	Name of Mother	Year	County
1	James Hudson	Dead	Eagle	Ah-ho-bo-tema	Dead	Eagle
2	S. H. Bohanan	1896	Wade	Margaret Bohanan	1896	Wade
3	No 1			No 2		
4	No 1			No 2		
5	No 1			No 2		
6	No 1			No 2		
7						
8	No.6 Enrolled May 23, 1901					
9	No 1 is guardian of Enoch Willis and Isham Hudson on Choctaw					
10	card #732. Letters of guardianship filed December 15, 1902					
11						
12	For child of Nos 1&2 see NB (Apr 26-06) Card #714					
13	"　"　"　"　"　"　" (Mar 3-05)　"　#1025					
14						
15				#1 to 2		
16				Date of Application for Enrollment. 5/22/99		
17	P.O. Tuskahoma, I.T.					

12/8/02

RESIDENCE: Wade	COUNTY.							
POST OFFICE: Talihina, I.T.	**Choctaw Nation**					**Choctaw Roll** (Not Including Freedmen)	CARD No. FIELD No. **1924**	

Dawes' Roll No.	NAME	Relationship to Person	AGE	SEX	BLOOD	TRIBAL ENROLLMENT		
						Year	County	No.
5489	1 Anderson, Crawford J³⁴	First Named	31	M	1/4	1896	Wade	158
5490	2 " Esther L ³⁰	Wife	27	F	Full	1896	"	159
5491	3 " Alice M ¹¹	Dau	8	"	5/8	1896	"	160
5492	4 " Bethel E ⁷	Son	4	M	5/8	1896	"	161
5493	5 " Myrtle ⁴	Dau	8mo	F	5/8			
5494	6 Bell, Elsie A ²⁰	Ward	17	"	1/4	1896	Wade	1033
5495	7 Anderson, Nellie ¹	Dau	3wks	F	5/8			
	8							

HIP CERTIFICATE
R NO 2-3-4-5-7
AUG 27 1903
10

NSHIP CERTIFICATE
FOR NO 1
AUG 31 1903
13

14

HIP CERTIFICATE
R NO
AR 30 1904

	ENROLLMENT
	OF NOS. 1 2 3 4 5 6 and 7 HEREON
	APPROVED BY THE SECRETARY
	OF INTERIOR JAN 16 1903

17

TRIBAL ENROLLMENT OF PARENTS

	Name of Father	Year	County	Name of Mother	Year	County
1	John Anderson	Dead	Wade	Betsey Anderson	Dead	Non Citz
2	Billy Beams	"	"	Hannah Beams	"	Wade
3	No 1			Serena Anderson	"	"
4	No 1			" "	"	"
5	No 1			No 2		
6	George Bell	1896	Non Citz	Phoebe Bell	Dead	Wade
7	No 1			No 2		
8						
9	No 1 is now guardian of Mary R and Abigail Burney on Choctaw Card #2124					
10	As to marriage of parents of No1 see testimony of Wesley Anderson					
11						
12	No 6 on 1896 roll as Elsie Ann Bell					
13						
14	No 5 Affidavit of birth to be supplied Recd May 23/99					
15	No 7 Born Sept 7 1902: Enrolled Sept. 27, 1902					
16					5/22/99	
17						

Choctaw By Blood Enrollment Cards 1898-1914

RESIDENCE: Jacks Fork COUNTY. **Choctaw Nation** Choctaw Roll CARD NO.
POST OFFICE: Tushkahomma[sic] I.T. (Not Including Freedmen) FIELD NO. **1925**

Dawes' Roll No.		NAME		Relationship to Person First Named	AGE	SEX	BLOOD	TRIBAL ENROLLMENT		
								Year	County	No.
5496	1	Anderson Wesley	53	First Named	50	M	1/2	1896	Jacks Fork	507
~~5497~~	2	" ~~Elsie E~~	37	~~Wife~~	~~34~~	~~F~~	~~Full~~	~~1896~~ DIED PRIOR TO SEPTEMBER 25, 1902		~~388~~
5498	3	" Park J	15	Son	12	M	5/8	1896	" "	510
	4									
	5									
	6									
	7									
	8									
	9	ENROLLMENT								
	10	OF NOS. 1 2 and 3 HEREON ~~APPROVED BY THE SECRETARY~~								
	11	OF INTERIOR JAN 16 1903								
	12									
	13									
	14									
	15									
	16									
	17									

TRIBAL ENROLLMENT OF PARENTS

	Name of Father	Year	County	Name of Mother	Year	County
1	Silas Anderson	Dead	Wade	Mary Anderson	Dead	Wade
2	~~Austin Cravotte~~	"	~~Jackson~~	~~Ellen Cravotte~~	"	~~Jackson~~
3	No 1			Micey Anderson	"	Jacks Fork
4						
5						
6	No.2 Died Feb. 18, 1900. Enrollment cancelled by Department July 8, 1904					
7						
8						
9	No 2 on 1896 roll as Eliza E Anderson					
10						
11						
12						
13						
14						
15						
16						5/22/99
17						

125

Choctaw By Blood Enrollment Cards 1898-1914

RESIDENCE: Jacks Fork   COUNTY.
POST OFFICE: Tushkahomma[sic], I.T.   **Choctaw Nation**   **Choctaw Roll** *(Not Including Freedmen)*   CARD NO.   FIELD NO. **1926**

Dawes' Roll No.	NAME		Relationship to Person First Named	AGE	SEX	BLOOD	TRIBAL ENROLLMENT		
							Year	County	No.
5499	1 Wall Edwin	63	First Named	60	M	1/4	1896	Wade	13119
5500	2 " Agnes	41	Wife	38	F	1/2	1896	"	13120
5501	3 " Tandy	23	Son	20	M	1/2	1896	"	13121
5502	4 " Thomas	22	"	19	"	1/2	1896	"	13122
5503	5 " Sinie	21	Dau	18	F	1/2	1896	"	13123
5504	6 " Columbus	15	Son	12	M	1/2	1896	"	13124
5505	7 " Delilah	14	Dau	11	F	1/2	1896	"	13125
5506	8 " Margaret	12	"	9	"	1/2	1896	"	13126
5507	9 " Emiline	11	"	8	"	1/2	1896	"	13127
5508	10 " Peter	10	Son	7	M	1/2	1896	"	13128
5509	11 " Laura	7	Dau	4	F	1/2	1896	"	13129
5510	12 " Victor R	4	Son	1	M	3/8			

SHIP CERTIFICATE
OR NO 1-2-3-4-5-6-7-8-9- 10-11-12
JUL 27 1903

ENROLLMENT
OF NOS. 1 2 3 4 5 6 7 8 9 10 11 and 12 HEREON
APPROVED BY THE SECRETARY
OF INTERIOR JAN 16 1903

TRIBAL ENROLLMENT OF PARENTS

	Name of Father	Year	County	Name of Mother	Year	County
1	Jesse Wall	Dead		Delilah Wall	Dead	Cedar
2	Ervin Anderson	"	Wade		"	Wade
3	No 1			No 2		
4	No 1			No 2		
5	No 1			No 2		
6	No 1			No 2		
7	No 1			No 2		
8	No 1			No 2		
9	No 1			No 2		
10	No 1			No 2		
11	No 1			No 2		
12	No 1			No 2		
13						
14	No 11 on 1896 roll as Sarah Wall					
15	No.3 is now the husband of Phoebe A Bohanan Choctaw card #2002					5/22/99
16				Nov. 20, 1901		
17						

126

Choctaw By Blood Enrollment Cards 1898-1914

| RESIDENCE: Jacks Fork | COUNTY. | **Choctaw Nation** | | | | **Choctaw Roll** | CARD NO. | |
| POST OFFICE: Tushkahomma[sic] IT | | | | | | *(Not Including Freedmen)* | FIELD NO. | **1927** |

Dawes' Roll No.	NAME			Relationship to Person	AGE	SEX	BLOOD	TRIBAL ENROLLMENT		
								Year	County	No.
5511	1	Bohanan Ellis	57	First Named	54	M	1/2	1896	Jacks Fork	1959
5512	2	" Susan	40	Wife	37	F	Full	1896	" "	1960
5513	3	" Green	19	Son	16	M	1/2	1896	" "	1961
5514	4	" Dora	17	Dau	14	F	1/2	1896	" "	1962
5515	5	" Kitty	15	"	12	"	1/2	1896	" "	1963
5516	6	" Wilson	12	Son	9	M	1/2	1896	" "	1964
5517	7	" Wesley	6	"	3	"	3/4	1896	" "	1965
5518	8	Bohanan Anna B	19	S Dau	16	F	3/4	1896	" "	502
5519	9	Anderson Emma	15	" "	12	"	3/4	1896	" "	503
5520	10	" Nona	11	" "	8	"	3/4	1896	" "	504
5521	11	" Alice	9	" "	6	"	3/4	1896	" "	505
~~5522~~	~~12~~	~~Bohanan John~~	~~3~~	~~Son~~	~~2mo~~	~~M~~	~~3/4~~	DIED PRIOR TO SEPTEMBER 25, 1902		
5523	13	"		Dau of No 8	1mo	F	7/8			
	14	ENROLLMENT OF NOS. 1 2 3 4 5 6 7 8 9 10 11 12 and 13 HEREON APPROVED BY THE SECRETARY OF INTERIOR JAN 16 1903								
	15									
	16									

No12 Died Feb 26,1900. Enrollment cancelled by Department July 8, 1904

TRIBAL ENROLLMENT OF PARENTS

	Name of Father	Year	County	Name of Mother	Year	County
1	Wm Bohanan	Ded	Jacks Fork	Betsy Bohanan	Ded	Wade
2	Thomas Benton	"	Sugar Loaf	Silptria Benton	"	Sugar Loaf
3	No 1			Patsy Bohanan	"	Wade
4	No 1			" "	"	" "
5	No 1			" "	"	" "
6	No 1			" "	"	" "
7	No 1			Susan Bohanan	1896	Jacks Fork
8	Solomon Anderson	Ded	Jacks Fork	No 2		
9	" "	"	" "	No 2		
10	" "	"	" "	No 2		
11	" "	"	" "	No 2		
12	~~No 1~~			~~No 2~~		
13	Julius H Bohanan	1893	Wade	No 8		
14	No 8 on 1896 rolls as Arebelle Anderson					
15	No 12 died Feb 26, 1900; proof of death filed Dec 12, 1902					
16	~~No8 is now the wife of Julius H Bohanan on Choctaw card #2002 Evidence of marriage requested July 23, 1902~~					5/22/99
17	No 13 Born June 12, 1902: enrolled July 23, 1902.			No 12 enrolled Oct. 6/99		

Choctaw By Blood Enrollment Cards 1898-1914

RESIDENCE: Wade   COUNTY.
POST OFFICE: Tushkahomma[sic], I.T.   **Choctaw Nation**   **Choctaw Roll** (Not Including Freedmen)   CARD NO.
FIELD NO. **1928**

Dawes' Roll No.	NAME	Relationship to Person First Named	AGE	SEX	BLOOD	TRIBAL ENROLLMENT Year	County	No.
5524	1 Spring, David J. ³²	Named	29	M	3/4	1896	Wade	11341
5525	2 " Ada ³¹	Wife	28	F	3/4	1896	"	11342
5526	3 " Levena ⁸	Dau	5	"	3/4	1896	"	11343
5527	4 " Daisy ⁴	"	5mo	"				
	5							
	6 CITIZENSHIP CERTIFICATE ISSUED FOR NO. 1 MAY 1 1903							
	7							
	8							
	9 ENROLLMENT							
	10 OF NOS. 1 2 3 and 4 HEREON APPROVED BY THE SECRETARY							
	11 OF INTERIOR JAN 16 1903							
	12							
	13							
	14							
	15							
	16							
	17							

	TRIBAL ENROLLMENT OF PARENTS					
	Name of Father	Year	County	Name of Mother	Year	County
1	Edward Spring	Ded	Wade	Siny Spring	1896	Wade
2	Wm King	Ded	Jacks Fork	Sophia King	1896	Jacks Fork
3	No 1			No 2		
4	No 1			No 2		
5						
6						
7						
8						
9						
10						
11						
12						
13						
14						
15						
16						5-22-99
17						

Choctaw By Blood Enrollment Cards 1898-1914

RESIDENCE: Wade	COUNTY:	Choctaw Nation	Choctaw Roll	CARD No.
POST OFFICE: Tushkahomma[sic], I.T.			(Not Including Freedmen)	FIELD No. **1929**

Dawes' Roll No.	NAME	Relationship to Person First Named	AGE	SEX	BLOOD	TRIBAL ENROLLMENT		
						Year	County	No.
15528	1 Williams, Jack	First Named	35	M	1/2	1896	Wade	13114
15763	2 " Amos	Son	11	"	1/4	1896	"	13115
15764	3 " Ora	Dau	5	F	1/4			
15765	4 " Clarence	Son	3	M	1/4			
15766	5 " Dora	Dau	1	F	1/4			
	6							
	7							
	8							
	9	ENROLLMENT OF NOS. 2,3,4 and 5 HEREON APPROVED BY THE SECRETARY OF INTERIOR Dec 23 1904						
	10							
	11							
	12							
	13	ENROLLMENT OF NOS. 1 HEREON APPROVED BY THE SECRETARY OF INTERIOR Jan 16 1903						
	14							
	15							
	16							
	17							

TRIBAL ENROLLMENT OF PARENTS

	Name of Father	Year	County	Name of Mother	Year	County
1	Sylvester Williams	1896	Colored	Isabelle Beams	Dead	Tobucksy
2	No 1	1896	Wade	Mary J Williams	"	Colored woman
3	No 1	1896	"	" " "	"	" " "
4	No 1	1896	"	" " "	"	" " "
5	No 1	1896	"	" " "	"	" " "
6						
7	Ages given hereon for Nos 2,3,4 and 5 are [remainder illegible]					
8						
9	No. 1 the husband of Mary Jane Williams Choctaw Freed card D 31					
10	No.1 is father of children on Choctaw card #D 176					
11	Nos 2 and 3 originally listed for enrollment May 22/99; No.4 Nov 1/99 and No.5 March [illegible] Choctaw card #D 176. transferred to this card Dec. 15, 1904. See decision of					
12	Nov. 28, 1904					
13	For child of No.1 see NB (March 3, 1905) #641					
14						#1
15						Date of Application for Enrollment
16						5/22/99
17	P.O. Spiro I.T.					

Choctaw By Blood Enrollment Cards 1898-1914

RESIDENCE: Jacks Fork	COUNTY.	**Choctaw Nation**	**Choctaw Roll**	CARD NO.	
POST OFFICE: Tushkahomma[sic], I.T.			(Not Including Freedmen)	FIELD NO. **1930**	

Dawes' Roll No.	NAME	Relationship to Person First Named	AGE	SEX	BLOOD	TRIBAL ENROLLMENT Year	TRIBAL ENROLLMENT County	TRIBAL ENROLLMENT No.
1	Jones, Sim Out		26	M	Full	1896	Jacks Fork	7350
2								
3								
4								
5								
6								
7								
8								
9								
10								
11								
12								
13								
14								
15								
16								
17								

Void Duplicate of No 464

CANCELLED

TRIBAL ENROLLMENT OF PARENTS

	Name of Father	Year	County	Name of Mother	Year	County
1	Jones Hoteka	Dead	Jacks Fork	Peggy	Dead	Jacks Fork
2						
3						
4						
5						
6						
7						
8						
9						
10						
11						
12						
13						
14						
15						
16					5/22/99	
17						

Choctaw By Blood Enrollment Cards 1898-1914

RESIDENCE: Jacks Fork COUNTY. **Choctaw Nation** **Choctaw Roll** CARD NO.
POST OFFICE: Tushkahomma[sic], I.T. *(Not Including Freedmen)* FIELD NO. **1931**

Dawes' Roll No.	NAME	Relationship to Person First Named	AGE	SEX	BLOOD	TRIBAL ENROLLMENT		
						Year	County	No.
DEAD. 1	Moore, Austin C DEAD.	First Named	28	M	Full	1896	Jacks Fork	8865
5529 2	" Lena	Wife	22	F	"	1896	Cedar	1073
3								
4								
5								
6								
7	ENROLLMENT OF NOS. 2 HEREON							
8	APPROVED BY THE SECRETARY							
9	OF INTERIOR JAN 16 1903							
10								
11								
12								
13								
14								
15								
16								
17								

TRIBAL ENROLLMENT OF PARENTS

	Name of Father	Year	County	Name of Mother	Year	County
1	Dallas Moore	Dead	Jacks Fork	Selina Carnes	1896	Jacks Fork
2	Isom Bohanan	Dead	Red River	Eliza Ann	Dead	Red River
3						
4						
5						
6		No 1 died in May 1900				
7						
8						
9						
10		No1 On 1896 roll as Oston C More				
11		No2 " " " " Lena Bohanan				
12						
13						
14						
15						
16						5/22/99
17						

131

Choctaw By Blood Enrollment Cards 1898-1914

RESIDENCE: Jacks Fork COUNTY.
POST OFFICE: Tushkahomma[sic] I.T.

Choctaw Roll (Not Including Freedmen)   FIELD NO. 1932

	NAME	Relationship to Person	AGE	SEX	BLOOD	Year	TRIBAL ENROLLMENT County	No.
5530	1 Anderson Mary ²⁴	First Person Named	21	F	Full	1893	Jackson	P.R. 200
5531	2 " Maggie ⁵	Dau	1	"	3/4			
5532	3 DIED PRIOR TO SEPTEMBER 25, 1902 Flora	Dau	1	F	3/4			
5533	4 " Lejah ¹	Son	8mo	M	3/4			
	5							
	6							
	7							
	8 For child of No.1 see NB (Apr 26-01) Card #512							
	9 " " " " " " (Mar 3-05) " #859							
	10							
	11							
	12							
	13							
	14							
	15 ENROLLMENT OF NOS. 1,2,3,4 HEREON							
	16 APPROVED BY THE SECRETARY OF INTERIOR JAN 16 1903							
	17							

TRIBAL ENROLLMENT OF PARENTS

	Name of Father	Year	County	Name of Mother	Year	County
1	Esias[sic] Peter	Ded	Jackson	Molsey Peter	Ded	Jackson
2	Norton Anderson	1896	Jacks Fork	No 1		
3	" "	"	Chick. roll	No 1		
4	" "	1896	" "	Nº1		
5						
6						
7						
8						
9						
10			No1 on 1893 Pay roll as Mary Peter			
11			No.1 is the wife of Norton Anderson on Chickasaw card #1081.			
12			No.3 Enrolled Feby 21st, 1901			
13			Nº4 Born Dec 26, 1901; enrolled Sept 10, 1902			
13			No 3 died Feb 2, 1902; proof of death filed Dec 12, 1902			
14			No.3 died Feb 2, 1902: Enrollment cancelled by Department July 8, 1904.			
15						#1&2
16				Date of Application for Enrollment	5/22/99	
17						

132

Choctaw By Blood Enrollment Cards 1898-1914

RESIDENCE: Jacks Fork COUNTY. **Choctaw Nation** **Choctaw Roll** CARD No.
POST OFFICE: Kosoma, I.T. (Not Including Freedmen) FIELD No. **1933**

Dawes' Roll No.	NAME	Relationship to Person	AGE	SEX	BLOOD	TRIBAL ENROLLMENT		
						Year	County	No.
5534	1 Bond, Eliza 63	First Named	60	F	Full	1896	Jacks Fork	1924
	2							
	3							
	4							
	5							
	6							
	7							
P CERT FICATE	8							
NO 1								
28 1903	9							
	10							
	11	ENROLLMENT						
	12	OF NOS. 1 HEREON APPROVED BY THE SECRETARY						
	13	OF INTERIOR JAN 16 1903						
	14							
	15							
	16							
	17							

TRIBAL ENROLLMENT OF PARENTS

	Name of Father	Year	County	Name of Mother	Year	County
1	Ya-tah	Ded	Jacks Fork	Ma-to-na	Ded	Cedar
2						
3						
4						
5						
6						
7						
8						
9						
10						
11						
12						
13						
14						
15						
16						5-22-99
17						

RESIDENCE: Jacks Fork
POST OFFICE: Kosoma I.T.

COUNTY. **Choctaw Nation**

Choctaw Roll
(Not Including Freedmen)

CARD No.
FIELD No. 1934

Dawes' Roll No.	NAME	Relationship to Person	AGE	SEX	BLOOD	TRIBAL ENROLLMENT		
						Year	County	No.
5535	1 Pool, Summie B 23	First Named	20	F	Full	1896	Jacks Fork	1952
5536	2 " Ike 2	Son	2wks	M	1/2			
I.W. 182	3 " Ike K	husband	34	M	I.W.			
	4							
	5							
	6							
	7							
	8							
	9							
	10							
	11	ENROLLMENT OF NOS. 3 HEREON						
	12	APPROVED BY THE SECRETARY OF INTERIOR JUN 13 1903						
	13							
	14							
	15	ENROLLMENT OF NOS. 1, 2 HEREON						
	16	APPROVED BY THE SECRETARY OF INTERIOR JAN 16 1903						
	17							

TRIBAL ENROLLMENT OF PARENTS

	Name of Father	Year	County	Name of Mother	Year	County
1	Wilson Bob	1896	Jacks Fork	Tennessee Bob	1896	Jacks Fork
2	Ike Pool		white man	Summie B. Pool		
3	Mitchell Pool	Dead	non-citz	Lucinda Pool	Dead	non-citz
4						
5						
6						
7			See D 179 Choctaw Rolls for Husband			
8						
9			On 1896 roll as Summie Bob			
10			No.2 Enrolled Dec. 8th 1900			
11			No 3 transferred from Choctaw card #D179			
12			See decision of May 5, 1903.			
13						
14						
15					#1	
16				Date of Application for Enrollment	5/22/99	
17						

P.O. Nail IT 3/20/05

Choctaw By Blood Enrollment Cards 1898-1914

RESIDENCE: Jacks Fork   COUNTY. **Choctaw Nation**   **Choctaw Roll**   CARD NO.
POST OFFICE: Tushkohamma[sic] I.T.   *(Not Including Freedmen)*   FIELD NO. 1935

Dawes' Roll No.	NAME		Relationship to Person First Named	AGE	SEX	BLOOD	TRIBAL ENROLLMENT		
							Year	County	No.
5537	1 Colbert Washington	24	First Named	21	M	Full	1896	Jack's Fork	3040
[illegible]	2 " Jincy	37	Wife	34	F	"	1896	" "	525
	3								
	4								
	5								
	6								
	7								
	8								
	9								
	10								
	11								
	12								
	13								
	14								
	15								
	16								
	17								

ENROLLMENT OF NOS. 1 HEREON APPROVED BY THE SECRETARY OF INTERIOR JAN 16 1903

ENROLLMENT OF NOS. 2 HEREON APPROVED BY THE SECRETARY OF INTERIOR MAY 20 1903

TRIBAL ENROLLMENT OF PARENTS

Name of Father	Year	County	Name of Mother	Year	County
1 Billy Colbert	1896	Jack's Fork	Martha Colbert	1896	Jack's Fork
2 Jonas Hoteka	Dead	" "	Peggy Hoteka	Dead	" "
3					
4					
5					
6					
7					
8					
9					
10					
11					
12					
13					
14					
15					
16					
17					

No 2 On 1896 roll as Jincy Anderson

Nos 1 and 2 are divorced and Nº 1 is now the husband of Sallie Benton on Choctaw card #54855, Oct. 22, 1902.

Date of Application for Enrollment. 5/22/99

135

Choctaw By Blood Enrollment Cards 1898-1914

Dawes' Roll No.	NAME		Relationship to Person	AGE	SEX	BLOOD	TRIBAL ENROLLMENT		
							Year	County	No.
5538	1 Hardy, Thomas	30	First Named	27	M	1/2	1893	Nashoba	287
5539	2 " Emily	25	Wife	22	F	Full	1893	Wade	499
5540	3 " Dickey	3	Son	5mo	M	3/4			
14699	4 " Delphi	1	Son	5mo	M	3/4			
	5								
	6								
	7								
	8								
	9								
	10								
	11								
	12								
	13								
	14								
	15	ENROLLMENT OF NOS. 1,2,3 HEREON				ENROLLMENT OF NOS. 4 HEREON			
	16	APPROVED BY THE SECRETARY				APPROVED BY THE SECRETARY			
	17	OF INTERIOR JAN 16 1903				OF INTERIOR MAY 20 1903			

TRIBAL ENROLLMENT OF PARENTS

	Name of Father	Year	County	Name of Mother	Year	County
1	Gilbert Cooper	Dead	Cedar	Jane Cooper	1896	Cedar
2	Amos Bohanan	1896	Wade	Listie Bohanan	Dead	Nashoba
3	No.1			No.2		
4	No 1			No 2		
5						
6	No 1 on 1893 Pay roll as Thomas Hardy Page 24 No 287 Nashoba Co.					
7	No 2 " 1893 " " " Emily Wells " 68 No 499 Wade Co					
8	No.3 Enrolled June 25, 1900					
9	No.4 born July 27, 1901: enrolled December 15, 1902					
	For child of Nos 1&2 see NB (March 3, 1905) #1427					
10						
11	3/19/18 Nos 1&2 are duplicates of Nos 1&2 on Choctaw					
12	Card No 4878					
13						
14					#1 to 2 inc	
15					Date of Application for Enrollment.	
16					5/22/99	
17						

| RESIDENCE: | Jack's Fork | COUNTY. | **Choctaw Nation** | **Choctaw Roll** | CARD NO. |
| POST OFFICE: | Stringtown I.T. | | | *(Not Including Freedmen)* | FIELD NO. 1937 |

Dawes' Roll No.		NAME		Relationship to Person	AGE	SEX	BLOOD	TRIBAL ENROLLMENT		
								Year	County	No.
5541	1	Frazier Lizzie	33	First Named	30	F	Full	1896	Jack's Fork	4517
5542	2	McClure Willis	17	Cousin	14	M	"	1896	" "	9466
	3									
	4									
	5									
	6									
	7									
	8									
	9									
	10									
	11									
	12									
	13									
	14									
	15	ENROLLMENT OF NOS. 1, 2 HEREON								
	16	APPROVED BY T HE SECRETARY OF INTERIOR JAN 16 1903								
	17									

TRIBAL ENROLLMENT OF PARENTS

	Name of Father	Year	County	Name of Mother	Year	County
1	Sam Frazier	Dead	Cedar	Tona Frazier	Dead	Jack's Fork
2	Sam McClure	"	Sugar Loaf	Misa McClure	Dead	Sugar Loaf
3						
4						
5						
6						
7						
8						
9						
10						
11						
12						
13						
14						
15						
16				Date of Application for Enrollment.	5/22/99	
17						

137

Choctaw By Blood Enrollment Cards 1898-1914

RESIDENCE: Cedar   COUNTY.   **Choctaw Nation**   **Choctaw Roll**   CARD NO.
POST OFFICE: Tushkahomma[sic], I.T.   (Not Including Freedmen)   FIELD NO. **1938**

Dawes' Roll No.	NAME	Relationship to Person	AGE	SEX	BLOOD	TRIBAL ENROLLMENT		
						Year	County	No.
5543	1 Ben Lucy ³⁰	First Named	27	F	Full	1896	Cedar	1061
5544	2 " Malena ¹¹	Dau	8	F	"	1896	"	1063
5545	3 " Amy ⁶	Dau	2	F	"	1896	"	
	4							
	5							
	6							
	7							
	8							
	9							
	10	ENROLLMENT OF NOS. 1 2 and 3 HEREON APPROVED BY THE SECRETARY OF INTERIOR JAN 16 1903						
	11							
	12							
	13							
	14							
	15							
	16							
	17							

TRIBAL ENROLLMENT OF PARENTS

	Name of Father	Year	County	Name of Mother	Year	County
1	Nelson Smith	Dead	Cedar	Melissa Smith	Dead	Cedar
2	German Ben	"	"	No 1		
3	" "	"	"	No 1		
4						
5						
6			No 2 on 1896 roll as Melliney Ben			
7			No 1 wife of Sumplin Frazier Choctaw card #1951			
8						
9						
10						
11						
12						
13						
14						
15						
16			5/22/99			
17						

138

Choctaw By Blood Enrollment Cards 1898-1914

RESIDENCE: Jack's Fork	COUNTY.							
POST OFFICE: Tushkahomma[sic], I.T.	**Choctaw Nation**					**Choctaw Roll** *(Not Including Freedmen)*	CARD NO. FIELD NO.	**1939**

Dawes' Roll No.	NAME	Relationship to Person First Named	AGE	SEX	BLOOD	TRIBAL ENROLLMENT		
						Year	County	No.
DEAD.	1 Anderson Benjamin	First Named	31	M	1/2	1896	Jack's Fork	515
14700	2 Fobb Louisa ²⁸	Wife	25	F	Full	1896	" "	14108
5546	3 Anderson Virgil ⁸	Boy	5	M	1/4	1896	" "	516
14701	4 Fobb Lily ¹	Dau of No 2	6mo	F	Full			
	5							
	6							
	7							
	8							
	9	ENROLLMENT OF NOS. 3 HEREON APPROVED BY THE SECRETARY OF INTERIOR JAN 16 1903						
	10							
	11							
	12	ENROLLMENT OF NOS. 2 and 4 HEREON APPROVED BY THE SECRETARY OF INTERIOR MAY 20 1903						
	13							
	14							
	15							
	16							
	17							

TRIBAL ENROLLMENT OF PARENTS

	Name of Father	Year	County	Name of Mother	Year	County
1	Stephen Anderson	1896	Jacks Fork	Wisey Anderson	Dead	Jack's Fork
2	Edwin Wall	1896	" "	Lavina Anderson	Dead	" "
3	No 1			May Anderson	Dead	Non Citz
4	Benjamin Fobb			No 2		
5						
6						
7	No 2 on 1896 roll as Louisa Walt					
8	No 3 " " " " Virgil Anderson					
9	Evidence of marriage between father and mother of Virgil Anderson, see testimony of Wm B Anderson					
10	No 1 died Oct 3, 1900; proof of death filed Dec 12, 1902 filed Dec 30, 1902					
11	No 2 is wife of Benjamin Fobb Choctaw card #1646 Evidence					
12	of marriage filed January 22, 1903					
13	No4 Born June 28,1902; Enrolled Dec 11 1902					
14						
15						
16					5/22/99	
17	P.O. Kosoma I.T. 12/8/02					

139

RESIDENCE:	Wade	COUNTY.	**Choctaw Nation**	**Choctaw Roll**	CARD NO.	
POST OFFICE:	Tushkahomma[sic], I.T.			(Not Including Freedmen)	FIELD NO.	1940

Dawes' Roll No.	NAME	Relationship to Person Named	AGE	SEX	BLOOD	TRIBAL ENROLLMENT		
						Year	County	No.
5547	1 McKinney, Silas 52	First Named	49	M	1/2	1896	Wade	9248
5548	2 " Nancy 46	Wife	43	F	Full	1896	"	9249
5549	3 Bell, Silas 13	Neph	10	M	1/4	1896	"	1035
5550	4 " Martha 15	Niece	12	F	1/4	1896	"	1034
5551	5 Bohanan Catherine 15	Ward	12	"	Full	1896	"	967
DEAD.	6 Artemus Meashintubby	"	5	M	"	1896	"	8577
	7							
	8							
	9	ENROLLMENT						
	10	OF NOS. 1 2 3 4 and 5 HEREON APPROVED BY THE SECRETARY						
	11	OF INTERIOR JAN 16 1903						
	12							
	13							
	14							
	15							
	16							
	17							

TRIBAL ENROLLMENT OF PARENTS

	Name of Father	Year	County	Name of Mother	Year	County
1	Jesse McKinney	Ded	Jacks Fork	Elsie McKinney	Ded	Cedar
2	Jefferson Bacon	"	Red River	Frazier	"	Red River
3	George Bell		Non Citz	Phoebe Bell	"	Wade
4	" "		" "	" "	"	"
5	Amos Bohanan	1896	Wade	Listy Bohanan	Ded	Nashoba
6	Meashintubby	1896	"	Wilsy Meashintubby	"	Wade
7						
8						
9	No 6 on 1896 Roll as Timothy Meashintubby					
10	No 6 Died August 15, 1899. Evidence of death filed April 16, 1901					
11						
12						
13						
14						
15						
16					5-22-99	
17						

RESIDENCE: Cedar **COUNTY.** **Choctaw Nation** **Choctaw Roll** CARD NO.
POST OFFICE: Tushkahomma[sic] I.T. *(Not Including Freedmen)* FIELD NO. 1941

Dawes Roll No.	NAME		Relationship to Person First Named	AGE	SEX	BLOOD	TRIBAL ENROLLMENT		
							Year	County	No.
5552	1 Philip Jacob	28		25	M	Full	1896	Cedar	10326
5553	2 " Winnie	36	Wife	33	F	"	1896	"	10327
5554	3 Bacon Esias	18	Stepson	15	M	"	1896	"	1064
	4								
	5								
	6								
	7								
	8								
	9								
	10								
	11								
	12								
	13								
	14								
	15	ENROLLMENT OF NOS. 1,2,3 HEREON APPROVED BY THE SECRETARY OF INTERIOR JAN 16 1903							
	16								
	17								

TRIBAL ENROLLMENT OF PARENTS

	Name of Father	Year	County	Name of Mother	Year	County
1	James Philip	Ded	Cedar	Bessie Philip	1896	Cedar
2	Gilbert Cooper	"	"	Mary Cooper	Ded	"
3	George Bacon	1896	"	No 2		
4						
5						
6						
7						
8			No 3 on 1896 roll as Esiah Bacon			
9						
10			Surname of Nos 1-2 on 1896 roll as Phillip			
11						
12						
13						
14						
15					Date of Application for Enrollment.	
16					5-22-99	
17						

RESIDENCE:	Wade		COUNTY.	**Choctaw Nation**		**Choctaw Roll**		CARD NO.	
POST OFFICE:	Tushkahomma[sic] I.T.					*(Not Including Freedmen)*		FIELD NO.	1942

Dawes' Roll No.	NAME	Relationship to Person	AGE	SEX	BLOOD	TRIBAL ENROLLMENT		
						Year	County	No.
5555	1 Bryant William ~~DIED PRIOR TO SEPTEMBER 25 1902~~	First Named	31	M	Full	1896	Wade	1044
	2							
	3							
	4							
	5							
	6							
	7							
	8							
	9							
	10							
	11							
	12							
	13							
	14							
	15	ENROLLMENT OF NOS. 1 HEREON APPROVED BY THE SECRETARY						
	16	OF INTERIOR JAN 16 1903						
	17							

TRIBAL ENROLLMENT OF PARENTS

	Name of Father	Year	County	Name of Mother	Year	County
1	Nathan Bryant	Ded	Wade	Lucinda Bryant	Ded	Wade
2						
3						
4						
5						
6	Nº1 was the husband of Nancy Spring Choctaw card #1903					
7						
8	~~No 1 died July 27, 1902; proof of death filed Dec 12, 1902~~					
9	No.1 died July 27. 1902: Enrollment cancelled by Department July 8, 1904					
10						
11						
12						
13						
14					Date of Application for Enrollment.	
15					5-22-99	
16						
17						

Choctaw By Blood Enrollment Cards 1898-1914

RESIDENCE: Cedar   COUNTY. **Choctaw Nation**   **Choctaw Roll**   CARD NO.

POST OFFICE: Tushkahomma[sic] I.T.   *(Not Including Freedmen)*   FIELD NO. **1943**

Dawes' Roll No.	NAME		Relationship to Person First Named	AGE	SEX	BLOOD	TRIBAL ENROLLMENT		
							Year	County	No.
5556	1	McFarland Israel 27	First Named	24	M	Full	1896	Cedar	9256
5557	2	" Polly 23	Wife	20	F	"	1896	"	9257
5558	3	" Mary 4	Dau	2/3	"	"			
5559	4	" Florence 1	Dau	3mo	F	"			
	5								
	6								
	7								
	8								
	9								
	10								
	11								
	12								
	13								
	14								
	15	ENROLLMENT OF NOS. 1,2,3,4 HEREON							
	16	APPROVED BY THE SECRETARY							
	17	OF INTERIOR Jan 16 1903							

TRIBAL ENROLLMENT OF PARENTS

	Name of Father	Year	County	Name of Mother	Year	County
1	Sam McFarland	Ded	Nashoba	Listy McFarland	Ded	Cedar
2	Lewis Noahatubi	"	Cedar	Silin Noahtubi[sic]	1896	"
3	No 1			No 2		
4	Nº1			Nº2		
5						
6						
7	No3 "Died prior to Sept 25, 1902: not entitled to land or money"					
8	See copy of Indian Office Letter of Aug 4, 1908 (Land 45530-1908)					
9	Nº4 Born Feby 14, 1902; enrolled May 16, 1902.					
10						
11	For child of Nos 1&2 see NB (Apr 26-06) Card #335					
12						
13						
14						
15					#1 to 3 inc	
16				Date of Application for Enrollment.		
17	P.O. Dexter I.T.				5-22-99	

12/8/02

Choctaw By Blood Enrollment Cards 1898-1914

RESIDENCE: Cedar COUNTY. **Choctaw Nation** **Choctaw Roll** CARD NO.
POST OFFICE: Tushkahomma[sic], I.T. (Not Including Freedmen) FIELD NO. **1944**

Dawes' Roll No.	NAME	Relationship to Person First Named	AGE	SEX	BLOOD	TRIBAL ENROLLMENT		
						Year	County	No.
5560	1 McFarland, Andrew 29	First Named	26	M	Full	1893	Nashoba	P.R. 563
	2							
	3							
	4							
	5							
	6							
	7							
	8							
	9							
	10							
	11							
	12							
	13							
	14							
	15							
	16							
	17							

ENROLLMENT
OF NOS. 1 HEREON
APPROVED BY THE SECRETARY
OF INTERIOR JAN 16 1903

TRIBAL ENROLLMENT OF PARENTS

	Name of Father	Year	County	Name of Mother	Year	County
1	Sam McFarland	Ded	Nashoba	Listy McFarland	Ded	Cedar
2						
3						
4						
5		On 1893 Pay roll 563 page 47, Nashoba Co as Telo McFarlin				
6						
7		Also on 1896 roll Page No 233, No 9285, Nashoba Co as Fillo				
8		McFarland				
9						
10						
11						
12						
13						
14						
15						
16						5-22-99
17						

P.O. Lukfata I.T. 1/16-04

RESIDENCE: Nashoba COUNTY. **Choctaw Nation** Choctaw Roll CARD NO.
POST OFFICE: Tushkahoma[sic], I.T. (Not Including Freedmen) FIELD NO. **1945**

Dawes' Roll No.	NAME		Relationship to Person	AGE	SEX	BLOOD	TRIBAL ENROLLMENT		
							Year	County	No.
5561	1 Garland, William	58	First Named	55	M	Full	1896	Nashoba	4768
5562	2 " Delilah	43	Wife	40	F	"	1896	"	4769
5563	3 James, Betsy	21	Dau	18	"	"	1896	"	4770
~~5564~~	~~4 Garland, Robert~~ DIED PRIOR TO SEPTEMBER 25, 1902		~~Son~~	~~7~~	~~M~~	~~"~~	~~1896~~	~~"~~	~~4773~~
5565	5 " Sumner	8	"	5	"	"	1896	"	4774
5566	6 " Rachel	17	Dau	14	F	"	1896	Jacks Fork	14111
5567	7 Harrison, Sophie	17	Ward	14	"	"	1896	Nashoba	5550
5568	8 Morris Isham	18	Ward	15	M	"	1896	"	8626
5569	9 Garland, Rebecca	2	Gr Dau	2	F	"			
5570	10 James, Melvina	1	Gr Dau	7mo	F	"			
14702	11 Colbert, Webster	2	Son of No 7	2	M	1/2			
	12 No3 P.O. M°Millan Okla 1/8/10								
	13 For child of No.7 see NB (March 3'05) #974								
	" No 3 " " " #1326								
	14 No 11 born June 20,1900: Enrolled Dec 17, 1902								
	15 ENROLLMENT								
	16 OF NOS. 1,2,3,4,5,6,7,8,9,10 HEREON APPROVED BY THE SECRETARY								
	17 OF INTERIOR Jan 16 1903								

TRIBAL ENROLLMENT OF PARENTS

	Name of Father	Year	County	Name of Mother	Year	County
1	Lo-hubbee	Dead	Sugar Loaf	Si-e-mey	Dead	Nashoba
2	Alexander Bond	"	Wade	Fa-la-ma-huna	"	Wade
3	No 1			Adeline Garland	"	Nashoba
4	No 1			No 2		
5	No 1			No 2		
6	No 1			Netsie Ward	Dead	Jacks Fork
7	Sampson Tasahiya	Dead	Wade	Sukie Tasahiya	"	Wade
8	John Morris	"	Nashoba	Sillen Morris	"	Nashoba
9	Byington Battiest			N°3		
10	Joseph E James			N°3		
11	Charley Colbert			No 7		
12						
13	No6 on 1896 roll as Rachel[sic] Ward			ENROLLMENT OF NOS. HEREON APPROVED BY THE SECRETARY		
14	N°9 Born May 17, 1900: Enrolled July 29, 1902			OF INTERIOR May 20 1903		
15	N°9 is illegitimate (For child of No.7 see NB (Apr 26-06) Card #609					
16	N°3 is now the wife of Joseph B James			Date of Application for Enrollment. 5/22/99		
17	No10 Born Dec. 19, 1901: enrolled July 29, 1902.					
	No 4 died Sept 22, 1902: proof of death filed Dec 12, 1902			No 8 5/23/99		

No.4 died Sept 22, 1902: Enrollment cancelled by Department July 8, 1904

Choctaw By Blood Enrollment Cards 1898-1914

RESIDENCE: Nashoba COUNTY. **Choctaw Nation** **Choctaw Roll** CARD No.
POST OFFICE: Tushkahomma[sic] I.T. *(Not Including Freedmen)* FIELD No. **1946**

Dawes' Roll No.	NAME	Relationship to Person First Named	AGE	SEX	BLOOD	TRIBAL ENROLLMENT		
						Year	County	No.
5571	1 Frazier Rhoda 31	First Named	28	F	Full	1896	Nashoba	4154
5572	2 " Ben 10	Son	7	M	"	1896	"	4155
14703	3 Bohanan, Sophia 1	Dau	10m	F	"			
	4							
	5							
	6							
	7	ENROLLMENT OF NOS. 1 and 2 HEREON						
	8	APPROVED BY THE SECRETARY						
	9	OF INTERIOR JAN 16 1903						
	10							
	11							
	12							
	13							
	14	ENROLLMENT						
	15	OF NOS. 3 HEREON						
	16	APPROVED BY THE SECRETARY OF INTERIOR MAY 20 1903						
	17							

TRIBAL ENROLLMENT OF PARENTS

Name of Father	Year	County	Name of Mother	Year	County
1 Sampson Tasahiya	Dead	Wade	Sukie Tasahiya	Dead	Wade
2 Simon Frazier	1896	Nashoba	No 1		
3 Watson Bohanan			No 1		
4					
5					
6					
7		See Choc D 173			
8		No 3 born Feb 21, 1902, enrolled Dec 15, 1902			
9		No1 is wife of Watson Bohanan Choctaw card #1953 12/10/02			
10					
11					
12					
13					
14					
15					
16				5/22/99	
17					

146

Choctaw By Blood Enrollment Cards 1898-1914

Choctaw Nation
(Not Including Freedmen)

Choctaw Roll

CARD NO. FIELD NO. **1947**

Dawes' Roll No.	NAME		Relationship to Person First Named	AGE	SEX	BLOOD	TRIBAL ENROLLMENT Year	County	No.
5573	1 Cooper Cornelius	43	First Named	40	M	Full	1896	Cedar	2423
5574	2 " Lucy	41	Wife	38	F	"	1896	"	2424
5575	3 " Ellen	16	Dau	13	"	"	1896	"	2426
5576	4 " Allen	15	Son	12	M	"	1896	"	2427
~~5577~~	~~5 White, Beckie~~	~~17~~	~~S Dau~~	~~14~~	~~F~~	~~"~~	~~1896~~	DIED PRIOR TO SEPTEMBER 25, 1902	~~2425~~
14704	6 Cooper Nora	1	S Dau	1	F	"			
14705	7 Jones Leuian	2	Son of No 3	2	M	"			
14706	8 " Judea	1	Dau of No 3	6mo	F	"			
	9								
	10	ENROLLMENT OF NOS. 1 2 3 4 and 5 HEREON APPROVED BY THE SECRETARY OF INTERIOR JAN 16 1903							
	11								
	12								
	13								
	14	ENROLLMENT OF NOS. 6- 7- and 8 HEREON APPROVED BY THE SECRETARY OF INTERIOR MAY 20 1903							
	15								
	16								
	17								

TRIBAL ENROLLMENT OF PARENTS

	Name of Father	Year	County	Name of Mother	Year	County
1	Gilbert Cooper	Dead	Cedar	Man-te-huna	Dead	Nashoba
2	Edmond Bohanan	1896	"	Seley Bohanan	"	Cedar
3	No 1			No 2		
4	No 1			No 2		
5	~~Me-a-shin-tubbee~~	~~Dead~~	~~Wade~~	~~No 2~~		
6	No 1			No 1		
7	Charles Jones			No 3		
8	" "			No 3		
9	No5 Died Feb, 1900. Enrollment cancelled by Dept. July 8, 1904					
10	No 5 on 1896 roll as Beckie Cooper					
11	No6 born Sept 2, 1901 enrolled December 15, 1902 ~~No7 born Dec 18, 1900, enrolled December 15 1902~~					
12	No8 born June 24, 1902 enrolled December 15, 1902					
13	No 3 is now wife of Charley Jones on Choctaw card #1972. Evidence of marriage filed Dec 11, 1902.					
14	~~No 5 died in Feb, 1900; proof of death filed Dec 12, 1902~~					
15						
16					5/22/99	
17						

147

Choctaw By Blood Enrollment Cards 1898-1914

						TRIBAL ENROLLMENT		
RESIDENCE: Cedar		COUNTY.	**Choctaw Nation**			**Choctaw Roll**	CARD NO.	
POST OFFICE: Tushkahomma[sic] I.T.						*(Not Including Freedmen)*	FIELD NO.	**1948**

Dawes' Roll No.	NAME		Relationship to Person First Named	AGE	SEX	BLOOD	Year	County	No.
5578	1 Colbert, Johnson	52	First Named	49	M	Full	1896	Cedar	2416
5579	2 " Sinie	42	Wife	39	F	"	1896	"	2417
5580	3 " Charlie	26	Son	23	M	"	1896	"	2419
5581	4 " Bessie	21	Dau	18	F	"	1896	"	2420
5582	5 " Whitson	6	G Son	3	M	"	1896	DIED PRIOR TO SEPTEMBER 25, 1902	2421
	6								
	7								
	8								
	9	ENROLLMENT							
	10	OF NOS. 1 2 3 4 and 5 HEREON APPROVED BY THE SECRETARY							
	11	OF INTERIOR JAN 16 1903							
	12								
	13								
	14								
	15								
	16								
	17								

TRIBAL ENROLLMENT OF PARENTS

	Name of Father	Year	County	Name of Mother	Year	County
1	Ba-la-la	Dead	Nashoba	Ho-te-mi-o-na	Dead	Nashoba
2	James Hoka	"	"	Mollie Hoka	"	Cedar
3	No 1			Melissie Colbert	"	Nashoba
4	No 1			Celie Colbert	"	Cedar
5	Chimon Beam	Dead	Cedar	No 4		
6						
7	No.5 Died Sept. 1900. Enrollment cancelled by Dept. July 8, 1904					
8						
9						
10	No 5 on 1896 roll as Watson Colbert					
11	No 5 died Sept 1900; proof of death filed Dec 12, 1902					
12						
13						
14						
15						
16						5/22/99
17						

Choctaw By Blood Enrollment Cards 1898-1914

| RESIDENCE: Cedar | COUNTY. | **Choctaw Nation** | Choctaw Roll | CARD NO. |
| POST OFFICE: Tushkahomma[sic] I.T. | | | (Not Including Freedmen) | FIELD NO. 1949 |

Dawes' Roll No.	NAME	Relationship to Person First Named	AGE	SEX	BLOOD	Year	County	No.
5583	1 Bohanan Edmond *DIED PRIOR TO SEPTEMBER 25 1902*	First Named	68	M	Full	1896	Cedar	1056
5584	2 " Narcissa 25	Wife	22	F	"	1896	Nashoba	1057
5585	3 *DIED PRIOR TO SEPTEMBER 25 1902* Levisa	Dau	6mo	"	"			
	4							
	5							
	6							
	7							
	8							
	9							
	10							
	11							
	12							
	13							
	14							
	15	ENROLLMENT OF NOS. 1,2,3 HEREON APPROVED BY THE SECRETARY OF INTERIOR JAN 16 1903						
	16							
	17							

TRIBAL ENROLLMENT OF PARENTS

	Name of Father	Year	County	Name of Mother	Year	County
1	Nohambi	Ded	Eagle		Ded	Eagle
2	Anolitubbee	"	Nashoba	Basie Taylor	"	Nashoba
3	No 1			No 2		
4						
5						
6						
7	No 1 died Oct – 1900; proof of death filed Dec 16, 1902					
8	No.1 died Oct - 1900: Enrollment cancelled by Department July 8, 1904					
9	No 2 is now wife of James Ben on Choctaw card #4876. Evidence of marriage filed Dec 11/02					
10	No. 3 died before Sept 25, 1902: Enrollment cancelled by Department May 2, 1906					
11						
12						
13						
14						
15						
16				Date of Application for Enrollment.	5-22-99	
17						

Choctaw By Blood Enrollment Cards 1898-1914

RESIDENCE: Nashoba   COUNTY.   **Choctaw Nation**   **Choctaw Roll**   CARD NO.
POST OFFICE: Tushkahomma[sic] I.T.   *(Not Including Freedmen)*   FIELD NO. **1950**

Dawes' Roll No.	NAME		Relationship to Person	AGE	SEX	BLOOD	TRIBAL ENROLLMENT		
							Year	County	No.
5586	1 Bohanan Wade	42	First Named	39	M	Full	1896	Nashoba	1237
5587	2 " Elizabeth	32	Wife	29	F	"	1896	PRIOR TO SEPTEMBER 25, 1902	1238
5588	3 " Martin	10	Son	7	M	"	1896	"	1239
	4								
	5								
	6								
	7								
	8								
	9	ENROLLMENT							
	10	OF NOS. 1 2 and 3 HEREON APPROVED BY THE SECRETARY							
	11	OF INTERIOR JAN 16 1903							
	12								
	13								
	14								
	15								
	16								
	17								

TRIBAL ENROLLMENT OF PARENTS

	Name of Father	Year	County	Name of Mother	Year	County
1	Edmond Bohanan	1896	Cedar	Celia Bohanan	Ded	Cedar
2	Anolitubbee	Ded	Nashoba	Basie Taylor	"	Nashoba
3	No 1			No 2		
4						
5						
6	No. 2 Died Jan. 22, 1901. Enrollment cancelled by Dept. July 8, 1904					
7						
8						
9						
10						
11						
12						
13						
14						
15						
16					Date of Application for Enrollment.	5/22/99
17	P.O. Talihina I.T. 12/30/02					

Choctaw By Blood Enrollment Cards 1898-1914

RESIDENCE: Nashoba COUNTY. **Choctaw Nation** Choctaw Roll CARD No.
POST OFFICE: Tushkahomma[sic], I.T. (Not Including Freedmen) FIELD No. **1951**

Dawes' Roll No.	NAME	Relationship to Person	AGE	SEX	BLOOD	TRIBAL ENROLLMENT		
						Year	County	No.
5589	1 Frazier Sumplin 30	First Named	27	M	Full	1896	Nashoba	4153
5590	2 Smith Sallie 18	Ward	15	F	"	1896	"	11420
	3							
	4							
	5							
	6							
	7	ENROLLMENT						
	8	OF NOS. 1 and 2 HEREON APPROVED BY THE SECRETARY						
	9	OF INTERIOR JAN 16 1903						
	10							
	11							
	12							
	13							
	14							
	15							
	16							
	17							

TRIBAL ENROLLMENT OF PARENTS

	Name of Father	Year	County	Name of Mother	Year	County
1	Lewis Frazier	Ded	Eagle	Ataklantema	11896	Nashoba
2	Nelson Smith	"	Cedar	Malissa Smith	Ded	Cedar
3						
4						
5						
6						
7	~~No1 is husband of Lucy Ben Choctaw card #1938~~					
8	No1 is now guardian of Aben and Lucy Ann Frazier Choctaw					
9	card #2046. Evidence filed December 17, 1902.					
10						
11						
12						
13						
14						
15						
16					5-22-99	
17						

151

Choctaw By Blood Enrollment Cards 1898-1914

RESIDENCE: Cedar   COUNTY. **Choctaw Nation**   **Choctaw Roll**   CARD No.
POST OFFICE: Tushkahomma[sic] I.T.   (Not Including Freedmen)   FIELD No.   **1952**

Dawes' Roll No.	NAME	Relationship to Person Named	AGE	SEX	BLOOD	TRIBAL ENROLLMENT Year	County	No.
5591	1 Hampton Aaron ⁴⁸	First Named	45	M	Full	1896	Cedar	5427
5592	2 " Henry ¹⁹	Son	16	"	"	1896	"	5429
5593	3 " Levina ¹⁵	Dau	12	F	"	1896	DIED PRIOR TO SEPTEMBER 25, 1902	5430
5594	4 " Timothy ¹³	Son	10	M	"	1893	"	230
5								
6								
7								
8								
9	ENROLLMENT OF NOS. 1 2 3 and 4 HEREON							
10	APPROVED BY THE SECRETARY							
11	OF INTERIOR JAN 16 1903							
12								
13								
14								
15								
16								
17								

TRIBAL ENROLLMENT OF PARENTS

	Name of Father	Year	County	Name of Mother	Year	County
1	File-mon-tubbee	Dead	Nashoba	Tosh-pa-hu-na	Dead	Wade
2	No 1			Elisie Hampton	"	Cedar
3	No 1			" "	"	"
4	No 1			" "	"	"
5						
6						
7	No.3 Died March 4, 1902. Enrollment cancelled by Dept. July 8, 1904					
8						
9						
10	No4 on 1893 Pay roll Page 21 No 230, Cedar County					
11	No1 is the husband of Susan Battiest on Choc. card 1969, July 7			1902		
12	No3 died March 4, 1902; proof of death filed Dec 12, 1902					
13						
14						
15						
16						5/22/99
17	P.O. Dexter I.T.					

Choctaw By Blood Enrollment Cards 1898-1914

Choctaw Nation

Choctaw Roll *(Not Including Freedmen)*

CARD No. FIELD No. **1953**

Dawes' Roll No.	NAME		Relationship to Person First Named	AGE	SEX	BLOOD	TRIBAL ENROLLMENT Year	County	No.
5595	1 Bohanan Watson	32	First Named	29	M	Full	1896	Nashoba	1233
5596	2 " Eliza	33	Wife	30	F	"	1896	"	1234
5597	3 " Nicey	11	Dau	8	F	"	1896	"	1236
5598	⊕4 Lewis Simeon	15	Step Son	12	M	"	1896	"	1235
5									
6	⊕ 5/7/1917: No.4 hereon reported to be duplicate of No.3 on Choctaw card No. 652: under investigation								
7									WHA
8	ENROLLMENT								
9	OF NOS. 1,2,3,4 HEREON APPROVED BY THE SECRETARY								
10	OF INTERIOR Jan 16 1903								
11									
12									
13									
14									
15									
16									
17									

TRIBAL ENROLLMENT OF PARENTS

	Name of Father	Year	County	Name of Mother	Year	County
1	Edmund Bohanan	1896	Cedar	Celia Bohanan	Dead	Cedar
2	Joseph Meshaya	Dead	Kiamatia[sic]		Dead	Kiamatia[sic]
3	Joe Lewis	"	Towson	Liza Lewis	1896	Noshoba[sic]
4	" "	"	"	No 2		
5						
6						
7	No 3 On 1896 roll as Naisey Bohanan					
8	" 4 " " " " Simeon Bohanan					
9	For child of No.1 see NB (March 3 1905) #856					
10	Nos 1 and 2 have separated. No 1 is husband of Rhoda Frazier. Choctaw card #1946.					
11	12/10/02					
12						
13						
14						
15						
16			Date of Application for Enrollment.	5/22/99		
17						

Choctaw By Blood Enrollment Cards 1898-1914

RESIDENCE:	Cedar	COUNTY.									CARD NO.	
POST OFFICE:	Tushkahomma[sic], I.T.		**Choctaw Nation**				**Choctaw Roll** *(Not Including Freedmen)*			FIELD NO.	1954	

Dawes' Roll No.	NAME		Relationship to Person	AGE	SEX	BLOOD	TRIBAL ENROLLMENT		
							Year	County	No.
5599	₁ Colbert, John	28	First Named	25	M	Full	1896	Cedar	2418
	2								
	3								
	4								
	5								
	6								
	7								
	8								
	9								
	10								
	11								
	12								
	13								
	14								
	15	ENROLLMENT OF NOS. 1 HEREON APPROVED BY THE SECRETARY OF INTERIOR JAN 16 1903							
	16								
	17								

TRIBAL ENROLLMENT OF PARENTS

	Name of Father	Year	County	Name of Mother	Year	County
1	Johnson Colbert	1896	Cedar	Melissa Colbert	Dead	Nashoba
2						
3						
4						
5						
6			On 1896 roll as Johnnie Colbert			
7						
8						
9						
10						
11						
12						
13						
14					Date of Application for Enrollment.	
15						
16					5/22/99	
17						

Choctaw By Blood Enrollment Cards 1898-1914

RESIDENCE: Cedar COUNTY. **Choctaw Nation**
POST OFFICE: Tushkahomma[sic], I.T.

Choctaw Roll *(Not Including Freedmen)*

CARD NO.
FIELD NO. **1955**

Dawes' Roll No.	NAME		Relationship to Person	AGE	SEX	BLOOD	TRIBAL ENROLLMENT		
							Year	County	No.
5600	1 White, Robert	25	First Named	22	M	Full	1896	Cedar	13145
5601	2 " Jincy	30	Wife	27	F	"	1896	"	3358
5602	3 DIED PRIOR TO SEPTEMBER 25, 1902 Agnes		Dau	1	"	"			
5603	4 McKinzie, Kimpsey	11	S Dau	8	F	"	1893	Cedar	118"
5604	5 White, Sampson	3	Son	3mo	M	"			
5605	6 " , Willis	1	Son	3mo	M	"			
	7								
	8								
	9								
	10								
	11								
	12								
	13								
	14	ENROLLMENT OF NOS. 1,2,3,4,5,6 HEREON							
	15	APPROVED BY THE SECRETARY OF INTERIOR Jan 16 1903							
	16								
	17								

TRIBAL ENROLLMENT OF PARENTS

	Name of Father	Year	County	Name of Mother	Year	County
1	Willis White	Dead	Gaines	Susan White		Cedar
2	Jack Battiest		Cedar	Miley Battiest		"
3	No 1			No 2		
4	Goodman McKinzie	"	Cedar	No 2		
5	No.1			No.2		
6	No1			No2		
7						
8						
9						
10			No4 Sex changed from "M" to "F" under Departmental authority of			
11			September 17, 1896 (I.T. 17130-1896) D.C. 40868-1906.			
			No2 on 1896 Roll as Jinsie Durant			
12			No4 " 1893 Pay Roll, Cedar Col No 118			
13			No.5 Enrolled June 11, 1900			
14			No6 Born Feby. 4, 1902; enrolled May 24, 1902			Date of Application for Enrollment.
15	No.3 died January 12, 1900; proof of death filed Dec 15, 1902					May 22/99
16	No.3 died Jan. 12, 1900: Enrollment cancelled by Department July 8, 1904					
			For child of Nos 1&2 see NB (Apr 26-06) card 430			
17			Date of application for enrollment			

Dexter I.T. seems to be present P.O. 5/24/02

155

Choctaw By Blood Enrollment Cards 1898-1914

RESIDENCE: Jacks Fork	COUNTY.						CARD NO.	
POST OFFICE: Stringtown, I.T.	**Choctaw Nation**				**Choctaw Roll** (Not Including Freedmen)		FIELD NO.	1956

Dawes' Roll No.	NAME		Relationship to Person First Named	AGE	SEX	BLOOD	TRIBAL ENROLLMENT		
							Year	County	No.
5606	1 Williams, Joe B	28		25	M	Full	1896	Jacks Fork	14097
14707	2 " Amanda	5	Dau	2	F	1/2			
	3								
	4								
	5								
	6								
	7								
	8								
	9								
	10								
	11								
	12								
	13								
	14								
	15	ENROLLMENT OF NOS. 1 HEREON APPROVED BY THE SECRETARY OF INTERIOR JAN 16 1903		ENROLLMENT OF NOS. 2 HEREON APPROVED BY THE SECRETARY OF INTERIOR MAY 20 1903					
	16								
	17								

TRIBAL ENROLLMENT OF PARENTS

	Name of Father	Year	County	Name of Mother	Year	County
1	Bill Williams	Dead	Jacks Fork	Emma Williams	Dead	Jacks Fork
2	No 1			Carrie Williams	Dead	Chickasaw roll
3						
4						
5						
6	Has a child whose name appears					
7	on Chickasaw Card No 1436 (same as No 2)					
8	No 2 transferred from Chickasaw card #1436 December 31, 1902					
9						
10						
11						
12						
13						
14						Date of Application for Enrollment.
15						
16						5/22/99
17						

Choctaw By Blood Enrollment Cards 1898-1914

RESIDENCE: Jacks Fork	COUNTY.		Choctaw Roll	CARD No.
POST OFFICE: Stringtown, I.T.	**Choctaw Nation**		(Not Including Freedmen)	FIELD No. 1957

Dawes' Roll No.	NAME	Relationship to Person First Named	AGE	SEX	BLOOD	TRIBAL ENROLLMENT		
						Year	County	No.
5607	₁ Williams, Eastman ²⁰	First Named	17	M	Full	1896	Blue	13919
	2							
	3							
	4							
	5							
	6							
	7							
	8							
	9							
	10							
	11							
	12							
	13							
	14							
	15	ENROLLMENT OF NOS. 1 HEREON APPROVED BY THE SECRETARY OF INTERIOR JAN 16 1903						
	16							
	17							

TRIBAL ENROLLMENT OF PARENTS

	Name of Father	Year	County	Name of Mother	Year	County
1	Bill Williams	Dead	Jacks Fork	Emma Williams	Dead	Jacks Fork
2						
3						
4						
5						
6		Also on 1896 roll Page 319, No 14099, as				
7		Eastman William Jacks Fork Co.				
8						
9						
10						
11						
12						
13						
14					Date of Application for Enrollment.	
15						
16					5/22/99	
17						

Choctaw By Blood Enrollment Cards 1898-1914

RESIDENCE: Nashoba   COUNTY.
POST OFFICE: Tushkahomma[sic], I.T.

Choctaw Nation

Choctaw Roll
(Not Including Freedmen)

CARD NO.
FIELD NO. 1958

Dawes' Roll No.	NAME	Relationship to Person First Named	AGE	SEX	BLOOD	TRIBAL ENROLLMENT Year	County	No.
5608	1 Ben, Wallace DIED PRIOR TO SEPTEMBER 25 1902		70	M	Full	1896	Nashoba	1225
5609	2 " Lina ²⁹	Wife	26	F	"	1896	"	1226
5610	3 " Salina ¹⁰	Dau	7	"	"	1896	"	1227
5611	4 " Elem ³	Son	9mo	M	"			
	5							
	6							
	7							
	8							
	9							
	10							
	11							
	12							
	13							
	14							
	15	ENROLLMENT OF NOS. 1,2,3,4 HEREON APPROVED BY THE SECRETARY OF INTERIOR JAN 16 1903						
	16							
	17							

TRIBAL ENROLLMENT OF PARENTS

	Name of Father	Year	County	Name of Mother	Year	County
1	A thle po tubbee	Dead	in Mississippi	Ish ta hu na	Dead	
2	Dennis Posh	"	Nashoba	Linney Posh	"	Nashoba
3	No 1			No 2		
4	No.1			No.2		
5						
6						
7			No2 on 1896 roll as Linie Ben			
8			No.4 Enrolled January 2, 1901.			
9			Proof of birth of No.4 filed Dec. 23, 1902 as Elum "Bean"			
			No.1 died before Sept 25, 1902. Enrollment cancelled by Department May 2, 1906			
10						
11						
12						
13						
14					#1 to 3	
15					Date of Application for Enrollment.	
16					5/22/99	
17			P. O. Nashoba I.T. 11/12/07			

158

Choctaw By Blood Enrollment Cards 1898-1914

| RESIDENCE: Cedar | COUNTY. | Choctaw Nation | Choctaw Roll | CARD No. |
| POST OFFICE: Tushkahomma[sic], I.T. | | | (Not Including Freedmen) | FIELD No. 1959 |

Dawes' Roll No.	NAME	Relationship to Person First Named	AGE	SEX	BLOOD	TRIBAL ENROLLMENT		
						Year	County	No.
5612	1 Choate, Lummy 55	First Named	52	M	Full	1896	Wade	11332
5613	2 DIED PRIOR TO SEPTEMBER 25 1902 Cornelia	Wife	35	F	"	1896	"	11333
5614	3 " Millie 11	Dau	8	"	"	1896	"	11335
5615	4 " Stephen 7	Son	4	M	"	1896	"	11336
	5							
	6							
	7							
	8							
	9							
	10							
	11							
	12							
	13							
	14							
	15	ENROLLMENT OF NOS. 1,2,3,4 HEREON APPROVED BY THE SECRETARY OF INTERIOR JAN 16 1903						
	16							
	17							

TRIBAL ENROLLMENT OF PARENTS

	Name of Father	Year	County	Name of Mother	Year	County
1	Pesa-chubbee	Dead	Wade	Ho-lich-na	Dead	Nashoba
2	Davison	1896	Nashoba	Jinsey Davison	"	"
3	No 1			No 2		
4	No 1			No 2		
5						
6						
7			No1 on 1896 roll as Limmy Shoat			
8			Surnames on 1896 roll as Shoat			
9			No.2 died Jany 4, 1902. Proof of death filed Dec 30, 1902			
10			aNo.2 died Jan 4, 1902: Enrollment cancelled by Department July 8, 1904			
11						
12						
13						
14						
15						
16			Date of Application for Enrollment.	5/22/99		
17						

159

Choctaw By Blood Enrollment Cards 1898-1914

RESIDENCE: Nashoba   COUNTY. **Choctaw Nation**   **Choctaw Roll** CARD NO.
POST OFFICE: Tushkahomma[sic] I.T.   *(Not Including Freedmen)* FIELD NO. 1960

Dawes' Roll No.	NAME	Relationship to Person	AGE	SEX	BLOOD	TRIBAL ENROLLMENT Year	County	No.
5616	1 Attuklantema ~~DIED PRIOR TO SEPTEMBER 25, 1902~~	First Named	78	F	Full	1896	Nashoba	236
	2							
	3							
	4							
	5							
	6							
	7							
	8							
	9							
	10							
	11							
	12							
	13							
	14							
	15	ENROLLMENT OF NOS. 1 HEREON						
	16	APPROVED BY THE SECRETARY OF INTERIOR JAN 16 1903						
	17							

TRIBAL ENROLLMENT OF PARENTS

	Name of Father	Year	County	Name of Mother	Year	County
1	Tuno-la	Ded	Eagle	Pis-a-tima	Ded	Eagle
2						
3						
4						
5						
6						
7		On 1896 roll as Antuk-lan-tema				
8						
9		No1 died Sept 16, 1902; proof of death filed Dec 15, 1902				
10		No.1 died Sept. 16, 1902: Enrollment cancelled by Department July 8, 1904				
11						
12						
13						
14					Date of Application for Enrollment.	
15						
16					5-22-99	
17						

160

Choctaw By Blood Enrollment Cards 1898-1914

RESIDENCE: Cedar COUNTY. **Choctaw Nation** Choctaw Roll CARD NO.
POST OFFICE: Tushkahomma[sic] I.T. *(Not Including Freedmen)* FIELD NO. **1961**

Dawes' Roll No.	NAME	Relationship to Person First Named	AGE	SEX	BLOOD	TRIBAL ENROLLMENT		
						Year	County	No.
5617	1 Cooper, Jane 63		60	F	1/4	1896	Cedar	2448
5618	2 " Henry 16	G. Son	13	M	1/2	1896	"	2449
	3							
	4							
	5							
	6							
	7							
	8							
	9							
	10							
	11							
	12							
	13							
	14							
	15	ENROLLMENT OF NOS. 1,2 HEREON APPROVED BY THE SECRETARY OF INTERIOR JAN 16 1903						
	16							
	17							

TRIBAL ENROLLMENT OF PARENTS

	Name of Father	Year	County	Name of Mother	Year	County
1	Hardy	Dead	Non-Citz	Peggy Hardy	Dead	Bok Tuklo
2	King Hardy	"	Atoka	Lasen Hardy	1896	Red River
3						
4						
5						
6						
7						
8						
9						
10						
11						
12						
13						
14					Date of Application for Enrollment.	
15						
16					5/23/99	
17						

161

RESIDENCE: Cedar COUNTY.
POST OFFICE: Tushkahomma[sic] I.T. **Choctaw Nation**
Choctaw Roll (Not Including Freedmen)
CARD NO.
FIELD NO. **1962**

Dawes' Roll No.	NAME	Relationship to Person	AGE	SEX	BLOOD	Year	County	No.
5619	1 Hardy, Napoleon 60	First Named	57	M	1/4	1896	Cedar	5468
5620	2 " Emily 46	Wife	43	F	3/4	1896	"	5442
5621	3 " Nellie 19	Dau	16	"	1/2	1896	"	5445
5622	4 " Washington 18	Son	15	M	1/2	1896	"	5446
5623	5 " Annie 17	Dau	14	F	1/2	1896	"	5447
5624	6 " Polina 15	"	12	"	1/2	1896	"	5448
5625	7 " Elsine 14	"	11	"	1/2	1896	"	5449
5626	8 " Kennedy 10	Son	7	M	1/2	1896	"	5450
5627	9 " Meliney 6	Dau	3	F	1/2	1896	"	5451
	10							
	11							
	12							
	13							
	14							
	15							
	16							
	17							

(DIED PRIOR TO SEPTEMBER 25, 1902)

ENROLLMENT
OF NOS. 1,2,3,4,5,6,7,8,9 HEREON
APPROVED BY THE SECRETARY
OF INTERIOR Jan. 16 1903

TRIBAL ENROLLMENT OF PARENTS

	Name of Father	Year	County	Name of Mother	Year	County
1	Hardy	Dead	Non Citz	Peggy Hardy	Dead	Bok Tuklo
2	Reuben Calvin	"	Nashoba	Ta-nich-me	"	Cedar
3	No 1			No 2		
4	No 1			No 2		
5	No 1			No 2		
6	No 1			No 2		
7	No 1			No 2		
8	No 1			No 2		
9	No 1			No 2		
10	No 4 on 1896 roll as Wash Hardy					
11	No 5 on 1896 " " Ann "					
12	No 6 on 1896 " " Fannie "					
13	No 1 died Nov. 26, 1901: Proof of death filed Dec 12, 1902					
	No 3 is now the wife of Ben Benjamin Choctaw Card #1998					
14	No 1 died Nov. 26, 1901: Enrollment cancelled by Department July 8, 1904					
15	For child of No 3 see NB (Apr 26-06) Card #674					
16	" " No 5 " (Mar 3-05) " #855				Date of Application for Enrollment.	
17					5/23/99	

Choctaw By Blood Enrollment Cards 1898-1914

RESIDENCE: Jacks Fork   COUNTY. **Choctaw Nation**   **Choctaw Roll**   CARD No.
POST OFFICE: Stringtown, I.T.   *(Not Including Freedmen)*   FIELD No.   1963

Dawes' Roll No.	NAME	Relationship to Person	AGE	SEX	BLOOD	TRIBAL ENROLLMENT Year	County	No.
5628	1 Billy, Alexander DIED PRIOR TO SEPTEMBER 25, 1902	First Named	9	M	1/2	1896	Jacks Fork	1894
	2							
	3							
	4							
	5							
	6							
	7							
	8							
	9							
	10							
	11							
	12							
	13							
	14							
	15							
	16							
	17							

ENROLLMENT
OF NOS. 1 HEREON
APPROVED BY THE SECRETARY
OF INTERIOR JAN 16 1903

TRIBAL ENROLLMENT OF PARENTS

	Name of Father	Year	County	Name of Mother	Year	County
1	Simon Billy	1896	Chick Roll	Levina Billy	Dead	Jacks Fork
2						
3						
4						
5						
6	Father on Chickasaw Card No 707					
7	No. 1 died Aug. – 1901: Enrollment cancelled by Department Sept 16, 1904					
8						
9						
10						
11						
12						
13						
14				Date of Application for Enrollment.		
15						
16				5/23/99		
17						

Choctaw By Blood Enrollment Cards 1898-1914

RESIDENCE: Cedar   COUNTY.   **Choctaw Nation**   **Choctaw Roll**   CARD NO.

POST OFFICE: Tushkahomma[sic], I.T.   *(Not Including Freedmen)*   FIELD NO.   1964

Dawes' Roll No.		NAME		Relationship to Person	AGE	SEX	BLOOD	TRIBAL ENROLLMENT		
								Year	County	No.
5629	1	Hardy, Rogers	27	First Named	24	M	1/2	1896	Cedar	5444
	2									
	3									
	4									
	5									
	6									
	7									
	8									
	9									
	10									
	11									
	12									
	13									
	14									
	15									
	16									
	17									

ENROLLMENT
OF NOS. 1 HEREON
APPROVED BY THE SECRETARY
OF INTERIOR JAN 16 1903

TRIBAL ENROLLMENT OF PARENTS

	Name of Father	Year	County	Name of Mother	Year	County
1	Napoleon Hardy	1896	Cedar	Emily Hardy	1896	Cedar
2						
3						
4						
5						
6		Also on 1896 roll, Sugar Loaf Co, Page 128				
7		No 5242				
8						
9						
10						
11						
12						
13						
14						
15						
16					Date of Application for Enrollment.	5/23/99
17	P.O. Boswell, I.T.					

12/2/02

Choctaw By Blood Enrollment Cards 1898-1914

RESIDENCE: Nashoba   COUNTY. **Choctaw Nation**   **Choctaw Roll**   CARD NO.
POST OFFICE: Tushkahomma[sic], I.T.   (Not Including Freedmen)   FIELD NO. **1965**

Dawes' Roll No.	NAME		Relationship to Person	AGE	SEX	BLOOD	TRIBAL ENROLLMENT		
							Year	County	No.
5630	1 Noah, Ebenezer	50	First Named	47	M	Full	1896	Nashoba	9714
5631	2 " Ellen	24	Wife	21	F	"	1896	"	9715
5632	3 " Maggie	5	Dau	1	"	"			
5633	4 Battiest, Elizabeth	17	Ward	14	"	"	1896	Nashoba	1218
5634	5 Noah, Ellias	3	Son	4mo	M	"			
5635	6 " Rogers	1	Son	3mo	M	"			
	7								
	8								
	9								
	10								
	11								
	12								
	13								
	14								
	15	ENROLLMENT OF NOS. 1,2,3,4,5,6 HEREON APPROVED BY THE SECRETARY							
	16	OF INTERIOR Jan. 16, 1903							
	17								

TRIBAL ENROLLMENT OF PARENTS

	Name of Father	Year	County	Name of Mother	Year	County
1	Lowin Noah	Dead	Nashoba	Mea-sho-to-na	Dead	Nashoba
2	Nicholas Pickens	1896	"	Pollie Pickens	1896	"
3	No 1			No 2		
4	Calvin Battiest	Dead	Cedar	Sillie Ann Battiest	Dead	Cedar
5	No 1			No.2		
6	No 1			No.2		
7						
8						
9	For child of Nos 1&2 see N.B. (Apr 26-06) Card #737					
10	" " " " " " " " " #934					
11	No.5 Enrolled June 11, 1900					
	No 6 Born May 30, 1902, enrolled Aug 23, 1902					
12	No 4 is wife of Roberson Choate Choctaw Card #5618 certificate of					
13	marriage filed Dec. 10, 1901					
14						
15						
16						
17						

P.O. Nashoba I.T. 4/2/06

Choctaw By Blood Enrollment Cards 1898-1914

| RESIDENCE: Cedar | COUNTY. | | | | |
| POST OFFICE: Tushkahomma[sic], I.T. | | | | | |

Choctaw Nation

Choctaw Roll (Not Including Freedmen)

CARD NO. FIELD NO. 1966

Dawes' Roll No.	NAME	Relationship to Person Named	AGE	SEX	BLOOD	TRIBAL ENROLLMENT		
						Year	County	No.
5636	1 Battiest, Jackson *DIED PRIOR TO SEPTEMBER 25, 1902*	First Named	91	M	Full	1896	Cedar	1070
5637	2 " Mila ⁵⁵	Wife	52	F	"	1896	"	1071
5638	3 " Kimsey ¹³	Ward	10	"	"	1896	"	1072
	4							
	5							
	6							
	7							
	8							
	9							
	10							
	11							
	12							
	13							
	14	ENROLLMENT						
	15	OF NOS. 1,2,3 HEREON						
	16	APPROVED BY THE SECRETARY OF INTERIOR JAN 16 1903						
	17							

TRIBAL ENROLLMENT OF PARENTS

	Name of Father	Year	County	Name of Mother	Year	County
1	John Battiest	Dead		E ka na	Dead	Cedar
2	Lowin Noah	"	Nashoba	Mea-sho-to-na	"	Nashoba
3	Goodman M°Kinzie	1896	Cedar	Jinsey White	1896	Cedar
4						
5						
6						
7		No2 on 1896 roll as Mimy Battiest				
8		No3 " 1896 " " Kensey "				
9						
10		No1 died Oct. 1, 1900; proof of death filed Dec 15, 1902				
11		No1 died Oct. 1, 1900. Enrollment cancelled by Department July 8, 1904				
12		No.3 is duplicate of Kimpsey M°Kinzie on Choctaw card 1955. Enrollment cancelled un Departmental authority of September 17, 1896 (ITD 17130-1896)				
13		DC 40868-1906				
14						
15						
16				Date of Application for Enrollment.	5/23/99	
17						

Choctaw By Blood Enrollment Cards 1898-1914

RESIDENCE: Nashoba COUNTY **Choctaw Nation** Choctaw Roll CARD NO.
POST OFFICE: Alikchi, I.T. (Not Including Freedmen) FIELD NO. 1967

Dawes' Roll No.	NAME		Relationship to Person First Named	AGE	SEX	BLOOD	TRIBAL ENROLLMENT		
							Year	County	No.
5639	1 Bond, Ashford	23		20	M	Full	1896	Nashoba	1185
5640	2 " Hoppen	17	Bro	16	"	"	1896	"	1186
	3								
	4								
	5								
	6								
	7								
	8								
	9								
	10								
	11								
	12								
	13								
	14								
	15	ENROLLMENT OF NOS. 1,2 HEREON APPROVED BY THE SECRETARY OF INTERIOR JAN 16 1903							
	16								
	17								

TRIBAL ENROLLMENT OF PARENTS

	Name of Father	Year	County	Name of Mother	Year	County
1	Colone Bond	Dead	Nashoba	Larkie Bond	Dead	Nashoba
2	" "	"	"	" "	"	"
3						
4						
5						
6						
7						
8						
9						
10						
11						
12						
13						
14						
15						
16				Date of Application for Enrollment. 5/23/99		
17						

167

RESIDENCE: Jacks Fork COUNTY. **Choctaw Nation** Choctaw Roll CARD NO.
POST OFFICE: Tushkahomma[sic], I.T. *(Not Including Freedmen)* FIELD NO. **1968**

Dawes' Roll No.	NAME	Relationship to Person First Named	AGE	SEX	BLOOD	TRIBAL ENROLLMENT		
						Year	County	No.
5641	1 Colbert, Ellis 32	Named	29	M	1/2	1896	Jacks Fork	3038
~~5642~~	2 ~~Elsie~~ DIED PRIOR TO SEPTEMBER 24 1902	~~Wife~~	~~38~~	~~F~~	~~Full~~	~~1893~~	~~Sans Bois~~	~~215~~
5642	3 Cooper, George 12	S. Son	9	M	1/2	1893	" "	216
	4							
	5							
	6							
	7							
	8							
	9							
	10							
	11							
	12							
	13							
	14							
	15	ENROLLMENT OF NOS. 1,2,3 HEREON						
	16	APPROVED BY THE SECRETARY OF INTERIOR JAN 16 1903						
	17							

TRIBAL ENROLLMENT OF PARENTS

Name of Father	Year	County	Name of Mother	Year	County
1 Billie Colbert	1896	Chick Roll	Martha Colbert	1896	Jacks Fork
2 ~~Mickie King~~	~~Dead~~	~~Sans ABois~~	~~Susan King~~	~~Dead~~	~~Sans Bois~~
3 Morris Cooper	1896	Chick Roll	No 2		
4					
5					
6					
7					
8					
9		No2 on 1893 Pay roll, Page 21, No 215, Sans Bois Co as Elsy Cooper			
10		No3 " 1893 " " " 21 " 216 " " "			
11		For child of No.1 see NB (March 3, 1905) #833			
12		~~No2 died Oct, 1899; proof of death filed Dec 12, 1902~~			
13		No 1 is now husband of No 3 on Choctaw card #4156			
14		No.2 died Oct - 1899: Enrollment cancelled by Department July 8, 1904			
15			Date of Application for Enrollment.		
16			5/23/99		
17					

168

Choctaw By Blood Enrollment Cards 1898-1914

RESIDENCE: Cedar COUNTY. **Choctaw Nation** Choctaw Roll CARD NO.
POST OFFICE: Tushkahomma[sic], I.T. *(Not Including Freedmen)* FIELD NO. 1969

Dawes' Roll No.	NAME		Relationship to Person First Named	AGE	SEX	BLOOD	TRIBAL ENROLLMENT		
							Year	County	No.
5644	1 Hampton, Susan	40	First Named	37	F	Full	1896	Cedar	1065
5645	2 Battiest, Houston	19	Son	16	M	"	1896	"	1066
5646	3 " Lena	12	Dau	9	F	"	1896	"	1067
5647	4 " Sema	10	Dau	7	F	"	1896	"	1068
5648	5 Hampton, Wilmon	1	Son	8mo	M	"			
	6								
	7								
	8								
	9								
	10								
	11								
	12								
	13								
	14								
	15								
	16								
	17								

ENROLLMENT
OF NOS. 1,2,3,4,5 HEREON
APPROVED BY THE SECRETARY
OF INTERIOR JAN 16 1903

TRIBAL ENROLLMENT OF PARENTS

	Name of Father	Year	County	Name of Mother	Year	County
1	Gilbert Cooper	Dead	Cedar	Montahona	Dead	Gaines
2	Calvin Battiest	"	"	No 1		
3	" "	"	"	No 1		
4	" "	"	"	No 1		
5	Aaron Hampton		Choc. card 1952	No 1		
6						
7						
8	No4 On 1896 roll as Sena Battiest					
9	No1 " 1896 " " Susie Battiest					
10	No.1 is the wife of Aaron Hampton on Choc. card 1952. Evidence of marriage filed July 7, 19012.					
11	No.5 born November 9, 1901: Enrolled July 7, 1902.					
12	For child of No.4 see NB (March 3, 1905) #1407					
13						
14						
15					#1 to 4	
16				Date of Application for Enrollment:		5/23/99
17						

169

Choctaw By Blood Enrollment Cards 1898-1914

RESIDENCE: Cedar COUNTY.
POST OFFICE: Tushkahomma[sic], I.T.

Choctaw Nation

Choctaw Roll (Not Including Freedmen)

CARD NO.
FIELD NO. 1970

Dawes' Roll No.	NAME	Relationship to Person First Named	AGE	SEX	BLOOD	TRIBAL ENROLLMENT Year	County	No.
5649	1 Eyachubbe, Thompson	Named	18	M	Full	1896	Cedar	3713
5650	2 DIED PRIOR TO SEPTEMBER 25, 2902 Sissie	Wife	23	F	"	1896	"	4724
5651	3 DIED PRIOR TO SEPTEMBER 25, 1902 Lita	Dau	8mo	"	"			
5652	4 DIED PRIOR TO SEPTEMBER 25, 1902 Green, Isaac	S.Son	9	M	"	1896	Cedar	4725
5653	5 " Joe	"	3	"	"	1896	"	4726
	6							
	7							
	8							
	9							
	10							
	11 No.2 died July – 1899; No.3 died Aug 1 1899;							
	12 No.4 died Jan - 1900; Enrollment cancelled by							
	13 Department July 8, 1904							
	14							
	15 ENROLLMENT OF NOS. 1,2,3,4,5 HEREON							
	16 APPROVED BY THE SECRETARY							
	17 OF INTERIOR JAN 16 1903							

TRIBAL ENROLLMENT OF PARENTS

Name of Father	Year	County	Name of Mother	Year	County
1 Wm Eyachabbe[sic]		Cedar	Jincy Eyachabbe	Dead	Cedar
2 Gilbert Cooper	Dead	"	Ka-ni-he-ma	"	Nashoba
3 No 1			No 2		
4 Arben Green	Dead	Cedar	No 2		
5 " "	"	"	No 2		
6					
7					
8 No2 on 1896 Roll as Sissie Green					
9 No4 died January – 1900; proof of death filed Dec 16, 1902					
10 No2 " July – 1899; " " " " " 17, "					
11 No3 " Aug – 1899; " " " " " 17, "					
12 No 1 is now husband of Polly Morris Choctaw card #1894.					
13					
14				Date of Application for Enrollment.
15				
16				May 23/99
17 No.5 Dexter I.T.				

P.O. Antlers, I.T.   12/12/02

Choctaw By Blood Enrollment Cards 1898-1914

RESIDENCE: Cedar COUNTY. **Choctaw Nation** **Choctaw Roll** CARD No.
POST OFFICE: Tushkahomma[sic], I.T. *(Not Including Freedmen)* FIELD No. 1971

Dawes' Roll No.	NAME	Relationship to Person First Named	AGE	SEX	BLOOD	TRIBAL ENROLLMENT		
						Year	County	No.
5654	1 White Susan ⁴⁸	First Named	45	F	Full	1896	Cedar	9265
	2							
	3							
	4							
	5							
	6							
	7							
	8							
	9							
	10							
	11							
	12							
	13							
	14							
	15							
	16							
	17							

ENROLLMENT
OF NOS. 1 HEREON
APPROVED BY THE SECRETARY
OF INTERIOR JAN 16 1903

TRIBAL ENROLLMENT OF PARENTS

	Name of Father	Year	County	Name of Mother	Year	County
1	Makintubbe	Dead	Red River		Dead	Red River
2						
3						
4						
5						
6	On 1896 roll as Susan McFarland					
7						
8						
9						
10						
11						
12						
13						
14						
15					DATE OF APPLICATION FOR ENROLLMENT.	
16						
17						

Choctaw By Blood Enrollment Cards 1898-1914

RESIDENCE: Wade   COUNTY.   **Choctaw Nation**   **Choctaw Roll**   CARD NO.
POST OFFICE: Clayton I.T.   *(Not Including Freedmen)*   FIELD NO.   1972

Dawes' Roll No.	NAME	Relationship to Person Named	AGE	SEX	BLOOD	TRIBAL ENROLLMENT		
						Year	County	No.
5655	1 Jones Charley 32	First Named	29	M	Full	1896	Wade	6699
5656	2 Amanda DIED PRIOR TO SEPTEMBER 25,1902	Dau	4	F	"	1896	"	6701
5657	3 Solomon DIED PRIOR TO SEPTEMBER 23,1903	Nephew	16	M	"	1896	"	6705
	4							
	5							
	6							
	7							
	8							
	9							
	10							
	11							
	12							
	13							
	14							
	15	ENROLLMENT OF NOS. 1,2,3 HEREON						
	16	APPROVED BY THE SECRETARY OF INTERIOR JAN 16 1903						
	17							

TRIBAL ENROLLMENT OF PARENTS

	Name of Father	Year	County	Name of Mother	Year	County
1	Thomas Jones	Dead	Wade	Mehatona	Dead	Wade
2	No 1			Jenny Jones	"	"
3	Jamson[sic] Jones	Dead	Wade	Ina Jones	"	"
4						
5						
6						
7	No2 died May 6, 1902; proof of death filed Dec 16, 1902					
8	No3 " February-1900; " " " " " "					
9	No1 is now husband of Ellen Cooper on Choctaw card #1947					
10	No.2 died May6,1902. No.3 died Feb-1900. Enrollment cancelled by Department July 8, 1904					
11	For child of No1 see NB (Apr 26-06) Card #557					
12	" " " " " " (Mar 3-05) " #852					
13						
14						
15					Date of Application for Enrollment.	
16					5/23/99	
17						

172

Choctaw By Blood Enrollment Cards 1898-1914

RESIDENCE: Cedar   COUNTY.
POST OFFICE: Tushkahomma I.T.

Choctaw Nation

Choctaw Roll   CARD NO.
(Not Including Freedmen)   FIELD NO. 1973

Dawes' Roll No.	NAME	Relationship to Person First Named	AGE	SEX	BLOOD	TRIBAL ENROLLMENT Year	County	No.
5658	1 Kincade Rayson DIED PRIOR TO SEPTEMBER 25 1902		28	M	Full	1896	Cedar	7521
5659	2 " Anna 45	Wife	42	F	"	1896	"	7522
5660	3 Wright Allen 15	Ward	12	M	"	1896	"	13134
	4							
	5							
	6							
	7							
	8							
	9							
	10							
	11							
	12							
	13							
	14							
	15	ENROLLMENT OF NOS. 1,2,3, [sic] HEREON APPROVED BY THE SECRETARY OF INTERIOR JAN 16 1903							
	16							
	17							

TRIBAL ENROLLMENT OF PARENTS

	Name of Father	Year	County	Name of Mother	Year	County
1	George Kincade	1896	Red River	Wiley Kincade	Dead	Red River
2	Simon McFarland	Dead	Nashoba	Inlahima	"	Nashoba
3	John Wright	"	Red River	Kittie	"	Red River
4						
5						
6			No1 On 1896 roll as Rayson Kinkade			
7			No2 " " " " Anna Kinkade			
8						
9			No1 died May 7, 1900; proof of death filed Dec 15, 1902			
10		No1 died May 7, 1900: Enrollment cancelled by Department July 8, 1904				
11						
12						
13						
14						
15					Date of Application for Enrollment.	
16					5/23/99	
17						

173

RESIDENCE: Cedar COUNTY. **Choctaw Nation** **Choctaw Roll** CARD NO.
POST OFFICE: Tushkahomma[sic] I.T. *(Not Including Freedmen)* FIELD NO. 1974

Dawes' Roll No.	NAME		Relationship to Person First Named	AGE	SEX	BLOOD	TRIBAL ENROLLMENT			
							Year	County		No.
5661	1 Wall Sam	31		28	M	Full	1896	Jacks Fork		14134
14708	2 " Sibbel	18	Wife	15	F	"	1896	"	"	3025
	3									
	4									
	5									
	6									
	7									
	8									
	9									
	10									
	11									
	12									
	13									
	14									
	15	ENROLLMENT OF NOS. 1 HEREON APPROVED BY THE SECRETARY OF INTERIOR JAN 16 1903			ENROLLMENT OF NOS. 2 HEREON APPROVED BY THE SECRETARY OF INTERIOR MAY 20 1903					
	16									
	17									

TRIBAL ENROLLMENT OF PARENTS

	Name of Father	Year	County	Name of Mother	Year	County
1	Edwin Wall	1896	Wade	Elizabeth Wall	Dead	Jack's Fork
2	Joshua Calvin	1896	Jack's Fork	Lucy	"	" " "
3						
4						
5						
6			No.2 on 1896 Choctaw roll as Libby Calvin			
7			No.2 Transferred from Card #37 to this card 5/23/99			
8			For child of Nos 1-2 see NB (March 3 1905) #832			
9						
10						
11						
12						
13						
14						
15					#1	
16				Date of Application for Enrollment.		5/23/99
17						

Choctaw By Blood Enrollment Cards 1898-1914

RESIDENCE: Jack's Fork COUNTY. **Choctaw Nation**   **Choctaw Roll**   CARD NO.

POST OFFICE: Tushkahomma[sic] I.T.   *(Not Including Freedmen)*   FIELD NO. **1975**

Dawes' Roll No.	NAME		Relationship to Person First Named	AGE	SEX	BLOOD	TRIBAL ENROLLMENT		
							Year	County	No.
5662	₁ Tupper, Thomas	59		56	M	Full	1893	Jack's Fork	P.R. 685
5663	₂ " Alford	12	Son	9	M	"	1893	" "	P.R. 687
5664	₃ " Jolum	10	Son	7	M	"	1893	" "	689
	4								
	5								
	6								
	7								
	8								
	9								
	10								
	11								
	12								
	13								
	14								
	15	ENROLLMENT OF NOS. 1,2,3 HEREON APPROVED BY THE SECRETARY OF INTERIOR Jan 16, 1903							
	16								
	17								

TRIBAL ENROLLMENT OF PARENTS

	Name of Father	Year	County	Name of Mother	Year	County
₁	Bashpotapa	Dead	Jack's Fork	Notona	1896	Nashoba
₂	No 1			Sissie Tupper	Dead	Jack's Fork
₃	No 1			" "	"	" " "
4						
5			No1 also on 1896 Choctaw roll page 223 #8894 as Thomas More			
6			No3 " " " " " " " #8895 " John More			
7						
8						
9			No1 On 1893 payroll page 77, No 685 Jack's Fork Co			
10			No2 " " " " 77 No 687 " "			
11			No3 " " " 78 No 689 " " "			
11			No2 on 1896 Choctaw roll as Alfred T More; page 222 #8860			
12			No1 is now husband of No1 on Choctaw card #1437			
13					12/11/02	
14						
15						
16				Date of Application for Enrollment.	5/23/99	
17						

175

Choctaw By Blood Enrollment Cards 1898-1914

RESIDENCE: Nashoba   COUNTY.   **Choctaw Nation**   **Choctaw Roll**   CARD NO.
POST OFFICE: Tushkahomma[sic] I.T.   (Not Including Freedmen)   FIELD NO.   1976

Dawes' Roll No.	NAME	Relationship to Person	AGE	SEX	BLOOD	TRIBAL ENROLLMENT Year	County	No.
5665	1 Mom's Nelson (DIED PRIOR TO SEPTEMBER 23 1902)	First Named	45	M	Full	1896	Nashoba	8631
5666	2 " Sibbie ⁴⁶	Wife	43	F	"	1896	"	8632
5667	3 " Mila (DIED PRIOR TO SEPTEMBER 25 1902)	Dau	20	F	"	1896	"	8633
5668	4 " Silas ¹³	Son	10	M	"	1896	"	8636
	5							
	6							
	7							
	8							
	9							
	10							
	11							
	12							
	13							
	14							
	15							
	16							
	17							

ENROLLMENT
OF NOS. 1,2,3,4   HEREON
APPROVED BY THE SECRETARY
OF INTERIOR JAN 16 1903

TRIBAL ENROLLMENT OF PARENTS

	Name of Father	Year	County	Name of Mother	Year	County
1	Ahabe	Dead	Nashoba	Lucy Ahabe	Dead	Nashoba
2	Ahnabe	"	"	Onahoke	"	"
3	No 1			Celia Mom's	"	"
4	No 1			No 2		
5						
6						
7	No 3 On 1896 roll as Mailin Mom's					
8	No.2 died February 7, 1904					
9	No1 died May 26, 1901; proof of death filed Dec 15, 1902					
10	No.3 " Jany 1, 1901; " " " " " " "					
11	No.1 died May 26, 1901; No.3 died Jan 1, 1901; Enrollment cancelled by Department July 8, 1904					
12						
13						
14						
15						
16				Date of Application for Enrollment.		5/23/99
17						

Choctaw By Blood Enrollment Cards 1898-1914

RESIDENCE: Wade	COUNTY.					
POST OFFICE: Albion I.T.						

Choctaw Nation

Choctaw Roll (Not Including Freedmen)

CARD NO.

FIELD NO. 1977

Dawes' Roll No.	NAME	Relationship to Person First Named	AGE	SEX	BLOOD	TRIBAL ENROLLMENT		
						Year	County	No.
5669	1 Alexander Ned ^38	First Named	35	M	Full	1896	Wade	164
DEAD.	2 " Tuna	Wife	45	F		1896	"	165
	3							
	4							
	5							
	6							
	7							
	8							
	9							
	10							
	11 No. 2 HEREON DISMISSED UNDER							
	12 ORDER OF THE COMMISSION TO THE FIVE							
	13 CIVILIZED TRIBES OF MARCH 31, 1905.							
	14							
	15 ENROLLMENT OF NOS. 1 HEREON							
	16 APPROVED BY THE SECRETARY							
	17 OF INTERIOR JAN 16 1903							

TRIBAL ENROLLMENT OF PARENTS

	Name of Father	Year	County	Name of Mother	Year	County
1		Dead	Sugar Loaf	Sayimmi	Dead	Nashoba
2		Dead	Wade		Dead	"
3						
4						
5						
6			No1 On 1896 roll as Nelson Alexander			
7			No2 " " " " Luna Alexander			
8						
9						
10						
11			No2 died January 23, 1902; proof of death filed Dec 15, 1902			
12			No1 husband of Ellen Wright Choctaw card #2183			
13						
14						
15						
16				Date of Application for Enrollment.	5/23/99	
17						

Choctaw By Blood Enrollment Cards 1898-1914

RESIDENCE: Cedar COUNTY. **Choctaw Nation** **Choctaw Roll** CARD No.
POST OFFICE: Tushkahomma[sic] I.T. *(Not Including Freedmen)* FIELD No. 1978

Dawes' Roll No.	NAME	Relationship to Person First Named	AGE	SEX	BLOOD	TRIBAL ENROLLMENT		
						Year	County	No.
5670	1 McFarland, Silas 43	First Named	40	M	Full	1896	Cedar	9264
5671	2 " Susan 26	Wife	23	F	3/4	1896	Jacks Fork	522
	3							
	4							
	5							
	6							
	7							
	8							
	9							
	10							
	11							
	12							
	13							
	14							
	15							
	16							
	17							

ENROLLMENT
OF NOS. 1,2 HEREON
APPROVED BY THE SECRETARY
OF INTERIOR JAN 16 1903

TRIBAL ENROLLMENT OF PARENTS

	Name of Father	Year	County	Name of Mother	Year	County
1	Simon Tahubbee	Dead	Nashoba	En-la-he-ma	Dead	Nashoba
2	Graham Anderson	"	Jacks Fork	Susan Bond	"	Wade
3						
4						
5						
6			No2 on 1896 roll as Susan Anderson			
7						
8						
9						
10						
11						
12						
13						
14						
15						
16			Date of Application for Enrollment.	5/23/99		
17						

178

Choctaw By Blood Enrollment Cards 1898-1914

RESIDENCE: Cedar COUNTY.
POST OFFICE: Tushkahomma[sic] I.T.

Choctaw Nation

Choctaw Roll
(Not Including Freedmen)

CARD NO.
FIELD NO. 1979

Dawes' Roll No.	NAME	Relationship to Person First Named	AGE	SEX	BLOOD	TRIBAL ENROLLMENT		
						Year	County	No.
5672	1 Williams, Harris 27		24	M	Full	1893	Nashoba	887
	2							
	3							
	4							
	5							
	6							
	7							
	8							
	9							
	10							
	11							
	12							
	13							
	14							
	15	ENROLLMENT OF NOS. 1 HEREON APPROVED BY THE SECRETARY OF INTERIOR JAN 16 1903						
	16							
	17							

TRIBAL ENROLLMENT OF PARENTS

	Name of Father	Year	County	Name of Mother	Year	County
1	Tomplis William	1896	Nashoba	Elsie Battiest	1896	Cedar
2						
3						
4						
5						
6						
7			On 1893 Pay roll, Page 76, No 887 Nashoba Co. as Hollis Williams			
8			Died prior to September 25, 1902; not entitled to land or money			
9			See Indian Office letter Nov 2, 1910			
10						
11						
12						
13						
14						
15						
16				Date of Application for Enrollment.	5/23/99	
17						

179

Choctaw By Blood Enrollment Cards 1898-1914

RESIDENCE: Wade   COUNTY. **Choctaw Nation**   Choctaw Roll 1980 FIELD NO.
POST OFFICE: Lyceum I.T.   *(Not Including Freedmen)*

Dawes' Roll No.	NAME	Relationship to Person First Named	AGE	SEX	BLOOD	TRIBAL ENROLLMENT		
						Year	County	No.
5673	1 Hudson, Peter W 24		21	M	Full	1896	Eagle	5585
I.W. **711**	2 " Myrtle 20	Wife	20	F.	I.W.			
	3							
	4							
	5							
	6							
	7							
	8							
	9							
	10							
	11	ENROLLMENT OF NOS. 2 HEREON APPROVED BY THE SECRETARY OF INTERIOR MAY -7 1904						
	12							
	13							
	14	ENROLLMENT OF NOS. 1 HEREON APPROVED BY THE SECRETARY OF INTERIOR JAN 16 1903						
	15							
	16							
	17							

TRIBAL ENROLLMENT OF PARENTS

	Name of Father	Year	County	Name of Mother	Year	County
1	Wash Hudson	Dead	Eagle	Frances Hudson	1896	Eagle
2	William Campbell	dead	non-citizen	Mary Campbell		non-citizen
3						
4						
5						
6	No 1 On 1896 roll as Peter Hudson					
7	No.1 is now the husband of Myrtle Hudson on Choctaw card #D.740					
8	No.2 transferred from Choctaw card #D.740; see decision of Feby 27, 1904				July 10, 1901	
9						
10	For child of Nos 1&2 see NB (March 3, 1905 #1034					
11						
12						
13						
14						Date of Application for Enrollment.
15						
16						5/23/99
17						

PO Tuskahoma IT 4/11/05

Choctaw By Blood Enrollment Cards 1898-1914

RESIDENCE: **Wade** COUNTY. **Choctaw Nation** **Choctaw Roll** CARD NO.
POST OFFICE: **Tushkahomma**[sic] I.T. *(Not Including Freedmen)* FIELD NO. #1981

Dawes' Roll No.	NAME		Relationship to Person First Named	AGE	SEX	BLOOD	TRIBAL ENROLLMENT		
							Year	County	No.
I.W. 149	1 Holman, Tuck D	35	First Named	32	M	I.W.	1896	Wade	14621
5674	2 " Mattie	26	Wife	23	F	1/4	1896	Wade	5411
5675	3 " Aline	5	Dau	2	"	1/8			
5676	4 " Gladys	3	"	3 wks	"	1/8			
	5								
	6								
	7								
	8								
	9								
	10								
	11								
	12								
	13								
	14								
	15								
	16								
	17								

ENROLLMENT OF NOS. 2,3,4 HEREON APPROVED BY THE SECRETARY OF INTERIOR JAN 16 1903

ENROLLMENT OF NOS. 1 ~~~~ HEREON APPROVED BY THE SECRETARY OF INTERIOR JUN 13 1903

TRIBAL ENROLLMENT OF PARENTS

	Name of Father	Year	County	Name of Mother	Year	County
1	Dan Holman	1896	Non-citizen	Mary A Holman	1896	Non-citizen
2	Mike Gleason	1896	" "	Minnie Gleason	dead	Gaines
3	No.1			No.2		
4	No.1			No.2		
5						
6						
7			No.1 on 1896 roll as Tucker Holman			
8			No.1 admitted by Dawes Commission in 1896 as an			
9			intermarried citizen: Choctaw case #1361: no appeal			
10			For child of Nos 1&2 see NB (Apr 26-06) Card #615			
11						
12						
13						
14						Date of Application for Enrollment.
15						
16						5/23/99
17						

181

Choctaw By Blood Enrollment Cards 1898-1914

RESIDENCE: Jacks Fork COUNTY. **Choctaw Nation**   Choctaw Roll   CARD NO.
POST OFFICE: Tushkahomma[sic] I.T.   (Not Including Freedmen) FIELD NO. 1982

Dawes' Roll No.	NAME	Relationship to Person First Named	AGE	SEX	BLOOD	TRIBAL ENROLLMENT		
						Year	County	No.
5677	1 Anderson, Edmond 65	Named	62	M	Full	1896	Jacks Fork	533
5678	2 " Nancy 63	Wife	60	F	"	1896	" "	534
5679	3 Hoklotubbe, Ben 20	Ward	17	M	"	1896	" "	5291
5680	4 " George 18	"	15	"	"	1896	" "	5292
5681	5 " Standley 15	"	12	"	"	1896	" "	5928
5682	6 " Joe 10	"	7	"	"	1896	" "	6142
	7							
	8							
	9							
	10							
	11							
	12							
	13							
	14							
	15	ENROLLMENT OF NOS. 1,2,3,4,5,6 HEREON APPROVED BY THE SECRETARY OF INTERIOR JAN 16 1903						
	16							
	17							

TRIBAL ENROLLMENT OF PARENTS

	Name of Father	Year	County	Name of Mother	Year	County
1	John Anderson	Dead	Wade	Sophie Anderson	Dead	Wade
2	Haka-lo-tubbee	"	Gaines	Wy-o-key	"	Gaines
3	Joe Hoklotubbe	"	"	Lucy A Hoklotubbe	"	"
4	" "	"	"	" " "	"	"
5	" "	"	"	" " "	"	"
6	" "	"	"	" " "	"	"
7						
8	No 2 on 1896 roll as Nicey Anderson					
9	No 5 " 1896 " " Standley Hoklotubbe					
10	No 4 " 1896 " " Geo. "					
11						
12	It is claimed that the mother of the Hoklotubbe					
13	children is a Chickasaw, but cannot be					
14	identified as such					Date of Application for Enrollment.
15	No.6 died June 14, 1906 Reported by N.S. Indian Sup't 7/31/11					
16						5/23/99
17						

182

Choctaw By Blood Enrollment Cards 1898-1914

RESIDENCE:	Nashoba	COUNTY.						
POST OFFICE:	Alikchi, I.T.							

Choctaw Nation

Choctaw Roll *(Not Including Freedmen)*

CARD NO. FIELD NO. **1983**

Dawes' Roll No.	NAME	Relationship to Person First Named	AGE	SEX	BLOOD	TRIBAL ENROLLMENT Year	County	No.
5683	1 Noah, Storden 28	First Named	25	M	Full	1896	Nashoba	9704
5684	2 " Summe 29	Wife	26	F	"	1896	"	9705
5685	3 " Isom 3	Son	7mo	M	"			
	4							
	5							
	6							
	7							
	8							
	9							
	10							
	11							
	12							
	13							
	14							
	15	ENROLLMENT OF NOS. 1,2,3 HEREON APPROVED BY THE SECRETARY OF INTERIOR JAN 16 1903						
	16							
	17							

TRIBAL ENROLLMENT OF PARENTS

	Name of Father	Year	County	Name of Mother	Year	County
1	[Illegible] Noah	Dead	Nashoba	Lucy Noah	Dead	Nashoba
2	Colone Bond	"	"	Larkie Bond	"	"
3	No.1			No.2		
4						
5						
6						
7						
8			No2 on 1896 roll as Samie Noah			
9			No.3 Enrolled June 11, 1900.			
10						
11						
12						
13						
14						
15				#1&2 Date of Application for Enrollment. 5/23/99		
16						
17						

183

Choctaw By Blood Enrollment Cards 1898-1914

RESIDENCE: Jacks Fork   COUNTY. **Choctaw Nation**   **Choctaw Roll**   CARD NO.

POST OFFICE: Lyceum, I.T.   *(Not Including Freedmen)*   FIELD NO.   1984

Dawes' Roll No.	NAME	Relationship to Person First Named	AGE	SEX	BLOOD	TRIBAL ENROLLMENT Year	County	No.
5686	1 Anderson, Millie ²¹	First Named	18	F	Full	1896	Jacks Fork	6130
5687	2 Anderson, Frank L ~~DIED PRIOR TO SEPTEMBER 25, 1902~~ Son		1	M	7/8			
5688	3 " James R ²	Son	3mo	M	7/8			
5689	4 " Peter M ¹	Son	2mo	M	7/8			
	5							
	6							
	7							
	8							
	9							
	10							
	11							
	12							
	13							
	14							
	15	ENROLLMENT OF NOS. 1,2,3,4 HEREON						
	16	APPROVED BY THE SECRETARY OF INTERIOR JAN 16 1903						
	17							

TRIBAL ENROLLMENT OF PARENTS

Name of Father	Year	County	Name of Mother	Year	County
1 Louis Carnes	Dead	Jacks Fork	Miney Byington	Dead	Jacks Fork
2 ~~Mack Anderson~~	1896	" "	~~No 1~~		
3 James Anderson	1896	" "	No.1		
4 " " "		" "	No.1		
5					
6					
7 No.1 is the wife of James D Anderson on Choctaw card #1986					
8 Evidence of marriage to be supplied. Filed June 11, 1901.					
9					
10					
11 No1 on 1896 roll as Millie Holson					
12 No.3 Enrolled March 1st, 1901					
13 No.4 born Nov 24th, 1901: Enrolled Jany 31st 1902					
~~No.2 died Feb 28, 1900. Enrollment cancelled by Department July 8, 1904~~					
14				Date of Application for Enrollment.	
15					
16				5/23/99	
17					

Choctaw By Blood Enrollment Cards 1898-1914

Dawes' Roll No.	NAME	Relationship to Person First Named	AGE	SEX	BLOOD	TRIBAL ENROLLMENT		
						Year	County	No.
5690	1 Bryant, Lucy ²⁵	First Named	22	F	Full	1896	Wade	1037
15572	2 Reed, Chicago ⁶	Son	2	M	"			
5691	3 Bryant, Mamie ²	Dau	1	F	"			
	4							
	5							
	6							
	7							
	8							
	9							
	10							
	11	ENROLLMENT						
	12	OF NOS. ~~ 2 ~~ HEREON APPROVED BY THE SECRETARY						
	13	OF INTERIOR SEP 22 1904						
	14							
	15	ENROLLMENT OF NOS. 1,3 HEREON						
	16	APPROVED BY THE SECRETARY						
	17	OF INTERIOR JAN 16 1903						

TRIBAL ENROLLMENT OF PARENTS

Name of Father	Year	County	Name of Mother	Year	County
1 Nathan Bryant	Dead	Wade	Lucinda Bryant	Dead	Wade
2 Joshua Reed	"	"	No 1		
3 Rodgers Jones	1896	Jackson	No.1		
4					
5					
6					
7	No.3 illegitimate child of No.1; born Dec. 20, 1902; Enrolled Jany 13, 1902				
8	N⁰2 Proof of birth received and filed Oct. 30, 1902				
9	N⁰2 Born Feby 20, 1897. See affidavits of N⁰1 and Lila McKinney filed June 3, 1904				
10					
11					
12					
13					
14					
15			#1&2		
16			Date of Application for Enrollment.	5/23/99	
17					

Choctaw By Blood Enrollment Cards 1898-1914

RESIDENCE: Jacks Fork COUNTY. **Choctaw Nation** **Choctaw Roll** CARD No.
POST OFFICE: Lyceum I.T. (Not Including Freedmen) FIELD No. 1986

Dawes' Roll No.	NAME	Relationship to Person First Named	AGE	SEX	BLOOD	TRIBAL ENROLLMENT		
						Year	County	No.
5692	1 Anderson James D ³¹	First Named	28	M	3/4	1896	Jacks Fork	500
	2							
	3							
	4							
	5							
	6							
	7							
	8							
	9							
	10							
	11							
	12							
	13							
	14							
	15							
	16							
	17							

ENROLLMENT
OF NOS. 1 HEREON
APPROVED BY THE SECRETARY
OF INTERIOR JAN 16 1903

TRIBAL ENROLLMENT OF PARENTS

	Name of Father	Year	County	Name of Mother	Year	County
1	Stephen Anderson		out of country	Wicey Anderson	Ded	Jacks Fork
2						
3						
4						
5						
6	No. 1 is the husband of Millie Carnes on Choctaw card #1984					
7						
8						
9						
10	On 1896 roll as J.D. Anderson					
11						
12						
13						
14					Date of Application for Enrollment.	
15						
16					5-23-99	
17						

Choctaw By Blood Enrollment Cards 1898-1914

RESIDENCE: Jacks Fork COUNTY. **Choctaw Nation**   **Choctaw Roll**   CARD No.
POST OFFICE: Tushkahomma[sic] I.T.   *(Not Including Freedmen)*   FIELD No.   1987

Dawes' Roll No.	NAME	Relationship to Person	AGE	SEX	BLOOD	TRIBAL ENROLLMENT		
						Year	County	No.
5693	1 King, Sophia 63	First Named	60	F	1/2	1896	Wade	7520
	2							
	3							
	4							
	5							
	6							
	7							
	8							
	9							
	10							
	11							
	12							
	13							
	14							
	15	ENROLLMENT OF NOS. 1 HEREON						
	16	APPROVED BY THE SECRETARY						
	17	OF INTERIOR JAN 16 1903						

TRIBAL ENROLLMENT OF PARENTS

	Name of Father	Year	County	Name of Mother	Year	County
1	Horace Woods	Dead	Non Citz	No-wa-te-ma	Dead	Wade
2						
3						
4						
5						
6			On 1896 roll as Sophire King			
7						
8						
9						
10						
11						
12						
13						
14					Date of Application for Enrollment.	
15						
16					5/23/99	
17						

Choctaw By Blood Enrollment Cards 1898-1914

RESIDENCE: Jacks Fork   COUNTY. **Choctaw Nation**   **Choctaw Roll**   CARD NO.

POST OFFICE: Tushkahomma[sic] I.T.   (Not Including Freedmen)   FIELD NO. 1988

Dawes' Roll No.	NAME	Relationship to Person First Named	AGE	SEX	BLOOD	Year	County	No.
5694	1 Henderson, Ida 26	First Named	23	F	1/2	1896	Wade	13063
5695	2 " Stanford M 2	Son	2mo	M	5/16			
I.W. 1294	3 " Samuel N 33	Husband	33	M	I.W.			
	4							
	5							
	6 No.3 was denied by Com. in '96, by blood, Case #425							
	7 No3 " admitted by U.S. Court at So. McAlester,							
	8 Jan. 18, 98 by blood – Case #44							
	9 On April 30, 1904 No.3 was denied by C.C.CC. by blood Case #112M							
	10 Nos. 1 and 3 were married May 9| 1899.							
	11 No.3 originally listed for enrollment ^ on Choctaw card D-987 Dec. 23, 1902; transferred as a citizen by marriage							
	12 to this card Jan. 29, 1905 See decision of Jan. 13, 1905							
	13 For child of Nos 1 and 3 see NB (Mar 3'05) #449							
	14							
	15	ENROLLMENT OF NOS. 1, 2 HEREON APPROVED BY THE SECRETARY OF INTERIOR JAN 16 1903			ENROLLMENT OF NOS. 3 HEREON APPROVED BY THE SECRETARY OF INTERIOR MAR 14 1905			
	16							
	17							

TRIBAL ENROLLMENT OF PARENTS

	Name of Father	Year	County	Name of Mother	Year	County
1	C. B. Wade	1896	Wade	Ellen Wade	Dead	Non Citz
2	Sam Henderson		Court citizen	No.1		
3	B. P. Henderson		non citz	Nancy Henderson		non citz
4						
5						
6						
7						
8						
9			Enrolled as Ida Wade on 1896 roll. Mother			
10			was a white woman. As to marriage			
11			of parents see testimony of G. W. Dukes			
12			For child of Nos. 1 and 3 see NB (Apr 26'06) No.538			
13			No.1 wife of Saml. Henderson on Choctaw Card #4745			
14			Evidence of divorce between Jefferson and Ida Bacon filed Feby. 5, 1903			
15			No.2 Enrolled June 25, 1900		Date of Application for Enrollment.	
16					5/23/99	
17						

188

Choctaw By Blood Enrollment Cards 1898-1914

RESIDENCE: Cedar COUNTY. **Choctaw Nation** Choctaw Roll CARD NO.
POST OFFICE: Tushkahomma[sic] I.T. *(Not Including Freedmen)* FIELD NO. 1989

Dawes' Roll No.	NAME	Relationship to Person First Named	AGE	SEX	BLOOD	TRIBAL ENROLLMENT Year	County	No.
5696	1 Anderson, Colbert 70	First Named	67	M	Full	1896	Jacks Fork	491
5697	2 " Lizzie 57	Wife	54	F	"	1896	" "	492
5698	3 DIED PRIOR TO SEPTEMBER 25 2002 Mary Ann	Dau	17	"	"	1896	" "	493
15786	4 Morris, Artiamissia	Dau	21	"	"	1896	" "	494
	5							
	6							
	7							
	8							
	9							
	10							
	11	ENROLLMENT						
	12	OF NOS. 4 HEREON						
	13	APPROVED BY THE SECRETARY OF INTERIOR MAR 15 11905						
	14							
	15	ENROLLMENT						
	16	OF NOS. 1,2,3 HEREON APPROVED BY THE SECRETARY						
	17	OF INTERIOR JAN 16 1903						

TRIBAL ENROLLMENT OF PARENTS

	Name of Father	Year	County	Name of Mother	Year	County
1	Reuben Anderson	Dead	Jacks Fork	Ho-te-ma	Dead	Wade
2	Simon Tahubbee	"	Nashoba	En-la-he-ma	"	Nashoba
3	No 1			No 2		
4	No.1			No.2		
5						
6	No4 is the mother of McKinly T. Morris on Choctaw card #2054					
7						
8	For child of No4 see NB (Apr 26-06) Card No 724					
9						
10	No 3 died July, 1900; proof of death filed Dec 12, 1902					
11	No.4 placed on this card March 16, 1904: apparently no application for her enrollment having been made prior t that date.					
12						
13						
14	No.3 died July - 1900: Enrollment cancelled by Department July 8, 1904					
15			#1,2 & 3			
16				Date of Application for Enrollment.	5/23/99	
17						

189

Choctaw By Blood Enrollment Cards 1898-1914

RESIDENCE: Jacks Fork   COUNTY.   **Choctaw Nation**   **Choctaw Roll**   CARD NO.
POST OFFICE: Tushkahomma[sic] I.T.   *(Not Including Freedmen)*   FIELD NO.   1990

Dawes' Roll No.	NAME	Relationship to Person	AGE	SEX	BLOOD	TRIBAL ENROLLMENT		
						Year	County	No.
5699	1 Gibson, Mary	First Named	68	F	Full	1896	Jacks Fork	5007
	2							
	3							
	4							
	5							
	6							
	7							
	8							
	9							
	10							
	11							
	12							
	13							
	14							
	15	ENROLLMENT OF NOS. 1 HEREON APPROVED BY THE SECRETARY OF INTERIOR JAN 16 1903						
	16							
	17							

TRIBAL ENROLLMENT OF PARENTS

	Name of Father	Year	County	Name of Mother	Year	County
1	She-mon-ta	Dead	Kiamitia	Pisa-he-ma-ya	Dead	Kiamitia
2						
3						
4						
5						
6	No.1 died November – 1900. Enrollment cancelled by Department May 2, 1906					
7						
8						
9						
10						
11						
12						
13						
14					Date of Application for Enrollment.	
15						
16					5/23/99	
17						

190

Choctaw By Blood Enrollment Cards 1898-1914

RESIDENCE: Wade   COUNTY. **Choctaw Nation**   **Choctaw Roll** (Not Including Freedmen)   CARD NO.

POST OFFICE: Talihina, I.T.   FIELD NO. 1991

Dawes' Roll No.	NAME		Relationship to Person	AGE	SEX	BLOOD	TRIBAL ENROLLMENT		
							Year	County	No.
5700	1 Lewis, Josiah	22	First Named	19	M	Full	1896	Wade	7892
	2								
	3								
	4								
	5								
	6								
	7								
	8								
	9								
	10								
	11								
	12								
	13								
	14								
	15	ENROLLMENT OF NOS. 1 HEREON							
	16	APPROVED BY THE SECRETARY							
	17	OF INTERIOR JAN 16 1903							

TRIBAL ENROLLMENT OF PARENTS

	Name of Father	Year	County	Name of Mother	Year	County
1	Simpson Lewis	1896	Wade	Leona Lewis	Dead	Wade
2						
3						
4						
5						
6	On 1896 roll as Josie Lewis					
7						
8						
9						
10						
11						
12						
13						
14						
15						
16				Date of Application for Enrollment.	5/23/99	
17						

Choctaw By Blood Enrollment Cards 1898-1914

RESIDENCE: Cedar   COUNTY.   **Choctaw Nation**   **Choctaw Roll**   CARD NO.
POST OFFICE: Tushahomma[sic], I.T.   *(Not Including Freedmen)*   FIELD NO.   **1992**

Dawes' Roll No.	NAME	Relationship to Person	AGE	SEX	BLOOD	TRIBAL ENROLLMENT		
						Year	County	No.
5701	1 Ben, Byington 27	First Named	24	M	Full	1896	Jacks Fork	1953
	2							
	3							
	4							
	5							
	6							
	7							
	8							
	9							
	10							
	11							
	12							
	13							
	14							
	15							
	16							
	17							

ENROLLMENT OF NOS. 1 APPROVED BY THE SECRETARY OF INTERIOR Jan. 16, 1903 HEREON

TRIBAL ENROLLMENT OF PARENTS

Name of Father	Year	County	Name of Mother	Year	County
1 Davis Ben	Dead	Nashoba	Emily Ben	Dead	Nashoba
2					
3					
4					
5					
6 N⁰1 is now the husband of Sophia Burris on Choctaw card #2004 June 9, 1902					
7					
8					
9					
10					
11					
12				Date of Application for Enrollment.	5/23/99	
13					
14					
15					
16					
17					

Choctaw By Blood Enrollment Cards 1898-1914

RESIDENCE: Jacks Fork COUNTY. **Choctaw Nation** **Choctaw Roll** CARD NO.
POST OFFICE: Tushkahomma[sic] I.T. (Not Including Freedmen) FIELD NO. 1993

Dawes' Roll No.	NAME	Relationship to Person First Named	AGE	SEX	BLOOD	TRIBAL ENROLLMENT		
						Year	County	No.
5702	1 Hotubbee, Joseph 45	First Named	42	M	Full	1896	Jacks Fork	6127
5703	2 Anderson, Lyles 19	Dau	16	F	"	1896	" "	6128
5704	3 Hotubbee Asie 17	"	14	"	"	1896	" "	6129
5705	4 Anderson, Bedford 1	Gr Son	15mo	M	3/4			
I.W. 1657	5 Hotubbee, Nancy	Wife	24	F	I.W.			
	6							
	7	ENROLLMENT						
	8	OF NOS. ~~~ 5 ~~~ HEREON APPROVED BY THE SECRETARY						
	9	OF INTERIOR MAR 4 1907						
	10							
	11	GRANTED						
	12	FEB 25 1907						
	13							
	14							
	15	ENROLLMENT OF NOS. 1,2,3,4, HEREON						
	16	APPROVED BY THE SECRETARY						
	17	OF INTERIOR JAN 16 1903						

TRIBAL ENROLLMENT OF PARENTS

	Name of Father	Year	County	Name of Mother	Year	County
1	Ho-tubbee	Dead	Nashoba	Amy Hotubbee	Dead	Nashoba
2	No 1			Mollie Hotubbee	"	Jacks Fork
3	No 1			" "	"	" "
4	Tandy Anderson	1896	Choctaw roll	Nº2		
5	Frank Freeman		Non citz	Mary Harrett	Dead	Non citz
6						
7	No 5 transferred from Chickasaw Card No D-236 Feby 25-1907					
8	See decision of same date					
9						
10	Nº2 is now the wife of Tandy Anderson on Chickasaw card #1082. Evidence					
11	of Marriage filed Sept. 12, 1902.					
12	Nº4 Born June 25, 1901 enrolled Sept. 12, 1902					
13	No 1 is the husband of Nancy Moore, Chickasaw D-236: Evidence of marriage filed Dec 17, 1902					
14	No 3 is now wife of No 1 on Choctaw card #37					
	12/9/02					
15	For child of No3 see NB (Mar 3-1905) Card #39				#1 to 3 inc	
16	" " " " 2 " " " " " #416			Date of Application for Enrollment	5/23/99	
17	" " " Nos 1&5 " " " " #1209					

193

RESIDENCE:	Wade	COUNTY.	**Choctaw Nation**				**Choctaw Roll**	CARD No.	
POST OFFICE:	Albion, I.T.						*(Not Including Freedmen)*	FIELD No.	1994

Dawes' Roll No.	NAME	Relationship to Person First Named	AGE	SEX	BLOOD	TRIBAL ENROLLMENT		
						Year	County	No.
DEAD.	₁ Hart, Cephus	Named	24	M	Full	1896	Wade	5412
DEAD	₂ " Betsy ~~DEAD~~	Sister	23	F	"	1896	"	5413
	3							
	4							
	5							
	6							
	7	No. 1 and 2 HEREON DISMISSED UNDER						
	8	ORDER OF THE COMMISSION TO THE FIVE CIVILIZED TRIBES OF MARCH 31, 1905.						
	9							
	10							
	11							
	12							
	13							
	14							
	15							
	16							
	17							

TRIBAL ENROLLMENT OF PARENTS

	Name of Father	Year	County	Name of Mother	Year	County
₁	Halis Hart		Wade	Phillis McKinney	1896	Wade
2	" "		"	" "	1896	"
3						
4						
5						
6						
7	No 1 Died June 14, 1900. Evidence of death filed April 16, 1901					
8	No 2 " January 23, 1901. Evidence of death filed May 1 of 1901.					
9						
10						
11						
12						
13						
14				Date of Application for Enrollment.		
15						
16				5/23/99		
17						

CANCELLED

died prior to Sept 25, 0?

Choctaw By Blood Enrollment Cards 1898-1914

	RESIDENCE: Wade		COUNTY. **Choctaw Nation**				**Choctaw Roll** *(Not Including Freedmen)*		CARD No.	
	POST OFFICE: Albion I.T.								FIELD No. 1995	

Dawes' Roll No.	NAME		Relationship to Person First Named	AGE	SEX	BLOOD	TRIBAL ENROLLMENT		
							Year	County	No.
5706	1 McKinney Egtill B	25	First Named	22	M	1/2	1896	Wade	9223
	2								
	3								
	4								
	5								
	6								
	7								
	8								
	9								
	10								
	11								
	12								
	13								
	14								
	15	ENROLLMENT OF NOS. 1 HEREON APPROVED BY THE SECRETARY OF INTERIOR JAN 16 1903							
	16								
	17								

TRIBAL ENROLLMENT OF PARENTS

	Name of Father	Year	County	Name of Mother	Year	County
1	Swinney McKinney	1896	Wade	Jincey McKinney	Dead	Wade
2						
3						
4						
5						
6	On 1896 Roll as Egleton B. McKinney					
7						
8						
9						
10						
11						
12						
13						
14					Date of Application for Enrollment.	
15						
16					5/23/99	
17						

195

Choctaw By Blood Enrollment Cards 1898-1914

RESIDENCE: Cedar   COUNTY. **Choctaw Nation**   **Choctaw Roll** CARD NO.
POST OFFICE: Kosoma I.T.   *(Not Including Freedmen)*   FIELD NO. **1996**

Dawes' Roll No.	NAME	Relationship to Person First Named	AGE	SEX	BLOOD	TRIBAL ENROLLMENT Year	County	No.
5707	1 Homer, Edward 30		27	M	Full	1896	Cedar	5434
5708	2 DIED PRIOR TO SEPTEMBER 25, 1902 Sophia	Wife	26	F	"	1896	"	5435
5709	3 DIED PRIOR TO SEPTEMBER 25, 1902 Jincey	Dau	2mo	"	"			
	4							
	5							
	6							
	7							
	8							
	9							
	10							
	11							
	12							
	13							
	14							
	15	ENROLLMENT OF NOS. 1,2,3 HEREON						
	16	APPROVED BY THE SECRETARY OF INTERIOR Jan. 16, 1903						
	17							

TRIBAL ENROLLMENT OF PARENTS

	Name of Father	Year	County	Name of Mother	Year	County
1	Im-pa-lam-be	Dead	Nashoba	Jinny	Dead	Nashoba
2	Lewis No-ata-be	Dead	Cedar	Cillin No-ata-be	1896	Cedar
3	No 1			No 2		
4						
5						
6	No 1 On 1896 roll as Edward Homma					
7	No 2 " " " " Sophia Homma					
8						
9						
10	No 2 died Feb. 9, 1901; proof of death filed Dec 15, 1902					
11	No 3 " Feb. 16, 1901; " " " " " "					
12	No 1 is now husband of Silvie Wesley Choctaw card #1730					
13	No.2 died Feb. 9, 1901. No.3 died Feb. 16 1901; Enrollment cancelled by Department Sept. 16, 1904					
14						
15					Date of Application for Enrollment.	
16					5/23/99	
17	Dexter I.T.			No3 Enrolled Nov. 1/99		

12/10/02

196

Choctaw By Blood Enrollment Cards 1898-1914

RESIDENCE: Jack's Fork   COUNTY. **Choctaw Nation**   **Choctaw Roll** *(Not Including Freedmen)*   CARD NO.

POST OFFICE: Standley I.T.   FIELD NO. **1997**

Dawes' Roll No.		NAME		Relationship to Person First Named	AGE	SEX	BLOOD	TRIBAL ENROLLMENT		
								Year	County	No.
5710	1	Battiest Stephen	25		22	M	Full	1896	Jack's Fork	1972
DEAD	2	" Martha		Wife	35	F	"	1896	" "	1973
5711	3	" Reiney DIED PRIOR TO SEPTEMBER 25, 1902		Step son	14	M	"	1896	" "	1974
5712	4	" Effie DIED PRIOR TO SEPTEMBER 25, 1902		Dau	7mo	F	"			
	5									
	6									
	7									
	8									
	9									

No. 2 Hereon Dismissed under order
of the Commission to the Five Civilized
Tribes of March 31, 1905.

ENROLLMENT
OF NOS. 1, 3, 4 HEREON
APPROVED BY THE SECRETARY
OF INTERIOR Jan. 16, 1903

TRIBAL ENROLLMENT OF PARENTS

	Name of Father	Year	County	Name of Mother	Year	County
1	Dixon Battiest	Dead	Cedar	Martha Wesley	1896	Cedar
2	Marlin Edward	1896	Jack's Fork	Louisiana Edward	Dead	"
3	Simon Garland	1896	Na-sho-ba	No 2		
4	No 1			No 2		
5						
6	No 3 on 1896 roll as Rena Battiest					
7	No1 the Husband of Frances Morris on Choctaw card #1894: Evidence of marriage filed July 19 1902					
8	No 2 died June 27, 1900: proof of death filed March 3, 1903					
	No 4 died Oct. 28, 1899: Enrollment cancelled by Department July 8, 1904					
9	* No 1 died in 1901: Enrollment cancelled by Department May 2, 1906					
10	For child of No1 see N.B. (March 3, 1905) #1227					
11						
12	* Notation as to date of death of No1 in error should be No3.					
13	ECF					
14						
15						
16	Date of Application for Enrollment.					
17	5/23/99					

Choctaw By Blood Enrollment Cards 1898-1914

RESIDENCE: Cedar COUNTY.	**Choctaw Nation**	**Choctaw Roll** (Not Including Freedmen)		CARD NO. FIELD NO. 1998			
POST OFFICE: Tushkahomma[sic] I.T.							

Dawes' Roll No.	NAME	Relationship to Person First Named	AGE	SEX	BLOOD	TRIBAL ENROLLMENT		
						Year	County	No.
5713	1 Benjamin, Ben ²⁹	First Named	26	M	Full	1896	Jacks Fork	1958
5714	2 ~~Nancy~~ DIED PRIOR TO SEPTEMBER 25 1902	Wife	40	F	"	1893	" "	176
	3							
	4							
	5							
	6							
	7							
	8							
	9							
	10							
	11							
	12							
	13							
	14							
	15	ENROLLMENT OF NOS. 1, 2 HEREON APPROVED BY THE SECRETARY OF INTERIOR JAN 16 1903						
	16							
	17							

TRIBAL ENROLLMENT OF PARENTS

Name of Father	Year	County	Name of Mother	Year	County	
1 Lawton Battiest	Dead	Cedar	Jane Battiest	Dead	Jacks Fork	
2 ~~Lo-ma-chubbee~~	"	"	~~Liza Frazier~~	"	" "	
3						
4						
5						
6						
7						
8		No2 on 1893 Pay roll, Page 17, No 176, Jacks Fork Co				
9		also on 1896 roll Page 12 No 468	"	"	"	
10		as Andy.				
11						
12						
13		No 2 died Oct, 1900; proof of death filed Dec 12, 1902				
14		~~No 1 husband of Nellie Hardy, Choctaw card #1962~~				Date of Application for Enrollment
15		No.2 died Oct – 1900 Enrollment cancelled by Department July 8, 1904				5/23/99
16						
17						

198

Choctaw By Blood Enrollment Cards 1898-1914

RESIDENCE: Cedar COUNTY. **Choctaw Nation** **Choctaw Roll** CARD No.
POST OFFICE: Tushkahomma[sic] I.T. *(Not Including Freedmen)* FIELD No. 1999

Dawes' Roll No.	NAME		Relationship to Person First Named	AGE	SEX	BLOOD	TRIBAL ENROLLMENT		
							Year	County	No.
5715	1 Bacon, George	46	First Named	43	M	Full	1896	Cedar	1058
	2								
	3								
	4								
	5								
	6								
	7								
	8								
	9								
	10								
	11								
	12								
	13								
	14								
	15								
	16								
	17								

ENROLLMENT
OF NOS. 1 HEREON
APPROVED BY THE SECRETARY
OF INTERIOR JAN 16 1903

TRIBAL ENROLLMENT OF PARENTS

	Name of Father	Year	County	Name of Mother	Year	County
1	Tunis Bacon	Dead	Cedar		Dead	Cedar
2						
3						
4						
5						
6						
7						
8						
9						
10						
11						
12						
13						
14						
15						
16				Date of Application for Enrollment.	5/22/99	
17						

Choctaw By Blood Enrollment Cards 1898-1914

RESIDENCE: Cedar   COUNTY.
POST OFFICE: Tushkahomma[sic] I.T.

Choctaw Nation

Choctaw Roll (Not Including Freedmen)

CARD NO. FIELD NO. 2000

Dawes' Roll No.	NAME	Relationship to Person First Named	AGE	SEX	BLOOD	TRIBAL ENROLLMENT Year	County	No.
5716	1 Shoat, Julius 39		36	M	Full	1896	Wade	11339
5717	2 " Lucy 23	Wife	20	F	"	1896	"	12927
5718	3 " Siball DIED PRIOR TO SEPTEMBER 25,1902	Dau	2	"	"			
5719	4 " Louie 3	Son	2mo	M	"			
15830	5 " Agnes	Dau	2	F	"			
	6							
	7							
	8							
	9							
	10							
	11							
	12							
	13							
	14							

ENROLLMENT
[The part of the page where this stamp is, was completely torn off the form]

ENROLLMENT OF NOS. 5 HEREON APPROVED BY THE SECRETARY OF INTERIOR JUN 12 1905

TRIBAL ENROLLMENT OF PARENTS

	Name of Father	Year	County	Name of Mother	Year	County
1	Lyman Shoat	1896	Cedar	Bitchie Shoat	Dead	Nashoba
2	Charles Wesley	1896	Sugar Loaf	Lottie Wesley	"	Gaines
3	No 1			No 2		
4	No 1			No 2		
5	No 1			No 2		
6						
7	No.2 On 1896 roll as Lucinda Wesley. Also on 1893 Pay Roll, Page 88					
8	No 816 as Lucy Wesley, Sugar Loaf County					
9						
10	No 3 died June, 1900; proof of death filed Dec 12, 1902					
11	No.3 died June - 1900: Enrollment cancelled by Department July 8, 1904					
12	No.5 was born Feb. 6, 1901; application received and No 5 placed					
13	on this card April 11, 1905, under Act of Congress approved March 3, 1905.					
14				#1 to 4		
15				Date of Application for Enrollment.		
16				5/23/99		
17				Nos 2-3-4 enrolled May 25/99		

200

Choctaw By Blood Enrollment Cards 1898-1914

RESIDENCE: Jack's Fork   COUNTY. **Choctaw Nation**   **Choctaw Roll**   CARD NO.
POST OFFICE: Stringtown, I.T.   Tushkahoma(?) I.T. 12/11 $\frac{02}{}$ (Not Including Freedmen)   FIELD NO. **2001**

Dawes' Roll No.	NAME	Relationship to Person Named	AGE	SEX	BLOOD	TRIBAL ENROLLMENT		
						Year	County	No.
5720	₁ Carnes, James A ²⁸	First Named	25	M	Full	1896	Jack's Fork	2988
5721	₂ " Mary Belle ²³	Wife	20	F	"	1896	PRIOR TO SEPTEMBER 25, 190?	2989
	₃							
	₄							
	₅							
	₆							
	₇							
	₈							
	₉							
	₁₀							
	₁₁							
	₁₂							
	₁₃							
	₁₄							
	₁₅	ENROLLMENT OF NOS. 1 and 2 HEREON						
	₁₆	APPROVED BY THE SECRETARY OF INTERIOR JAN 16 1903						
	₁₇							

TRIBAL ENROLLMENT OF PARENTS

	Name of Father	Year	County	Name of Mother	Year	County
₁	Harris Carnes	Dead	Jack's Fork	Adaline Carnes	Dead	Jack's Fork
₂	Billy William	"	" " "	Amy William	"	" " "
₃						
₄						
₅	No.2 Died Jan. 15, 1901: Enrollment cancelled by Dept July 8, 1904					
₆						
₇						
₈	No.2 on 1896 Roll as Belle Carnes					
₉	No.2 died Jany 15, 1901; Proof of death filed Dec 16, 1902					
₁₀						
₁₁						
₁₂						
₁₃						
₁₄						
₁₅						
₁₆					May 23, 1899	
₁₇						

Choctaw By Blood Enrollment Cards 1898-1914

	RESIDENCE: Jacks Fork	COUNTY.	**Choctaw Nation**		Choctaw Roll	CARD No.	
	POST OFFICE: Lyceum, I.T.				(Not Including Freedmen)	FIELD No.	2002

Dawes' Roll No.	NAME	Relationship to Person First Named	AGE	SEX	BLOOD	TRIBAL ENROLLMENT		
						Year	County	No.
5722	1 Bohanan, Samuel H [61]	First Named	58	M	1/2	1893	Wade	118
5723	2 " Margaret S [59]	Wife	56	F	1/2	1893	"	119
5724	3 Wall Phoebe A [25]	Dau	22	"	1/2	1893	"	120
5725	4 Bohanan Julius H [22]	Son	19	M	1/2	1893	"	121
5726	5 " Minnie A [19]	Dau	16	F	1/2	1893	"	122
5727	6 " Florence A [16]	"	13	"	1/2	1893	"	123
5728	7 Bacon, Judith A [10]	Ward	7	"	Full	1893	"	165
5729	8 Wall, Clarance H [1]	Grandson	5mo	M	1/2			
	9							
	10	ENROLLMENT OF NOS. 1,2,3,4,5,6,7,8 HEREON APPROVED BY THE SECRETARY OF INTERIOR JAN 16 1903						
	11							
	12							
	13	No.3 is now the wife of Tandy Wall on Choctaw card #1926						
	14							
	15	No.8 born June 30, 1901 and Enrolled Nov. 20, 1901.						
	16	N°4 is now husband of Anne B Anderson on						
	17	Choctaw card #1927 July 23 1902						

TRIBAL ENROLLMENT OF PARENTS

	Name of Father	Year	County	Name of Mother	Year	County
1	William Bohanan	Dead	Wade	Phoebe Bohanan	Dead	Wade
2	Oris Woods	"	Non Citz		"	"
3	No 1			No 2		
4	No 1			No 2		
5	No 1			No 2		
6	No 1			No 2		
7	Wilson Bacon	Dead	Wade	Louisa Bacon	Dead	Wade
8	Tandy Wall	1896	Wade	No.3		
9	For child of No4 see NB (Apr 26-06) Card #384					
10	" " " " 3 " (Mar 3-1905) " #825					
11	No1 on 1893 Pay roll, Page 12, No 118, Wade Co, as S.H. Bohanan					
12	No2 " 1893 " " " 12 " 119 " " " Margaret "					
13	No3 " 1893 " " " 12 " 120 " " " Phoebe "					
14	No4 " 1893 " " " 12 " 121 " " " "					
15	No5 " 1893 " " " 12 " 122 " " " "					
16	No6 " 1893 " " " 12 " 123 " " " Clarence A Bohanan					
17	No7 " 1893 " " " 16 " 165 " " " Judith					
	Ann Bacon				5/24/99 Date of Application for Enrollment.	

Choctaw By Blood Enrollment Cards 1898-1914

RESIDENCE: Wade   COUNTY. **Choctaw Nation**   **Choctaw Roll** (Not Including Freedmen)   CARD NO. FIELD NO. **2003**

POST OFFICE: Talihani[sic] I.T.

Dawes' Roll No.	NAME		Relationship to Person	AGE	SEX	BLOOD	TRIBAL ENROLLMENT		
							Year	County	No.
5730	1 Willis Albert	26	First Named	23	M	1/4	1896	Sugar Loaf	12876
	2								
	3								
	4								
	5								
	6								
	7								
	8								
	9								
	10								
	11								
	12								
	13								
	14								
	15	ENROLLMENT OF NOS. 1 HEREON							
	16	APPROVED BY THE SECRETARY OF INTERIOR JAN 16 1903							
	17								

TRIBAL ENROLLMENT OF PARENTS

	Name of Father	Year	County	Name of Mother	Year	County
1	Robert Willis		Non Citz	Sarah Willis	1896	Wade
2						
3						
4						
5						
6						
7						
8						
9						
10						
11						
12						
13						
14						
15						
16				Date of Application for Enrollment.	5/24/99	
17						

Choctaw By Blood Enrollment Cards 1898-1914

RESIDENCE: Jack's Fork COUNTY. **Choctaw Nation** **Choctaw Roll** CARD No.
POST OFFICE: Tushkahomma[sic] I.T. (Not Including Freedmen) FIELD No. 2004

Dawes' Roll No.	NAME	Relationship to Person First Named	AGE	SEX	BLOOD	TRIBAL ENROLLMENT		
						Year	County	No.
5731	₁ Ben, Sophia ²¹	First Named	18	F	Full	1896	Jack's Fork	1989
5732	₂ Ben, McKinney B ¹	Son	3mo	M	"			
	₃							
	₄							
	₅							
	₆							
	₇							
	₈							
	₉							
	₁₀							
	₁₁							
	₁₂							
	₁₃							
	₁₄							
	₁₅	ENROLLMENT OF NOS. 1,2 HEREON APPROVED BY THE SECRETARY OF INTERIOR JAN 16 1903						
	₁₆							
	₁₇							

TRIBAL ENROLLMENT OF PARENTS

Name of Father	Year	County	Name of Mother	Year	County
₁ Conway Burris	Dead	Tobucksey[sic]	Betsy Burris	Dead	Tobucksey[sic]
₂ Byington Ben	1896	Jacks Forks[sic]	N°1		
₃					
₄					
₅					
₆					
₇					
₈					
₉	N°1 is now the wife of Byington Ben on Choctaw card #1992: evidence				
₁₀	of marriage requested June 9, 1902				
₁₁	N°2 Born March 6, 1902: enrolled June 9, 1902 For child of No.1 see NB (Apr 26-06) Card #742				
₁₂					
₁₃					
₁₄					
₁₅					
₁₆			Date of Application for Enrollment.	5/24/99	
₁₇					

RESIDENCE: Jacks Fork   COUNTY. **Choctaw Nation**   Choctaw Roll   CARD No.
POST OFFICE: Tushkahomma[sic] I.T.   (Not Including Freedmen)   FIELD NO. 2005

Dawes' Roll No.	NAME	Relationship to Person First Named	AGE	SEX	BLOOD	TRIBAL ENROLLMENT		
						Year	County	No.
5733	1 Makintubee, Douglas 17	First Named	14	M	1/2	1896	Jacks Fork	8884
	2							
	3							
	4							
	5							
	6							
	7							
	8							
	9							
	10							
	11							
	12							
	13							
	14							
	15							
	16							
	17							

ENROLLMENT
OF NOS. 1 HEREON
APPROVED BY THE SECRETARY
OF INTERIOR JAN 16 1903

TRIBAL ENROLLMENT OF PARENTS

	Name of Father	Year	County	Name of Mother	Year	County
1	Ealon Makintubee	1896	Chick Roll	Wisey Makintubee	Dead	Jacks Fork
2						
3						
4	On 1896 roll as Douglas Makintubbi					
5						
6						
7						
8						
9						
10						
11						
12						
13						
14						
15						
16			Date of Application for Enrollment.	5/24/99		
17						

Choctaw By Blood Enrollment Cards 1898-1914

RESIDENCE: Atoka
POST OFFICE: Lehigh, I.T.

COUNTY. **Choctaw Nation**

Choctaw Roll
(Not Including Freedmen)

CARD NO.
FIELD NO. 2006

Dawes' Roll No.	NAME	Relationship to Person First Named	AGE	SEX	BLOOD	TRIBAL ENROLLMENT		
						Year	County	No.
5734	1 Clark Josephine	19 First Named	16	F	1/2	1896	Atoka	8809
5735	2 Murphy Jane	17 Sister	14	"	1/2	1896	"	8810
5736	3 Clark, Flossie May	1 Dau	3mo	F	1/4			
	4							
	5							
	6							
	7							
	8							
	9							
	10							
	11							
	12							
	13							
	14							
	15	ENROLLMENT OF NOS. 1,2,3 HEREON APPROVED BY THE SECRETARY OF INTERIOR JAN 16 1903						
	16							
	17							

TRIBAL ENROLLMENT OF PARENTS

Name of Father	Year	County	Name of Mother	Year	County
1 Ben Murphy	Dead	Jacks Fork	Mary Murphy	Dead	Atoka
2 " "	"	" "	" "	"	" "
3 Fount Clark		non citizen	No 1		
4					
5					
6					
7					
8					
9					
10					

11 No1 now the wife of Fount Clark, non citizen. Evidence of marriage filed July 1st 1902
12 No.3 Born April 22nd 1902: Enrolled July 14th 1902
13 No.2 is now the wife of O L Mitchell, a non citizen
   Evidence of marriage received and filed Dec 24, 1902
14 For child of No.2 see N.B. (Apr. 26, 1896) Card No. 149
15 "   "   "   "   1 "   "   "   "   " 747
16 "   "   "   "   1 " (Mar 3-1905) "   113
17 "   "   "   "   2 "   "   "   "   " " 787

Date of Application for Enrollment.
5/24/99

For Nos. 1 and 2

206

Choctaw By Blood Enrollment Cards 1898-1914

RESIDENCE: Sugar Loaf   COUNTY. **Choctaw Nation**   **Choctaw Roll** CARD NO.
POST OFFICE: Thomasville I.T.   *(Not Including Freedmen)*   FIELD NO. **2007**

Dawes' Roll No.	NAME		Relationship to Person	AGE	SEX	BLOOD	TRIBAL ENROLLMENT		
							Year	County	No.
5737	1 James, Benjamin	25	First Named	22	M	1/2	1896	Sugar Loaf	6544
5738	2 " Campbell	23	Bro	20	"	1/2	1896	" "	6556
5739	3 " Dock	20	"	17	"	1/2	1896	Blue	7241
16208	4 " George W	18	"	15	"	1/2	1896	Wade	6733
14709	5 " Campbell M	1	Son of No 2	4mo	"	1/4			
I.W. 817	6 " Edith	(17)	Wife of No 2	17	F	I.W.			

7 Father of No4 not Levi James 2/23/06

8 No4 notified to give further testimony as to parentage Nov. 17/03

9   ~~ENROLLMENT~~   No 1 on 1896 roll as Ben James
10 OF NOS. 6 HEREON   No 4 " 1896 " " George "
11 APPROVED BY THE SECRETARY
12 OF INTERIOR May 21, 1904   ~~ENROLLMENT~~
13 No 3 is Mayhew I.T. 12/2/02   OF NOS. 5 HEREON
14 No 2 is Poteau I.T. 2/18/02   APPROVED BY THE SECRETARY OF INTERIOR May 20, 1903
15   ENROLLMENT   ~~ENROLLMENT~~
16 OF NOS. 1,2,3 HEREON   OF NOS. 4 HEREON
17 APPROVED BY THE SECRETARY OF INTERIOR Jan. 16, 1903   APPROVED BY THE SECRETARY OF INTERIOR Mar. 4, 1907

TRIBAL ENROLLMENT OF PARENTS

	Name of Father	Year	County	Name of Mother	Year	County
1	Levi James	Dead	Sugar Loaf	Martha James	Dead	Non Citz
2	" "	"	" " "	" "	"	" " "
3	" "	"	" " "	" "	"	" " "
4	" "	"	" " "	" "	"	" " "
5	No 2			Edith James		" "
6	John Barley	Dead	noncitizen	Frank[sic] Barley		noncitizen
7						
8						

9 As to marriage of parents see testimony of
~~William Young and G.W. Thompson~~
10 No 6 transferred from Choctaw card D 959 April 15, 1904 See decision of March 15 1904
11 No 3 Also on 1896 census roll as Hodges James
12 #6557 page 161   May 16, 1900
13 No 2 is now the husband of Edith James, noncitizen. Evidence of marriage
No 5 Born June 18, 1902. Enrolled Nov. 4, 1902   filed Nov. 4, 1902 now on file in
14 Thomas & Lunsford Attys Talihina I.T.   7D-959
15
16   Date of Application for Enrollment.
17   5/24/99

Choctaw By Blood Enrollment Cards 1898-1914

RESIDENCE: Gaines   COUNTY. **Choctaw Nation**   **Choctaw Roll**   CARD NO.
POST OFFICE: Hartshorne, I.T.   *(Not Including Freedmen)*   FIELD NO.   2008

Dawes' Roll No.	NAME		Relationship to Person First Named	AGE	SEX	BLOOD	TRIBAL ENROLLMENT		
							Year	County	No.
5740	1 Thomas, Dave	43	First Named	40	M	Full	1896	Gaines	11990
5741	2 " Elsie	4	Dau	8mo	F	1/2			
5742	3 " Mary	3	Dau	5mo	F	1/2			
5743	4 " Lilian G	1	Dau	3mo	F	1/2			
I.W. 712	5 " Minnie	(23)	Wife	23	F	I.W.			
	6								
	7								
	8								
	9								
	10	ENROLLMENT OF NOS. ~~~ 5 ~~~ HEREON APPROVED BY THE SECRETARY							
	11	OF INTERIOR MAY -7 1904							
	12								
	13								
	14	ENROLLMENT OF NOS. 1,2,3,4 HEREON							
	15	APPROVED BY THE SECRETARY							
	16	OF INTERIOR JAN 16 1903							
	17								

TRIBAL ENROLLMENT OF PARENTS

	Name of Father	Year	County	Name of Mother	Year	County
1	Thos. Ponkin	Dead	Towson	Wa-hu-na	Dead	Red River
2	No 1			Minnie Thomas	1896	White woman
3	No.1			" "	"	" "
4	No.1			" "	"	" "
5	Norman		non-citz	Maggie Taylor	1896	non-citz
6						
7	For child of Nos 1&5 see NB (Mar 3-1905) ard #114					
8						
9	No5 admitted in '96 Case #76					
10	Wife of No1 on Card No D 182					
11						
12	Affidavit of birth of No2 to be supplied. Recd June 8/99					
13						
14	No.3 Enrolled June 15, 1900.					#1&2 inc
15	Jimmie Thomas as son of No.1 by Chickasaw wife on					Date of Application for Enrollment.
16	Chickasaw card #1440					5/24/99
17	No.4 born Oct. 19, 1901; Enrolled Jan. 10 1902.					
	No5 transferred from Choctaw card #D 182. See decision of Feby 27. 1904					

RESIDENCE: Jacks Fork   COUNTY.   **Choctaw Nation**   **Choctaw Roll**   CARD NO.
POST OFFICE: Stringtown, I.T.   *(Not Including Freedmen)*   FIELD NO. 2009

Dawes' Roll No.	NAME		Relationship to Person First Named	AGE	SEX	BLOOD	TRIBAL ENROLLMENT			
							Year	County		No.
5744	1 Doctor, Sissy DIED PRIOR TO SEPTEMBER 25, 1902		First Named	29	F	Full	1896	Jacks Fork		3630
5745	2 " Francis	11	Dau	8	"	1/2	1896	"	"	3631
5746	3 " Simon	9	Son	6	M	1/2	1896	"	"	3632
	4									
	5									
	6									
	7									
	8									
	9									
	10									
	11									
	12									
	13									
	14									
	15	ENROLLMENT OF NOS. 1,2,3 HEREON APPROVED BY THE SECRETARY OF INTERIOR JAN 16 1903								
	16									
	17									

TRIBAL ENROLLMENT OF PARENTS

	Name of Father	Year	County	Name of Mother	Year	County
1	Hefon Moore	Dead	Gaines	Lizzie Reed	1896	Jacks Fork
2	James Doctor	1896	Chick Roll	No 1		
3	" "	1896	" "	No 1		
4						
5						
6						
7						
8						
9	Is the husband of No 1 and father of Nos 2 and 3 the James					
10	Doctor on Chickasaw freedman card #970?					
11	No.1 died Sept 10, 1899: Enrollment cancelled by Department July 8, 1904					
12						
13						
14					Date of Application for Enrollment.	
15						
16					5/24/99	
17						

Choctaw By Blood Enrollment Cards 1898-1914

RESIDENCE: Wade   COUNTY. **Choctaw Nation**   **Choctaw Roll** *(Not Including Freedmen)*   CARD No.

POST OFFICE: Kiamitia, I.T.   FIELD No. 2010

Dawes' Roll No.	NAME	Relationship to Person First Named	AGE	SEX	BLOOD	TRIBAL ENROLLMENT		
						Year	County	No.
5747	1 Bryant, Daniel	29	26	M	Full	1896	Wade	1045
	2							
	3							
	4							
	5							
	6							
	7							
	8							
	9							
	10							
	11							
	12							
	13							
	14							
	15							
	16							
	17							

ENROLLMENT
OF NOS. 1 HEREON
APPROVED BY THE SECRETARY
OF INTERIOR JAN 16 1903

TRIBAL ENROLLMENT OF PARENTS

	Name of Father	Year	County	Name of Mother	Year	County
1	Nathan Bryant	Dead	Wade	Lucinda Bryant	Dead	Wade
2						
3						
4						
5						
6						
7						
8						
9						
10						
11						
12						
13						
14						
15						
16			Date of Application for Enrollment.	5/25/99		
17						

Choctaw By Blood Enrollment Cards 1898-1914

RESIDENCE: Wade COUNTY. **Choctaw Nation** **Choctaw Roll** CARD NO.
POST OFFICE: Tushkahomma[sic] I.T. *(Not Including Freedmen)* FIELD NO. 2011

Dawes' Roll No.	NAME		Relationship to Person First Named	AGE	SEX	BLOOD	TRIBAL ENROLLMENT		
							Year	County	No.
I.W. 564	1 McGee, John E	34	First Named	32	M	I.W.	1896	Wade	14868
5748	2 " Lillie J	25	Wife	22	F	1/4	1896	"	9228
5749	3 " Edgar	6	Son	3	M	1/8	1896	"	7519
5750	4 " Lillie B	5	Dau	1½	F	1/8			
5751	5 " William F	3	Son	1mo	M	1/8			
5752	6 " Effie	2	Dau	9mo	F	1/8			
14710	7 " Ora May	1	Dau	6mo	F	1/8			
	8								
	9	ENROLLMENT							
	10	OF NOS. ~~ 1 ~~ HEREON APPROVED BY THE SECRETARY OF INTERIOR FEB -8 1904							
	11								
	12								
	13	No.6 Enrolled July 15, 1901							
	14	No.7 born June 2,1902; enrolled Dec. 15, 1902							
	15	ENROLLMENT OF NOS. 2,3,4,5,6 HEREON APPROVED BY THE SECRETARY OF INTERIOR JAN 16 1903							
	16								
	17								

TRIBAL ENROLLMENT OF PARENTS

	Name of Father	Year	County	Name of Mother	Year	County
1	Fred McGee	Dead	Non Citz	Delitha A McGee	Dead	Non Citz
2	William King	"	Jacks Fork	Sophia King	1896	Jacks Fork
3	No 1			No 2		
4	No 1		ENROLLMENT	No 2		
5	No 1		OF NOS. 7 HEREON APPROVED BY THE SECRETARY	No 2		
6	No 1		OF INTERIOR MAY 20 1903	No 2		
7	No 1			No 2		
8						
9	No1 on 1896 roll as John McGee Also admitted as an					
10	intermarried citizen by Dawes Com., as John McGee,					
11	Case No 1270, No appeal.					
12						
13	No2 on 1896 roll as Lilly McGee					
14						
15	No3-4-5 Affidavits of birth to be supplied. Recd June 1/99					
16	No.3 also on 1896 census roll, as Webster Mc. King #7519, page 186			May 17, 1900	Date of Application for Enrollment.	5/25/99
17	Talihina I.T.					1 to 5

211

Choctaw By Blood Enrollment Cards 1898-1914

RESIDENCE: Jacks Fork COUNTY **Choctaw Nation** **Choctaw Roll** *(Not Including Freedmen)* CARD NO.

POST OFFICE: Dexter, I.T. FIELD NO. 2012

Dawes' Roll No.	NAME	Relationship to Person First Named	AGE	SEX	BLOOD	TRIBAL ENROLLMENT Year	County	No.
5753	1 Long, Rhoda 28	First Named	25	F	3/4	1896	Jacks Fork	8379
5754	2 " Julia May 10	Dau	7	"	3/8	1896	" "	8380
5755	3 DIED PRIOR TO SEPTEMBER 25 1902 Richard 1	Son	6	M	3/8	1896	" "	8381
5756	4 " Effie 7	Dau	4	F	3/8	1896	" "	8382
5757	5 " Frost 6	Son	2	M	3/8			
5758	6 " Willie A 4	Dau	6mo	F	3/8			
5759	7 " Wilson James 2	Son	10mo	M	3/8			
	8							
	9							
	10							
	11							
	12							
	13							
	14							
	15	ENROLLMENT OF NOS. 1,2,3,4,5,6,7 HEREON						
	16	APPROVED BY THE SECRETARY OF INTERIOR JAN 16 1903						
	17							

TRIBAL ENROLLMENT OF PARENTS

	Name of Father	Year	County	Name of Mother	Year	County
1	Silas Garland	Ded	Towson	Louisa Garland	Dead	Towson
2	Robert Long	1896	Non Citz	No 1		
3	" "	1896	" "	No 1		
4	" "	1896	" "	No 1		
5	" "	1896	" "	No 1		
6	" "	1896	" "	No 1		
7	" "		Cherokee	No 1		
8						
9						
10						
11						
12	No5-6 Affidavits of birth to be supplied. Recd June 1/99					
13	No.7 Enrolled Aug 20, 1901					
14	No.3 died Sept 9, 1902, proof of death filed Dec 16, 1902					
15	No.3 died Sept 9 1902; Enrollment cancelled by Department July 8, 1904				#1 to 6 inc	
16				Date of Application for Enrollment.	5/25/99	
17	Tuskahoma, I.T. 3/11/07					

212

Choctaw By Blood Enrollment Cards 1898-1914

RESIDENCE: Skullyville	COUNTY. **Choctaw Nation**		**Choctaw Roll** (Not Including Freedmen)	CARD NO.		
POST OFFICE: Cameron, I.T.				FIELD NO.	**2013**	

Dawes' Roll No.	NAME	Relationship to Person First Named	AGE	SEX	BLOOD	TRIBAL ENROLLMENT Year	County	No.
I.W. 565 ₁	Reynolds, James E 65	First Named	62	M	I.W.	1896	Skullyville	14961
14319 ₂	" Felicity L 55	Wife	52	F	3/8	1896	"	10701
14320 ₃	" James T 39	Son	36	M	3/16	1896	"	10702
14321 ₄	Murray Ida 32	Dau	29	F	3/16	1896	"	10703
14322 ₅	Reynolds Hugh A 29	Son	26	M	3/16	1896	"	10704
14323 ₆	" Alta G 16	Dau	13	F	3/16	1896	"	10706
14324 ₇	" Felicity L 15	"	12	"	3/16	1896	"	10707
14325 ₈	" Earl A 19	Son	16	M	3/16	1896	"	10705
15831 ₉	" William Jackson	Son of No 3	1	M	3/32			
₁₀			For child of No4 see NB (Mar 3-1905) Card #37					
₁₁	All admitted by Dawes							
₁₂	Commission Case No 65 No appeal							
₁₃	No4 is wife of Moses W Murray non-citizen evidence of marriage filed Dec 20,1902							
₁₄								
₁₅	ENROLLMENT OF NOS. 2 3 4 5 6 7 and 8 HEREON							
₁₆	APPROVED BY THE SECRETARY OF INTERIOR APR 11 1903							
₁₇								

TRIBAL ENROLLMENT OF PARENTS

	Name of Father	Year	County	Name of Mother	Year	County
₁	Bowen Reynolds	Dead	Non Citz	Sarah Reynolds	Dead	Non Citz
₂	Anthony Turnbull	"	Wade	Hannah Turnbull	"	Wade
₃	No1		ENROLLMENT	No2		
₄	No1	OF NOS ~~ 9 ~~ HEREON APPROVED BY THE SECRETARY		No2		
₅	No1	OF INTERIOR JUN 13 1905		No2		
₆	No1	ENROLLMENT		No2		
₇	No1	OF NOS ~~ 1 ~~ HEREON APPROVED BY THE SECRETARY		No2		
₈	No1	OF INTERIOR FEB -8 1904		No2		
₉	No1			Bessie Reynolds		Non citz
₁₀						
₁₁	No1 on 1896 roll as Jas.E. Reynolds. Also admitted by Dawes Com as James E Reynolds					
₁₂	No2 on 1896 roll as Felicity Reynolds. Admitted by Dawes Com as Felicity L Reynolds					
₁₃	No5 " 1896 " " Hugh "		" " " " "	Hugh A "		
₁₄	No6 " 1896 " " Grace "		" " " " "	A. Grace "		
₁₅	No7 " 1896 " " Felicity "		" " " " "	Felicity L. "		
₁₆	No8 " 1896 " " Earl "		" " " " "	Earl V. Reynolds	Date of Application for Enrollment.	5/25/99
₁₇	PO No4 is Poteau I.T. 12/17/02					

No.9 born Jan. 8, 1902: Application made and No 9 listed hereon March 30, 1905.

Choctaw By Blood Enrollment Cards 1898-1914

RESIDENCE:	Chickasaw Natn	COUNTY.					Choctaw Roll		CARD NO.	

RESIDENCE: Chickasaw Natn **COUNTY.** **Choctaw Nation** **Choctaw Roll** *(Not Including Freedmen)* **CARD NO.**
POST OFFICE: Pauls Valley, I.T. **FIELD NO.** 2014

Dawes' Roll No.	NAME	Relationship to Person	AGE	SEX	BLOOD	TRIBAL ENROLLMENT		
						Year	County	No.
I.W.566 ₁	Carr, Frederick H ³⁴	First Named	31	M	I.W.	1896	Skullyville	14373
14326 ₂	" Rosa O ³⁰	Wife	27	F	3/16	1896	"	2171
14671 ₃	" Ayleen ⁶	Dau	3	"	3/32	1896	"	2172
14327 ₄	" Weimer R ⁵	Son	2	M	3/32			
14328 ₅	" Winnie Irene ¹	Dau	2mo	F	3/32			
₆	ENROLLMENT							
₇	OF NOS. 2 4 and 5 HEREON APPROVED BY THE SECRETARY							
₈	OF INTERIOR APR 11 1903							
₉								
₁₀	ENROLLMENT							
₁₁	OF NOS. 5 HEREON APPROVED BY THE SECRETARY							
₁₂	OF INTERIOR MAY 20 1903							
₁₃								
₁₄	ENROLLMENT							
₁₅	OF NOS. ~~~ 1 ~~~ HEREON APPROVED BY THE SECRETARY							
₁₆	OF INTERIOR FEB -3 1 904							
₁₇								

TRIBAL ENROLLMENT OF PARENTS

	Name of Father	Year	County	Name of Mother	Year	County
₁	S.W. Carr	Dead	Non Citz	Samme A Spright	1896	Non Citz
₂	James E Reynolds	1896	Non Citz	Felicity L Reynolds	1896	Skullyville
₃	No1			No2		
₄	No1			No2		
₅	No 1			No 2		
₆						
₇	No1 was admitted by Dawes Com. as an Intermarried Citizen Case No 651					
₈	No2 " " " " " " Rosa A Carr and on 1896 roll					
₉	as Rosa Carr, Case No 651					
	No3 on 1896 roll as Alfred Carr					
₁₀	No 5 enrolled October 25 1902					
₁₁						
₁₂	Notify Albert Keimer Pauls Valley I.T. Attorney for No 1					
₁₃					#1 to 4	
₁₄					Date of Application for Enrollment.	
₁₅						
₁₆					5/25/99	
₁₇						

Choctaw By Blood Enrollment Cards 1898-1914

Dawes' Roll No.	NAME	Relationship to Person First Named	AGE	SEX	BLOOD	TRIBAL ENROLLMENT Year	County	No.
5760	1 Edwards, Tobias 77	Named	74	M	1/2	1893	Kiamitia	12
5761	2 " Lucy 45	Wife	42	F	Full	1896	Jacks Fork	4527
5762	3 Frazier, Jacob 20	S. Son	17	M	"	1896	" "	4528
5763	4 " Mary A 17	S. Dau	14	F	"	1893	" "	279
5764	5 DIED PRIOR TO SEPTEMBER 25, 1902 Ellen	"	4	"	"	1896	" "	4530
	6							
	7							
	8							
	9							
	10							
	11							
	12							
	13							
	14							
	15	ENROLLMENT OF NOS. 1,2,3,4,5 HEREON APPROVED BY THE SECRETARY OF INTERIOR Jan. 16 1903						
	16							
	17							

TRIBAL ENROLLMENT OF PARENTS

	Name of Father	Year	County	Name of Mother	Year	County
1	Ned Edwards	Dead	Freedman	Millie Edwards	Dead	Nashoba
2	Samintie Frazier	"	Jacks Fork		"	Jacks Fork
3	Henry Frazier	"	" "	No 2		
4	" "	"	" "	No 2		
5	" "	"	" "	No 2		
6						
7		No 2 died prior to Sept 25, 1901				
8						
9		No 1 on 1893 Pay roll Page 114 No 12 Kiamitia Co				
10		No 2 ' 1896 roll as Lucinda Frazier				
11		No 4 ' 1896 " " Wm " No 4529				
12						
13						
14		No 2 died Sept, 1902, proof of death filed Nov 26, 1902				
15		No 5 " in 1899; " " " " " " "			Date of Application for Enrollment.	
16		No.5 died -- 1899: Enrollment cancelled by Department July 8, 1904				
17		No 2 died prior to Sept. 25, 1902; not entitled to land or money; see Indian Office letter July 31, 1907 (I.T. 64827-1907)			5/25/99	

Choctaw By Blood Enrollment Cards 1898-1914

RESIDENCE: Nashoba COUNTY.
POST OFFICE: Smithville I.T.

Choctaw Nation

Choctaw Roll (Not Including Freedmen)

CARD NO.
FIELD NO. 2016

Dawes' Roll No.	NAME		Relationship to Person First Named	AGE	SEX	BLOOD	TRIBAL ENROLLMENT		
							Year	County	No.
5765	1 Carney, Payson	42	First Named	39	M	Full	1896	Nashoba	2533
5766	2 " Mary	35	Wife	32	F	"	1896	"	2534
5767	3 " Almis	12	Dau	9	F	"	1896	"	2535
5768	4 DIED PRIOR TO SEPTEMBER 25, 1902 Eastman		Son	4	M	"	1896	"	2536
4711	5 " Amanda	1	Dau	6mo	F	"			
	6								
	7								
	8								
	9								
	10								
	11								
	12								
	13								
	14								
	15	ENROLLMENT OF NOS. 1,2,3,4 HEREON APPROVED BY THE SECRETARY OF INTERIOR JAN 16 1903				ENROLLMENT OF NOS. 5 HEREON APPROVED BY THE SECRETARY OF INTERIOR MAY 20 1903			
	16								
	17								

TRIBAL ENROLLMENT OF PARENTS

	Name of Father	Year	County	Name of Mother	Year	County
1	Te-hlanotabe	Dead	Nashoba	Wallie	Dead	Nashoba
2	Bartin White	Dead	"	Lucy White	1896	Nashoba
3	No 1			No 2		
4	No 1			No 2		
5	Nº1			Nº2		
6						
7						
8						
9						
10						
11			No2 On 1896 Roll as Mele Carney			
12			Nº5 Born April 20, 1902; enrolled Oct. 20, 1902			
13			No4 died August 20, 1899: proof of death filed Dec 15, 1902			
14			No.4 died Aug 20 1899: Enrollment cancelled by Department July 8, 1904			
15			For child of Nos 1&2 see NB (March 3, 1905) #919			
16					Date of Application for Enrollment.	5/29/99
17						

Choctaw By Blood Enrollment Cards 1898-1914

RESIDENCE: Nashoba   COUNTY. **Choctaw Nation**   **Choctaw Roll**   CARD NO.
POST OFFICE: Smithville I.T.   *(Not Including Freedmen)*   FIELD NO. **2017**

Dawes' Roll No.	NAME		Relationship to Person First Named	AGE	SEX	BLOOD	TRIBAL ENROLLMENT		
							Year	County	No.
5769	1 Robert Daniel	54	First Named	51	M	Full	1896	Nashoba	10786
*5770	2 " Wynie	52	Wife	49	F	"	1896	"	10787
5771	3 " Raymond D	30	Son	27	M	"	1896	"	10788
5772	4 " Litsey	24	Niece	21	F	"	1896	"	10792
*5773	5 Jackson Silmon	20	Nephew	17	M	"	1896	"	6897
	6								
	7								
	8								
	9								
	10								
	11								
	12								
	13								
	14								
	15	ENROLLMENT OF NOS. 1,2,3,4,5 HEREON							
	16	APPROVED BY THE SECRETARY							
	17	OF INTERIOR Jan. 16, 1903							

TRIBAL ENROLLMENT OF PARENTS

	Name of Father	Year	County	Name of Mother	Year	County
1	Hemonabbe	Dead	Nashoba	Cha-fa-ho-na	Dead	Eagle
2	Opa-labbe	Dead	"		"	Bok Tuklo
3	No 1			No 2		
4	Robert, Morgan	Dead	Nashoba	Robert, Nancy	Dead	Nashoba
5	Joseph Jackson	Dead	"	Senale Jackson	Dead	"
6						
7						
8			No 4 On 1896 Roll as Lidsey Robert			
9						
10			For child of No 4 see N.B. (March 3rd 1905) Card No 942			
11			"	" " No 1 " "	" " " "	" 1066
12			* * Nos 2&5 "Died prior to Sept. 25, 1901, not entitled to land or money"			
13			(See Indian Office letter of August 2, 1911, No 1232-1911)			
14						
15				Date of application for enrollment		
16				Date of Application for Enrollment.	5/29/99	
17						

Choctaw By Blood Enrollment Cards 1898-1914

RESIDENCE: Wade   COUNTY. **Choctaw Nation**   **Choctaw Roll** (Not Including Freedmen)   CARD No.
POST OFFICE: Lenox I.T.   FIELD No. **2018**

Dawes' Roll No.	NAME		Relationship to Person	AGE	SEX	BLOOD	TRIBAL ENROLLMENT		
							Year	County	No.
5774	1 James William	29	First Named	26	M	Full	1896	Wade	6692
I.W. 1295	2 " Winnie	48	Wife	45	F	I.W.	1896	"	14692
5775	3 M'Intosh Ada	DIED PRIOR TO SEPTEMBER 25 1902	S. Dau	14	F	1/4	1896	"	13070
5776	4 Woods Henry	15	Step Son	12	M	1/4	1896	"	13071
5777	5 M'Intosh Carrie M	2	Dau of No 3	6mo	F	5/8			
	6								
	7								
	8 No1 is now divorced from No2 and								
	9 married to Rhoda Lewis on Choctaw								
	card #2111								
	10 No3 died -- 1901: Enrollment								
	11 cancelled by Department July 8, 1904 See testimony of William Janes								
	12								
	13								
	14								
	15 ENROLLMENT OF NOS. 1,3,4,5 HEREON					ENROLLMENT OF NOS. 2 HEREON			
	16 APPROVED BY THE SECRETARY OF INTERIOR Jan 16 1903					APPROVED BY THE SECRETARY OF INTERIOR Mar. 14, 1905			
	17								

TRIBAL ENROLLMENT OF PARENTS

	Name of Father	Year	County	Name of Mother	Year	County
1	P-sa-he-ka-be	Dead	Wade	Sally Ann James	1896	Wade
2	Hampden	"	Non Citz	Betsey Wade	Dead	Non Citz
3	Stephen Woods	"	Wade	No 2		
4	" "	"	"	No 2		
5	Alexander M'Intosh	1896	Wade	No 3		
6						
7	No 1 Evidence of marriage between William and Winnie James to					
8	be supplied. Recd May 29/99					
	For child of No 4 see N.B. (Apr 26,06) Card #1216					
9	No 2 Evidence of marriage between Stephen Woods and Winnie					
10	to be supplied. See evidence of G.W. Dukes					
11						
12						
13						
14						
15	No.3 is now the wife of Alexander M'Intosh No3 on Choctaw				#1 to 4	
16	Card #2058 Evidence of marriage filed this day May 17, 1901				Date of Application for Enrollment.	
	No 5 Enrolled May 17, 1901					
17	No.3 died in fall of 1901, proof of death filed Dec 15, 1[illegible]				5/29/99	

P.O. Talihina I.T.

Choctaw By Blood Enrollment Cards 1898-1914

RESIDENCE: Nashoba   COUNTY.   **Choctaw Nation**   Choctaw Roll   CARD No.

POST OFFICE: Smithville I.T.   (Not Including Freedmen)   FIELD No. 2019

Dawes' Roll No.	NAME		Relationship to Person	AGE	SEX	BLOOD	TRIBAL ENROLLMENT		
							Year	County	No.
5778	1 Whale Armis	41	First Named	38	M	Full	1896	Nashoba	13282
5779	2 " Martha	36	Wife	36	F	"	1896	"	13284
	3								
	4								
	5								
	6								
	7								
	8								
	9								
	10								
	11								
	12								
	13								
	14								
	15	ENROLLMENT OF NOS. 1, 2 HEREON APPROVED BY THE SECRETARY OF INTERIOR JAN 16 1903							
	16								
	17								

TRIBAL ENROLLMENT OF PARENTS

	Name of Father	Year	County	Name of Mother	Year	County
1	Werley Whale	Dead	Nashoba	Basey Whale	Dead	Eagle
2	Davison Peter	1896	"	Siney Ludlow	1896	Nasahoba
3						
4						
5						
6	No2 On 1896 roll as Mercie Whale					
7						
8						
9						
10						
11						
12						
13						
14					Date of Application for Enrollment.	
15						
16					5/29/99	
17						

Choctaw By Blood Enrollment Cards 1898-1914

RESIDENCE: Nashoba COUNTY. **Choctaw Nation** **Choctaw Roll** CARD NO.
POST OFFICE: Smithville, I.T. (Not Including Freedmen) FIELD NO. 2020

Dawes' Roll No.	NAME	Relationship to Person	AGE	SEX	BLOOD	TRIBAL ENROLLMENT		
						Year	County	No.
5780	1 Bohanan, Reed 50	First Named	47	M	Full	1896	Nashoba	1124
5781	2 " Viney 56	Wife	53	F	"	1896	"	1125
	3							
	4							
	5							
	6							
	7							
	8							
	9							
	10							
	11							
	12							
	13							
	14							
	15	ENROLLMENT OF NOS. 1, 2 HEREON APPROVED BY THE SECRETARY OF INTERIOR JAN 16 1903						
	16							
	17							

TRIBAL ENROLLMENT OF PARENTS

	Name of Father	Year	County	Name of Mother	Year	County
1	Ba-li-tubbee	De'd	Nashoba	Samey	de'd	Nashoba
2	John Wallace	"	Sugar Loaf	Ya-ko-te-ma	"	Eagle
3						
4						
5						
6	No 2 on 1896 roll as Fanny Bohanan					
7						
8						
9						
10						
11						
12						
13						
14					Date of Application for Enrollment.	
15						
16					May 29/99	
17						

Choctaw By Blood Enrollment Cards 1898-1914

RESIDENCE: Wade			COUNTY.						
POST OFFICE: Lenox I.T.			Choctaw Nation			Choctaw Roll (Not Including Freedmen)		CARD NO. FIELD NO. 2021	

Dawes' Roll No.	NAME		Relationship to Person First Named	AGE	SEX	BLOOD	TRIBAL ENROLLMENT		
							Year	County	No.
5782	1 Bacon Allen	35	First Named	32	M	Full	1896	Wade	1017
5783	2 " Sibbie	37	Wife	34	F	"	1896	"	1018
5784	3 " Odie	7	Dau	4	F	"	1896	"	1019
⊕5785	4 " Rosa	5	Son	1	M F	"			
	5								
	6								
	7								
	8								
	9								
	10								
	11								
	12								
	13								
	14								
	15 ENROLLMENT OF NOS. 1,2,3,4 HEREON								
	16 APPROVED BY THE SECRETARY OF INTERIOR Jan. 16, 1903								
	17								

TRIBAL ENROLLMENT OF PARENTS

	Name of Father	Year	County	Name of Mother	Year	County
1	Wilson Bacon	Dead	Wade	Im-ma	Dead	Wade
2	Yah-ma-kim-tah	"	"	On-te-ma-ho-na	"	"
3	No 1			No 2		
4	No 1			No 2		
5						
6						
7			No 3 On 1896 roll as Rhoda Bacon			
8			No 4 is a male see testimony of No1 of July 1, 1903			
9						
10	⊕ 3-31-33		Sex changed from "F" to "M" by authority of the Dept. dated 3-21-33.			
11					See letter 3-13-33	
12						
13						
14						
15						Date of Application for Enrollment.
16						5/29/99
17	Talihina I.T. 12/11/02					

RESIDENCE: Wade								
POST OFFICE: Talihina I.T.	COUNTY. **Choctaw Nation**				**Choctaw Roll** (Not Including Freedmen)	CARD NO. FIELD NO. **2022**		

Dawes' Roll No.	NAME		Relationship to Person	AGE	SEX	BLOOD	TRIBAL ENROLLMENT		
							Year	County	No.
5786	1 Frazier Hannah	57	First Named	54	F	Full	1896	Wade	4068
5787	2 " Thomas H	21	Son	18	M	3/4	1896	"	4069
5788	3 " Newton	14	Son	11	M	3/4	1896	"	4070
5789	4 " Verina	12	Dau	9	F	3/4	1896	"	4071
14712	5 Wade Esther	17	Niece	14	F	Full	1896	"	13130
14713	6 Alexander, Belle	1	Dau of Nº 5	8mo	F	"			
	7								
	8								
	9								
	10								
	11								
	12								
	13								
	14								
	15	ENROLLMENT OF NOS. 1,2,3,4, HEREON APPROVED BY THE SECRETARY OF INTERIOR JAN 16 1903			ENROLLMENT OF NOS. 5 and 6 HEREON APPROVED BY THE SECRETARY OF INTERIOR MAY 29 1903				
	16								
	17								

TRIBAL ENROLLMENT OF PARENTS

	Name of Father	Year	County	Name of Mother	Year	County
1	Alford Wade	Dead	Wade	A-ha-yo-te-ma	Dead	Wade
2	Thomas Frazier	"	"	No 1		
3	" "	"	"	No 1		
4	" "	"	"	No 1		
5	Leonidas Wade	"	"	Amy Wade	Dead	Wade
6	Henry Alexander	1896	"	Nº5		
7						
8						
9						
10	No2 On 1896 roll as Howard Frazier					
11	Nº6 Born March 23, 1902, enrolled Nov. 11, 1902.					
12	Nº6 illegitimate.					
13						
14					Date of Application for Enrollment.	#1 to 5
15						
16					5/29/99	
17						

RESIDENCE: Nashoba COUNTY. **Choctaw Nation** **Choctaw Roll** CARD No.
POST OFFICE: Smithville I.T. *(Not Including Freedmen)* FIELD No. **2023**

Dawes' Roll No.	NAME		Relationship to Person First Named	AGE	SEX	BLOOD	TRIBAL ENROLLMENT		
							Year	County	No.
5790	1 Harris Gilbert	41	First Named	38	M	Full	1896	Nashoba	5512
5791	2 " Jincey	50	Wife	47	F	"	1896	"	5513
5792	3 " Lucy Ann	13	Dau	10	F	"	1896	"	5514
5793	4 " Kissey	11	Dau	8	F	"	1896	"	5515
5794	5 " Nicey	19	Step Dau	16	F	"	1896	"	12140
14714	6 Homer, Weycia	1	Dau of No5	1	F	"			
	7								
	8								
	9								
	10								
	11								
	12								
	13								
	14								

ENROLLMENT OF NOS. 1,2,3,4,5 HEREON APPROVED BY THE SECRETARY OF INTERIOR Jan 16, 1903

ENROLLMENT OF NOS. 6 HEREON APPROVED BY THE SECRETARY OF INTERIOR May 20, 1903

TRIBAL ENROLLMENT OF PARENTS

	Name of Father	Year	County	Name of Mother	Year	County
1	James Harris	Dead	Nashoba	Betsy Harris	1896	Nashoba
2	Ka-nal-li-chu-bie	Dead	"	No-wat-i-ma	Dead	"
3	No 1			No 2		
4	No 1			No 2		
5	Calvin Taylor	Dead	Nashoba	Jincey Harris	1896	Nashoba
6	Byington Homer	1896	Nashoba	No 5		
7						
8						
9	No 3 On 1896 roll as Louisiana Harris					
10	No 5 " " " " Naisey Taylor					
11	No 6 Born July 6, 1901, transferred to this card from Choc Card 4252 Dec. 13, 1902					
12	No 5 is now the wife of Byington Homer on Choc Card 1386					
13	For child of No3 see N.B. (Apr 26-06) Card #730					
14	" " " " 5 " " (Mar 3-1905) " #798					#1 to 5
15						Date of Application for Enrollment.
16						5/29/99
17						

Choctaw By Blood Enrollment Cards 1898-1914

RESIDENCE: Nashoba   COUNTY. **Choctaw Nation**   **Choctaw Roll** CARD NO.
POST OFFICE: Smithville, I.T.   *(Not Including Freedmen)*   FIELD NO. **2024**

Dawes' Roll No.	NAME	Relationship to Person	AGE	SEX	BLOOD	TRIBAL ENROLLMENT		
						Year	County	No.
5795	1 ~~Lewis, Marini~~ DIED PRIOR TO SEPTEMBER 25 1902	First Named	49	M	Full	1896	Nashoba	7943
5796	2 " , Marsie ²⁵	Wife	22	F	"	1896	"	7944
5797	3 " , Jamison ¹⁸	Son	15	M	"	1896	"	7945
5798	4 " , Henry ¹⁵	Son	12	M	"	1896	"	7946
5799	5 " , Renda ⁸	Son	5	M	"	1896	"	7947
5800	6 " , Arrenie ⁴	Dau	9mo	F	"			
	7							
	8							
	9							
	10							
	11							
	12							
	13							
	14							
	15							
	16							
	17							

ENROLLMENT
OF NOS. 1,2,3,4,5,6 HEREON
APPROVED BY THE SECRETARY
OF INTERIOR Jan 16, 1903

TRIBAL ENROLLMENT OF PARENTS

	Name of Father	Year	County	Name of Mother	Year	County
1	Leuis[sic] Shoney	Dead	Red River	Nicey Shoney	Dead	Eagle
2	Morris Ward	1896	Nashoba	Yosten Ward	"	Nashoba
3	No.1			Lina Leuis	"	"
4	No.1			" "	"	"
5	No.1			No.2		
6	No.1			No.2		
7						
8						
9			No 5 on 1896 roll as Randy Leuis			
10			No.1 died April 10, 1901. Enrollment cancelled by Department July 8, 1904			
11			For child of No2 see NB (Apr 26-06) Card #868			
12			" " " No3 " " (Mar 3-05) " #965			
13						
14						
15						
16				Date of Application for Enrollment.	5/29/99	
17						

Choctaw By Blood Enrollment Cards 1898-1914

RESIDENCE: Nashoba   COUNTY. **Choctaw Nation**   Choctaw Roll   2025
POST OFFICE: Smithville, I.T.   (Not Including Freedmen)   CARD No.
FIELD NO. 2025

Dawes' Roll No.	NAME	Relationship to Person First Named	AGE	SEX	BLOOD	TRIBAL ENROLLMENT Year	County	No.
5801	1 Wilkin Delia 33		30	F	Full	1896	Nashoba	12177
5802	2 Push Thomas DIED PRIOR TO SEPTEMBER 25, 1902	Son	8mo	M	"			
5803	3 Wilkin, Lucy 1	Dau	5mo	F	"			
	4							
	5							
	6							
	7							
	8							
	9							
	10							
	11							
	12							
	13							
	14							
	15	ENROLLMENT OF NOS. 1,2,3 HEREON APPROVED BY THE SECRETARY OF INTERIOR Jan 16 1903						
	16							
	17							

TRIBAL ENROLLMENT OF PARENTS

	Name of Father	Year	County	Name of Mother	Year	County
1	Shuns Wallace	De'd	Nashoba	Beckey Wallace	De'd	Nashoba
2	Hickman Push	"	"	No 1		
3	John Wilkin	1896	Nashoba	No.1		
4						
5						
6						
7						
8						
9						
10	For child of No1 see NB (Apr 26-06) Card #735					
11	Not on 1896 Roll as Lillie Taylor					
	No.1 is now the wife of John Wilkin on Choctaw card #1873 Feby 13, 1902					
12	No.3 born Sept 7, 1901: Enrolled Feby 13, 1902 Evidence of marriage filed Dec 11, 1902					
13	No2 died Sept. 1900; proof of death filed Dec 16, 1902					
14	No.2 died Sept – 1900: Enrollment cancelled by Department July 8, 1904					
15				Date of Application for Enrollment.	For Nos 1 &2	
16					May 29/99	
17	Tushkahomma[sic] I.T. 12/11/02					

RESIDENCE: Nashoba   COUNTY.
POST OFFICE: Smithville I.T.

Choctaw Nation

Choctaw Roll
(Not Including Freedmen)

CARD NO.
FIELD NO. 2026

Dawes' Roll No.	NAME		Relationship to Person First Named	AGE	SEX	BLOOD	TRIBAL ENROLLMENT		
							Year	County	No.
5804	1 Push Solomon	50		47	M	Full	1896	Nashoba	10374
5805	2 " Louisa	57	Wife	54	F	"	1896	"	10375
5806	3 " Califlin	17	Son	14	M	"	1896	"	10376
5807	4 " Betsie	15	Dau	12	F	"	1896	"	10377
	5								
	6								
	7								
	8								
	9								
	10								
	11								
	12								
	13								
	14								
	15								
	16								
	17								

ENROLLMENT
OF NOS. 1,2,3,4   HEREON
APPROVED BY THE SECRETARY
OF INTERIOR   JAN 16 1903

TRIBAL ENROLLMENT OF PARENTS

	Name of Father	Year	County	Name of Mother	Year	County
1	Hai-nei	Dead	Nashoba	Pesa-hi-ma	Dead	Nashoba
2	Bob James	"	"		"	Eagle
3	No 1			No 2		
4	No 1			No 2		
5						
6						
7						
8			No3 On 1896 roll as Califlia Push			
9	No.4 ~~ Died prior to September 25-1902; not entitled to land or money;					
10	(See Indian Office letter September 22. 1910, D.C. #1301-1910)					
11						
12						
13						
14						
15						
16				Date of Application for Enrollment.		5/29/99
17						

RESIDENCE:	Nashoba		COUNTY.	**Choctaw Nation**				**Choctaw Roll**		CARD No.	
POST OFFICE:	Octeva[sic] I.T.							*(Not Including Freedmen)*		FIELD No.	2027

Dawes' Roll No.		NAME		Relationship to Person First Named	AGE	SEX	BLOOD	TRIBAL ENROLLMENT			
								Year	County		No.
5808	1	Ludlow	Willis	44	Named	41	M	Full	1896	Nashoba	7993
5809	2	"	Emma	29	Wife	26	F	"	1896	"	7994
5810	3	"	Meton	17	Son	14	M	"	1896	"	7995
5811	4	"	Watkin	16	Son	13	M	"	1896	"	8630
5812	5	"	Auis	6	Dau	3	F	"	1896	"	7996
5813	6	"	Caroline	4	Dau	10mo	F	"			
14715	7	"	Lillie	2	"	10 "	"	"			
	8										
	9										
	10										
	11										
	12										
	13										
	14										

ENROLLMENT
OF NOS. 1,2,3,4,5,6 HEREON
APPROVED BY THE SECRETARY
OF INTERIOR JAN 16 1903

ENROLLMENT
OF NOS. 7 HEREON
APPROVED BY THE SECRETARY
OF INTERIOR MAY 20 1903

TRIBAL ENROLLMENT OF PARENTS

	Name of Father	Year	County	Name of Mother	Year	County
1	Ma-kin-le	Dead	Nashoba	Hai-to-na	Dead	Nashoba
2	Anolatibe	"	"	Basey Taylor	"	"
3	No 1			Louissy Ludlow	"	"
4	No 1			" "	"	"d
5	No 1			No 1		
6	No 1			No 1		
7	No.1			No.1		
8						
9	No4 On 1896 roll as Watkin Miashintubbe					
10	No5 " " " " Ennie Ludlow					
11	No4 also on 1893 pay roll Wade Co No 371 page 46					
12	No7 Born Feby 27, 1902: Proof of birth filed Dec. 23, 1902					
13	No.6 = "Died prior to September 25, 1902; not entitled t land or money"					
	See Indian Office letter may 13, 1910, D.C. #657-1910					
14						
15					#1 to 6	
16				Date of Application for Enrollment.	5/29/99	
17						

Choctaw By Blood Enrollment Cards 1898-1914

RESIDENCE: Wade   COUNTY. **Choctaw Nation**   **Choctaw Roll** (Not Including Freedmen)   CARD NO.
POST OFFICE: Talihina, I.T.   FIELD NO. **2028**

Dawes' Roll No.	NAME	Relationship to Person First Named	AGE	SEX	BLOOD	Year	County	No.
						\multicolumn{3}{c}{TRIBAL ENROLLMENT}		
5814	1 Taylor, Solomon ⁴⁹	First Named	46	M	Full	1896	Nashoba	12167
5815	2 " Semie ¹⁶	Dau	13	F	"	1896	"	12170
5816	3 " Josephine ¹⁴	Dau	11	F	"	1896	"	12171
5817	4 " Rhoda Ann ¹⁰	Dau	7	F	"	1896	"	17172
5818	5 " Solomon Jr ⁸	Son	5	M	"	1896	"	12169
	6							
	7							
	8							
	9							
	10							
	11							
	12							
	13							
	14							
	15 ENROLLMENT OF NOS. 1,2,3,4,5 HEREON							
	16 APPROVED BY THE SECRETARY							
	17 OF INTERIOR Jan 16, 1903							

TRIBAL ENROLLMENT OF PARENTS

	Name of Father	Year	County	Name of Mother	Year	County
1	Ma-ta-be	Dead	Nashoba	Molly	Dead	Nashoba
2	No 1			Islin Taylor	"	"
3	No 1			" "	"	"
4	No 1			" "	"	"
5	No 1			" "	"	"
6						
7						
8	No2 on 1896 roll as Semi Taylor					
9	No3 " " " " Fannie Taylor					
10	No4 " " " " Lotiamie Taylor					
	No1 " 1896 " " Joseph Taylor					
11						
12						
13						
14					Date of Application for Enrollment.	
15						
16					5/29/99	
17						

228

Choctaw By Blood Enrollment Cards 1898-1914

RESIDENCE: Wade COUNTY. **Choctaw Nation** **Choctaw Roll** CARD No.
POST OFFICE: Talihini[sic] I.T. *(Not Including Freedmen)* FIELD No. 2029

Dawes' Roll No.	NAME	Relationship to Person First Named	AGE	SEX	BLOOD	TRIBAL ENROLLMENT		
						Year	County	No.
14716	1 Harkins Cornelia 58	First Named	55	F	Full	1896	Wade	5391
	2							
	3	ENROLLMENT						
	4	OF NOS. 1 HEREON APPROVED BY THE SECRETARY						
	5	OF INTERIOR MAY 20 1903						
	6							
	7							
	8							
	9							
	10							
	11							
	12							
	13							
	14							
	15							
	16							
	17							

TRIBAL ENROLLMENT OF PARENTS

	Name of Father	Year	County	Name of Mother	Year	County
1	Alex. Wade	Dead	Schuylerville	Ya-ha-pi	Dead	Schuylerville
2						
3						
4						
5						
6						
7						
8						
9						
10						
11						
12						
13						
14						Date of Application for Enrollment.
15						5-29-99
16						
17						

Choctaw By Blood Enrollment Cards 1898-1914

RESIDENCE: Wade	COUNTY.	**Choctaw Nation**	Choctaw Roll	CARD No.
POST OFFICE: Talihina I.T.			(Not Including Freedmen)	FIELD NO. 2030

Dawes' Roll No.	NAME	Relationship to Person First Named	AGE	SEX	BLOOD	TRIBAL ENROLLMENT		
						Year	County	No.
DEAD.	1 Anderson Davis		67	M	3/4	1896	Wade	170
5819	2 Anderson Levina ⁶⁸	Wife	65	F	Full	1896	"	171
5820	3 Willis Rosa ¹⁹	Ward	16	F	"	1896	"	13097
	4							
	5							
	6							
	7							
	8							
	9							
	10							
	11	NO. 1 HEREON DISMISSED UNDER						
	12	ORDER OF THE COMMISSION TO THE FIVE						
	13	CIVILIZED TRIBES OF MARCH 31, 1905.						
	14							
	15	ENROLLMENT OF NOS. 2,3 HEREON						
	16	APPROVED BY THE SECRETARY OF INTERIOR JAN 16 1903						
	17							

TRIBAL ENROLLMENT OF PARENTS

Name of Father	Year	County	Name of Mother	Year	County
1 John Anderson	Dead	Wade	A-tob-be	Dead	Jack's Fork
2 Alford Wade	"	"	A-ho-yo-tema	"	Wade
3 Thomas Willis	"	"	Mary Willis	"	"
4					
5					
6					
7	No 2 On 1896 roll as Melvina Anderson				
8	No.1 Died December 19, 1900. Evidence of death filed May 11, 1901				
9					
10					
11					
12					
13					
14					
15					
16				Date of Application for Enrollment.	5/29/99
17					

230

Choctaw By Blood Enrollment Cards 1898-1914

RESIDENCE: Nashoba   COUNTY.
POST OFFICE: Smithville, I.T.

Choctaw Nation
(Not Including Freedmen)

Choctaw Roll   CARD NO.
FIELD NO. 2031

Dawes' Roll No.	NAME		Relationship to Person First Named	AGE	SEX	BLOOD	TRIBAL ENROLLMENT Year	County	No.
5821	1 Samuel, Sampson	30	First Named	27	M	Full	1896	Nashoba	11398
5822	2 " Artie	34	Wife	31	F	"	1896	"	11399
5823	3 " Silas	12	S. Son	9	M	"	1896	"	11400
5824	4 " Jerry H	11	"	8	"	"	1896	"	11401
5825	5 " Emiline	8	Dau	5	F	"	1896	"	11402
5826	6 " Joel	4	Son	1	M	"			
	7								
	8								
	9								
	10								
	11								
	12								
	13								
	14								
	15								
	16								
	17								

ENROLLMENT
OF NOS. 1,2,3,4,5,6 HEREON
APPROVED BY THE SECRETARY
OF INTERIOR JAN 16 1903

TRIBAL ENROLLMENT OF PARENTS

	Name of Father	Year	County	Name of Mother	Year	County
1	Harris Samuel	Dead	Nashoba	Susan Samuel	Dead	Nashoba
2	Charley Bounce	1896	Eagle	Un-che-ya-luna	"	"
3	Allen James	1896	Nashoba	No 2		
4	Albert Harris	1896	"	No 2		
5	No 1			No 2		
6	No 1			No 2		
7						
8						
9	For two children of No 2 see N.B (Apr 26-06) Card #715					
10						
11						
12						
13						
14						
15				Date of Application for Enrollment.	5/29/99	
16						
17						

RESIDENCE:	Nashoba	COUNTY.	**Choctaw Nation**	**Choctaw Roll**	CARD No.	
POST OFFICE:	Smithville, I.T.			*(Not Including Freedmen)*	FIELD NO.	**2032**

Dawes' Roll No.	NAME		Relationship to Person First Named	AGE	SEX	BLOOD	TRIBAL ENROLLMENT		
							Year	County	No.
5827	1 Forbit, Singlynn	38	First Named	35	M	Full	1896	Nashoba	4140
5828	2 " , Cillen	48	Wife	45	F	"	1896	"	4141
5829	3 " , Henry	7	Son	4	M	"	1896	"	4142
5830	4 Thomas, Sim	19	S.Son	16	"	"	1896	"	12173
	5								
	6								
	7								
	8								
	9								
	10								
	11								
	12								
	13								
	14	ENROLLMENT							
	15	OF NOS. 1,2,3,4 HEREON							
	16	APPROVED BY THE SECRETARY							
	17	OF INTERIOR Jan 16, 1903							

TRIBAL ENROLLMENT OF PARENTS

	Name of Father	Year	County	Name of Mother	Year	County
1	Johnson Benjamin	Dead	Eagle	Alion Narlet	1896	Nashoba
2	Cus-tie	"	Cedar	A-lan-to-na	Dead	Cedar
3	No 1			No 2		
4	Seminton Thomas	Dead	Cedar	No 2		
5						
6						
7						
8						
9						
10						
11						
12						
13						
14					Date of Application for Enrollment.	
15						
16					5/29/99	
17						

Choctaw By Blood Enrollment Cards 1898-1914

RESIDENCE: Nashoba   COUNTY. **Choctaw Nation**   **Choctaw Roll** CARD NO.
POST OFFICE: Smithville, I.T.   *(Not Including Freedmen)*   FIELD NO. 2033

Dawes' Roll No.	NAME	Relationship to Person First Named	AGE	SEX	BLOOD	TRIBAL ENROLLMENT		
						Year	County	No.
5831	1 Wilson, Simpson ³³		30	M	Full	1896	Nashoba	13232
5832	2 " Sallie ⁴³	Wife	40	F	"	1896	"	13233
	3							
	4							
	5							
	6							
	7							
	8							
	9							
	10							
	11							
	12							
	13							
	14							
	15	ENROLLMENT OF NOS. 1, 2 HEREON APPROVED BY THE SECRETARY OF INTERIOR JAN 16 1903						
	16							
	17							

TRIBAL ENROLLMENT OF PARENTS

Name of Father	Year	County	Name of Mother	Year	County
1 Alex Wilson	1896	Nashoba	Liza Wilson	1896	Nashoba
2 Ta-sa-ha	Dead	Bok Tuklo	Na-sha-ho-ki	Ded	Bok Tuklo
3					
4					
5					
6					
7					
8					
9					
10					
11					
12					
13					
14					
15					
16			Date of Application for Enrollment.	5/29/99	
17					

233

Choctaw By Blood Enrollment Cards 1898-1914

RESIDENCE:	Nashoba	COUNTY.	**Choctaw Nation**		**Choctaw Roll**	CARD NO.	
POST OFFICE:	Smithville, I.T.				(Not Including Freedmen)	FIELD NO.	2034

Dawes' Roll No.	NAME		Relationship to Person	AGE	SEX	BLOOD	TRIBAL ENROLLMENT		
							Year	County	No.
5833	1 Narlett, Ellen	53	First Named	50	F	Full	1893	Cedar	27
	2								
	3								
	4								
	5								
	6								
	7								
	8								
	9								
	10								
	11								
	12								
	13								
	14								
	15	ENROLLMENT OF NOS. 1 HEREON							
	16	APPROVED BY THE SECRETARY OF INTERIOR Jan 16 1903							
	17								

TRIBAL ENROLLMENT OF PARENTS

	Name of Father	Year	County	Name of Mother	Year	County
1	Narlett	Dead	Eagle	Pa-he-ma	Dead	Eagle
2						
3						
4						
5						
6						
7						
8	On 1893 Pay Roll, Page 3, No 27, Cedar Co, as Ellen Billy					
9	No 1 married to Moses Loman on 7-7-27					
10						
11						
12						
13						
14						
15						
16				Date of Application for Enrollment.	5/29/99	
17						

234

Choctaw By Blood Enrollment Cards 1898-1914

RESIDENCE: Nashoba   COUNTY.   **Choctaw Nation**   **Choctaw Roll**   CARD NO.
POST OFFICE: Smithville, I.T.   *(Not Including Freedmen)*   FIELD NO. 2035

Dawes' Roll No.	NAME		Relationship to Person	AGE	SEX	BLOOD	TRIBAL ENROLLMENT		
							Year	County	No.
5834	1 Narlett, Adam	52	First Named	49	M	Full	1896	Nashoba	9677
5835	2 " Emma	28	Wife	25	F	"	1896	"	9678
5836	3 Ward, Bicey	10	S.Dau	7	"	"	1896	"	13276
5837	4 Narlett Carbin	3	Son	1mo	M	"			
14933	5 " Amanda	1	Dau	13mo	F	"			
	6								
	7								
	8								
	9								
	10								
	11								
	12								
	13								
	14								
	15								
	16								
	17								

ENROLLMENT OF NOS. ~~5~~ HEREON APPROVED BY THE SECRETARY OF INTERIOR OCT 15 1903

ENROLLMENT OF NOS. 1,2,3,4 HEREON APPROVED BY THE SECRETARY OF INTERIOR JAN 16 1903

TRIBAL ENROLLMENT OF PARENTS

	Name of Father	Year	County	Name of Mother	Year	County
1	Narlett	Dead	Eagle	Pa-he-ma	Dead	Eagle
2	Joseph Jackson	"	Nashoba	Phoebe Jackson	1896	Atoka
3	William Ward	1896	Eagle	No 2		
4	No 1			No 2		
5	No.1			No 2		
6						
7						
8	No 5 Born Nov 1, 1901; Proof of birth received and filed Dec 24, 1902					
9	No3 on 1896 roll as Baisey Ward					
10	For child of Nos 1&2 see NB (March 3-1905) #890					
11	Nº5 Affidavit of mother as to Birth filed Dec. 24, 1902					
12						
13						
14						
15					No4 enrolled Nov 24/99	
16			Date of Application for Enrollment	#1 to 3	5/29/99	
17						

RESIDENCE: Nashoba   COUNTY. **Choctaw Nation**   **Choctaw Roll**   CARD NO.

POST OFFICE: Smithville, I.T.   *(Not Including Freedmen)*   FIELD NO.   2036

Dawes' Roll No.	NAME	Relationship to Person First Named	AGE	SEX	BLOOD	TRIBAL ENROLLMENT		
						Year	County	No.
5838	1 Wallace, Jesse ²³	First Named	20	M	Full	1896	Nashoba	13294
DEAD.	2 " Elizabeth DEAD.	Wife	29	F	"	1896	Jacks Fork	6137
5839	3 " Amanda ⁶	Dau	1½	"	"			
15787	4 " Rena ¹	Dau	6mo	"	"			
	5							
	6							
	7							
	8							
	9							
	10							
	11	ENROLLMENT OF NOS. 4 HEREON APPROVED BY THE SECRETARY OF INTERIOR MAR 15 1905						
	12							
	13		No.	2	HEREON DISMISSED UNDER			
	14	Ludlow I.T.	ORDER OF THE COMMISSION TO THE FIVE					
	15	ENROLLMENT	CIVILIZED TRIBES OF MARCH 31, 1905.					
	16	OF NOS. 1, 3 HEREON APPROVED BY THE SECRETARY OF INTERIOR JAN 16 1903						
	17							

	TRIBAL ENROLLMENT OF PARENTS					
	Name of Father	Year	County	Name of Mother	Year	County
1	Lamus Wallace	Dead	Nashoba	Susan Wallace	1896	Nashoba
2	James Hudson	"	Jacks Fork	Selina Hudson	1896	Jacks Fork
3	No 1			No 2		
4	N°1			N°2		
5						
6						
7						
8	No2 on 1896 roll as Elizabeth Hudson					
9	N°2 Died March 26, 1902; proof of death filed Aug. 14, 1902					
10	N°4 Born March 26, 1902, affidavits to be supplied, Aug 14, 1902 Proof of birth filed Jan 21, 1905					
11						
12						
13						
14					Date of Application for Enrollment.	#1 to 3
15						
16					5/29/99	
17	P.O. Ludlow I.T. 11/17/05					

Choctaw By Blood Enrollment Cards 1898-1914

RESIDENCE: Nashoba   COUNTY. **Choctaw Nation**   **Choctaw Roll** *(Not Including Freedmen)*   CARD No. FIELD No. **2037**

POST OFFICE: Smithville, I.T.

Dawes' Roll No.	NAME	Relationship to Person First Named	AGE	SEX	BLOOD	Year	County	No.
5840	1 Ward, Achafatubbe 63		60	M	Full	1896	Nashoba	13252
5841	2 " Sealy 37	Wife	34	F	"	1896	"	13253
5842	3 " Minnie 9	Dau	6	"	"	1896	"	13254
	4							
	5							
	6							
	7							
	8							
	9							
	10							
	11							
	12							
	13							
	14							
	15							
	16							
	17							

ENROLLMENT
OF NOS. 1,2,3 HEREON
APPROVED BY THE SECRETARY
OF INTERIOR Jan 16 1903

TRIBAL ENROLLMENT OF PARENTS

	Name of Father	Year	County	Name of Mother	Year	County
1	A-fa-mun-tubby	Dead	Nashoba	Ma-la-le-huna	Dead	Nashoba
2	Thomas Jones	"	Wade	Me-ha-to-na	"	Wade
3	No 1			No 2		
4						
5						
6						
7						
8	No1 on 1896 roll as Archalatubbi Ward					
9	No2 ' 1896 " " Sallie Ward					
10						
11						
12						
13						
14						
15					Date of Application for Enrollment.	
16					5/29/99	
17						

No 1 lives in Wade Co

RESIDENCE:	Nashoba	COUNTY.					CARD NO.		
POST OFFICE:	Smithville, I.T.	Choctaw Nation				Choctaw Roll (Not Including Freedmen)	FIELD NO.	2038	

Dawes' Roll No.	NAME	Relationship to Person Named	AGE	SEX	BLOOD	TRIBAL ENROLLMENT		
						Year	County	No.
5843	1 Ward, Elias C. ³⁷	First Named	34	M	Full	1896	Nashoba	13290
5844	2 " Sina ²⁸	Wife	25	F	"	1896	"	13291
5845	3 " Henry E ¹¹	Son	8	M	"	1896	"	13292
5846	4 " Cornelius E ⁶	"	3	"	"	1896	"	13293
5847	5 " Celestie ¹	Dau	17mo	F	"			
	6							
	7							
	8							
	9							
	10							
	11							
	12							
	13							
	14	Ludlow I.T. 10/16/02						
	15	ENROLLMENT OF NOS. 1,2,3,4,5, HEREON						
	16	APPROVED BY THE SECRETARY OF INTERIOR JAN 16 1903						
	17							

TRIBAL ENROLLMENT OF PARENTS

	Name of Father	Year	County	Name of Mother	Year	County
1	Cornelius Ward	Dead	Nashoba	Selina Ward	Dead	Nashoba
2	Peter Johnson		"	Wilsey Johnson	"	"
3	No1			No2		
4	No1			No2		
5	N°1			N°2		
6						
7						
8						
9			No1 on 1896 Roll as Elias C. Word			
10			No2 " 1896 " " Sainer "			
			No4 " 1896 " " Cornelius E "			
11			N°5 Born April 11, 1901, enrolled Oct. 6, 1902.			
12						
13						
14						
15				Date of Application for Enrollment.	5/29/99	
16						
17	Talihina I.T. 8/31/06					

238

Choctaw By Blood Enrollment Cards 1898-1914

RESIDENCE: Nashoba   COUNTY.   **Choctaw Nation**   Choctaw Roll   CARD NO.
POST OFFICE: Smithville, I.T.   (Not Including Freedmen)   FIELD NO. 2039

Dawes' Roll No.	NAME	Relationship to Person First Named	AGE	SEX	BLOOD	TRIBAL ENROLLMENT		
						Year	County	No.
5848	1 Harris, Albert 39	First Named	36	M	Full	1896	Nashoba	5517
5849	2 " Silwy 46	Wife	43	F	"	1896	"	5518
	3							
	4							
	5							
	6							
	7							
	8							
	9							
	10							
	11							
	12							
	13							
	14							
	15	ENROLLMENT OF NOS. 1, 2 HEREON APPROVED BY THE SECRETARY OF INTERIOR JAN 16 1903						
	16							
	17							

TRIBAL ENROLLMENT OF PARENTS

	Name of Father	Year	County	Name of Mother	Year	County
1	Jim Harris	Dead	Nashoba	Betsey Harris	1896	Nashoba
2	"	"	Eagle	Silmey	Dead	Eagle
3						
4						
5						
6						
7	No2 died May 28 1900. Enrollment cancelled Dec. 12, 1896					
8	March 19, 1909 Department requests report as to No.2					
9	March 31, 1909 Report to Department					
10	June 14, 1909 Department holds case is not analogous to Golosby case and declares to take action looking to her enrollment					
11						
12						
13						
14						
15						
16			Date of Application for Enrollment.	5/29/99		
17						

Choctaw By Blood Enrollment Cards 1898-1914

RESIDENCE: Nashoba   COUNTY.   **Choctaw Nation**   **Choctaw Roll**   CARD NO.

POST OFFICE: Smithville, I.T.   *(Not Including Freedmen)*   FIELD NO.   2040

Dawes' Roll No.	NAME	Relationship to Person First Named	AGE	SEX	BLOOD	TRIBAL ENROLLMENT Year	County	No.
5850	1 Harris, Betsy 83	First Named	80	F	Full	1896	Nashoba	5516
	2							
	3							
	4							
	5							
	6							
	7							
	8							
	9							
	10							
	11							
	12							
	13							
	14							
	15							
	16							
	17							

ENROLLMENT
OF NOS. 1 HEREON
APPROVED BY THE SECRETARY
OF INTERIOR JAN 16 1903

TRIBAL ENROLLMENT OF PARENTS

	Name of Father	Year	County	Name of Mother	Year	County
1	Ne-ta-huma	Dead	Nashoba		Dead	
2						
3						
4						
5						
6						
7	L.S. Bohanon, Ludlow I.T. is kin to No 1					
8	* "Died prior to Sept. 25, 1902: not entitled to land or money." See D 997 June 9, 1911					
9						
10						
11						
12						
13						
14						
15						
16				Date of Application for Enrollment.	5/29/99	
17						

Choctaw By Blood Enrollment Cards 1898-1914

| RESIDENCE: Wade | COUNTY. | **Choctaw Nation** | **Choctaw Roll** | CARD No. |
| POST OFFICE: Lenox, I.T. | | | *(Not Including Freedmen)* | FIELD No. 2041 |

Dawes' Roll No.	NAME	Relationship to Person First Named	AGE	SEX	BLOOD	TRIBAL ENROLLMENT Year	County	No.
5851	1 Williams, Abel ⁵¹		48	M	Full	1896	Wade	13108
DEAD.	2 " Catherine **DEAD.**	Wife	26	F	"	1896	"	13109
	3							
	4							
	5							
	6							
	7							
	8							
	9							
	10							
	11 No. 2 HEREON DISMISSED UNDER							
	12 ORDER OF THE COMMISSION TO THE FIVE							
	12 CIVILIZED TRIBES OF MARCH 31, 1905.							
	13							
	14							
	15 ENROLLMENT OF NOS. 1 HEREON							
	16 APPROVED BY THE SECRETARY							
	17 OF INTERIOR JAN 16 1903							

TRIBAL ENROLLMENT OF PARENTS

Name of Father	Year	County	Name of Mother	Year	County
1 Jos Williams	Dead	Wade	Ema-spe-sa-huna	Dead	Wade
2 Alex Benton	"	"	Mollie Benton	"	"
3					
4					
5					
6	No1 on 1896 roll as Abel William				
7	No2 " 1896 " " Catherine "				
8	Nº2 Died June 9, 1901; proof of death filed May 8, 1902				
9					
10	For child of No1 see NB (Apr 26-06) Card #454				
11	" " " " " " (Mar 3-05) " #1408				
12					
13					
14					
15				Date of Application for Enrollment.	
16				5/29/99	
17					

Choctaw By Blood Enrollment Cards 1898-1914

RESIDENCE: Nashoba   COUNTY.   **Choctaw Nation**   **Choctaw Roll**   CARD NO.

POST OFFICE: Talihina, I.T.   (Not Including Freedmen)   FIELD NO.   2042

Dawes' Roll No.	NAME		Relationship to Person	AGE	SEX	BLOOD	TRIBAL ENROLLMENT		
							Year	County	No.
5852	1 Jackson Mary	32	First Named	29	F	Full	1896	Nashoba	6896
5853	2 " Loyd	10	Son	7	M	"	1896	"	6898
5854	3 " Melvina	7	Dau	4	F	"	1896	"	6899
	4								
	5								
	6								
	7								
	8								
	9								
	10								
	11								
	12								
	13								
	14								
	15								
	16								
	17								

ENROLLMENT
OF NOS. 1,2,3 HEREON
APPROVED BY THE SECRETARY
OF INTERIOR Jan 16 1903

TRIBAL ENROLLMENT OF PARENTS

	Name of Father	Year	County	Name of Mother	Year	County
1	Charles Potts	Dead	Wade	Martha James	Dead	Wade
2	Jos Jackson	"	"	No 1		
3	" "	"	"	No 1		
4						
5						
6						
7		No 3 on 1896 roll as Leviney Jackson				
8		No1 wife of Smallwood Frazier 7-2046				
9						
10						
11						
12						
13						
14						
15				Date of Application for Enrollment.		
16				5/29/99		
17						

Choctaw By Blood Enrollment Cards 1898-1914

RESIDENCE: Wade	COUNTY.	Choctaw Nation	Choctaw Roll (Not Including Freedmen)	CARD NO.
POST OFFICE: Lenox, I.T.				FIELD NO. 2043

Dawes' Roll No.	NAME		Relationship to Person	AGE	SEX	BLOOD	TRIBAL ENROLLMENT		
							Year	County	No.
5855	1 Johnson, Henry	44	First Named	41	M	Full	1896	Wade	6687
5856	2 " Eliza	60	Wife	57	F	"	1896	"	6688
5857	3 " Hickman	17	Son	14	M	"	1896	"	6691
	4								
	5								
	6								
	7								
	8								
	9								
	10								
	11								
	12								
	13								
	14								
	15								
	16								
	17								

ENROLLMENT
OF NOS. 1,2,3 HEREON
APPROVED BY THE SECRETARY
OF INTERIOR JAN 16 1903

TRIBAL ENROLLMENT OF PARENTS

	Name of Father	Year	County	Name of Mother	Year	County
1	Tisho-hambe	Dead	Wade	A-to-ba	Dead	Wade
2	Pe-sa-ubbe	"	"		"	"
3	No 1			No 2		
4						
5						
6						
7						
8						
9						
10						
11						
12						
13						
14						
15						
16				Date of Application for Enrollment.	5/29/99	
17						

Choctaw By Blood Enrollment Cards 1898-1914

RESIDENCE: Wade	COUNTY.					CARD NO.	
POST OFFICE: Lenox, I.T.	Choctaw Nation				Choctaw Roll (Not Including Freedmen)	FIELD NO. 2044	

Dawes' Roll No.	NAME	Relationship to Person	AGE	SEX	BLOOD	TRIBAL ENROLLMENT		
						Year	County	No.
5858	1 White, Jency 33	First Named	30	F	Full	1896	Wade	13067
5859	2 " Luther 6	Dau[sic]	3	"	"	1896	"	13068
	3							
	4							
	5							
	6							
	7							
	8							
	9							
	10							
	11							
	12							
	13							
	14							
	15	ENROLLMENT OF NOS. 1, 2 HEREON APPROVED BY THE SECRETARY OF INTERIOR JAN 16 1903						
	16							
	17							

TRIBAL ENROLLMENT OF PARENTS

	Name of Father	Year	County	Name of Mother	Year	County
1	Jerry White	1896	Wade	Mary White	Dead	Wade
2	Henry Johnson	1896	"	No 1		
3						
4						
5						
6						
7						
8						
9						
10						
11						
12						
13						
14						
15						
16			Date of Application for Enrollment	5/29/99		
17						

Choctaw By Blood Enrollment Cards 1898-1914

2045

RESIDENCE: Nashoba   COUNTY.   **Choctaw Nation**   Choctaw Roll   CARD No.
POST OFFICE: Smithville, I.T.   *(Not Including Freedmen)*   FIELD NO. 2045

Dawes' Roll No.		NAME		Relationship to Person First Named	AGE	SEX	BLOOD	TRIBAL ENROLLMENT		
								Year	County	No.
5860	1	Taylor Benjamin	29		26	M	Full	1896	Nashoba	12153
5861	2	" Hinnie	33	Wife	30	F	"	1896	"	12154
5862	3	" Lillie May	13	S.Dau	10	"	"	1896	"	12155
DEAD.	4	" Cornelius		S.Son	9	M	"	1896	"	12156
16115	5	" Josephine	10	Dau	7	F	"	1896	"	12157
5863	6	" Jordin *(DIED PRIOR TO SEPTEMBER 25, 1902)*		Son	3	M	"	1896	"	12158
5864	7	" Alixen	4	"	6mo	"	"			
	8									
	9									
	10	No. 4 HEREON DISMISSED UNDER								
	11	ORDER OF THE COMMISSIONER TO THE FIVE CIVILIZED TRIBES OF JULY 18, 1905.								
	12	ENROLLMENT								
	13	OF NOS. ~~ 5 ~~ HEREON								
	14	APPROVED BY THE SECRETARY OF INTERIOR FEB 21 1907								
	15	ENROLLMENT								
	16	OF NOS. 1,2,3,6,7 HEREON								
	17	APPROVED BY THE SECRETARY OF INTERIOR JAN 16 1903								

TRIBAL ENROLLMENT OF PARENTS

	Name of Father	Year	County	Name of Mother	Year	County
1	Sam Taylor	Dead	Cedar	A-che-ya	Dead	Nashoba
2	Ish-ta-che	"	Nashoba	A-he-thla-huna	"	Eagle
3	Chas Benjamin	1896	"	No 2		
4	Lewis Wade	1896	"	No 2		
5	No 1			No 2		
6	No 1			No 2		
7	No 1			No 2		
8						
9						
10	No2 died April 4 1901; No3 died April 3, 1900. Enrollment cancelled by Department March 2 1907					
11	No5 is still living. See testimony of witnesses taken June 27, 1896					12/14/06
12	No 6 on 1896 roll as Jerome Taylor					
13						
14	Proof of death of No.4 filed Feb. 5, 1896 No4 died April 15, 1900					
15	No.6 died April 1, 1900. Enrollment cancelled by Department May 2, 1896.					
16				Date of Application for Enrollment.	5/29/99	
17						

RESIDENCE: Nashoba
POST OFFICE: Smithville, I.T.

COUNTY. **Choctaw Nation**

Choctaw Roll *(Not Including Freedmen)*

CARD NO.
FIELD NO. 2046

Dawes' Roll No.	NAME		Relationship to Person	AGE	SEX	BLOOD	TRIBAL ENROLLMENT		
							Year	County	No.
5865	1 Frazier, Smallwood	22	First Named	19	M	Full	1896	Nashoba	4147
5866	2 DIED PRIOR TO SEPTEMBER 25 1902 Selina	29	Wife	26	F	"	1896	"	4150
5867	3 " Aben	10	S.Son	7	M	"	1896	"	4151
5868	4 " Lucy Ann	6	S.Dau	2	F	"			
	5								
	6								
	7								
	8								
	9								
	10								
	11								
	12								
	13								
	14								
	15	ENROLLMENT OF NOS. 1,2,3,4, HEREON							
	16	APPROVED BY THE SECRETARY							
	17	OF INTERIOR JAN 16 1903							

TRIBAL ENROLLMENT OF PARENTS

	Name of Father	Year	County	Name of Mother	Year	County
1	Lord Frazier	Dead	Nashoba	Alis Frazier	Dead	Nashoba
2	"	"	Cedar			
3	Still Frazier	"	"	No 2		
4	" "	"	"	No 2		
5						
6						
7						
8						
9						
10			No2 on 1896 roll as Selena Frazier			
11						
12			No4 Affidavit of birth to be supplied. Filed Nov 1/99			
13			Nos 2-3 are wards of Sumplin Frazier on Choctaw card #1951: evidence thereof filed December 17, 1902			Date of Application for Enrollment.
14			No2 is dead. Affidavit of death to be supplied.			
15			No2 evidence of death filed Dec 10, 1902			
			Not husband of Mary Jackson Choc 2042			5/29/99
16	No2 died Aug 17, 1900; Enrollment cancelled by Department July 8, 1904					
17						

246

Choctaw By Blood Enrollment Cards 1898-1914

RESIDENCE: Nashoba
POST OFFICE: Smithville, I.T.

COUNTY. **Choctaw Nation**

Choctaw Roll
(Not Including Freedmen)

CARD No.
FIELD No. **2047**

Dawes' Roll No.	NAME	Relationship to Person	AGE	SEX	BLOOD	TRIBAL ENROLLMENT		
						Year	County	No.
5869	1 Frazier, Lean ¹⁸	First Named	15	F	Full	1896	Nashoba	4148
	2							
	3							
	4							
	5							
	6							
	7							
	8							
	9							
	10							
	11							
	12							
	13							
	14							
	15							
	16							
	17							

ENROLLMENT
OF NOS. 1 HEREON
APPROVED BY THE SECRETARY
OF INTERIOR Jan 16, 1903

TRIBAL ENROLLMENT OF PARENTS

	Name of Father	Year	County	Name of Mother	Year	County
1	Lord Frazier	Dead	Nashoba	Alis Frazier	Dead	Nashoba
2						
3						
4						
5						
6						
7						
8		On 1896 roll as Lear Frazier				
9		No.1 is wife of Levi Wilkin on Choctaw Card #1873				
10		Evidence of marriage to be supplied 12/9/02				
11		For child of No.1 see NB (March 3, 1905) #793				
12						
13						
14						
15				Date of Application for Enrollment.		
16					5/29/99	
17						

P.O. Nashoba I.T. 4/7/05

Choctaw By Blood Enrollment Cards 1898-1914

RESIDENCE: Wade COUNTY.
POST OFFICE: Talihina, I.T.

Choctaw Nation

Choctaw Roll
(Not Including Freedmen)

CARD NO.
FIELD NO. 2048

Dawes' Roll No.	NAME	Relationship to Person First Named	AGE	SEX	BLOOD	TRIBAL ENROLLMENT		
						Year	County	No.
5870	1 Jones, Laymon 49		46	M	Full	1896	Wade	6726
	2							
	3							
	4							
	5							
	6							
	7							
	8							
	9							
	10							
	11							
	12							
	13							
	14							
	15							
	16							
	17							

ENROLLMENT
OF NOS. 1 HEREON
APPROVED BY THE SECRETARY
OF INTERIOR JAN 16 1903

TRIBAL ENROLLMENT OF PARENTS

	Name of Father	Year	County	Name of Mother	Year	County
1	Lo-ma-chubbee	Dead	Wade		Dead	Wade
2						
3						
4						
5						
6						
7			Also on 1896 roll, Wade Co, Page 165,			
8		No 6698				
9						
10						
11						
12						
13						
14						
15						
16			Date of Application for Enrollment	5/29/99		
17						

Choctaw By Blood Enrollment Cards 1898-1914

RESIDENCE: Nashoba		COUNTY. **Choctaw Nation**				**Choctaw Roll** *(Not Including Freedmen)*	CARD NO.	
POST OFFICE: Smithville, I.T.							FIELD NO.	2049

Dawes' Roll No.	NAME		Relationship to Person	AGE	SEX	BLOOD	TRIBAL ENROLLMENT		
							Year	County	No.
5871	1	Taylor, Phelen ⁲⁴	First Named	21	M	Full	1896	Nashoba	12147
	2								
	3								
	4								
	5								
	6								
	7								
	8								
	9								
	10								
	11								
	12								
	13								
	14								
	15	ENROLLMENT OF NOS. 1 HEREON APPROVED BY THE SECRETARY OF INTERIOR JAN 16 1903							
	16								
	17								

TRIBAL ENROLLMENT OF PARENTS

	Name of Father	Year	County	Name of Mother	Year	County
1	John Taylor	1896	Nashoba	Sarah Taylor	1896	Nashoba
2						
3						
4						
5						
6			On 1896 roll as Phalen Taylor			
7			For child of No.1 see NB (Mar 3, 1905) #482			
8						
9						
10						
11						
12						
13						
14						
15						
16				Date of Application for Enrollment.	5/29/99	
17						

Choctaw By Blood Enrollment Cards 1898-1914

RESIDENCE: Nashoba   COUNTY. **Choctaw Nation**   **Choctaw Roll**   CARD NO.

POST OFFICE: Smithville I.T.   *(Not Including Freedmen)*   FIELD NO. **2050**

Dawes Roll No.	NAME		Relationship to Person First Named	AGE	SEX	BLOOD	TRIBAL ENROLLMENT		
							Year	County	No.
5872	1 Samuel Austin C.	31	Named	28	M	Full	1896	Nashoba	11396
5873	2 " Silesie	25	Wife	22	F	"	1896	"	11397
5874	3 " Cillen	5	Dau	2	"	"			
5875	4 " Sophvin	3	Dau	4mo	"	"			
	5								
	6								
	7								
	8								
	9								
	10								
	11								
	12								
	13								
	14								
	15								
	16								
	17								

ENROLLMENT
OF NOS. 1,2,3,4, HEREON
APPROVED BY THE SECRETARY
OF INTERIOR JAN 16 1903

TRIBAL ENROLLMENT OF PARENTS

	Name of Father	Year	County	Name of Mother	Year	County
1	Charles Samuel	De'd	Nashoba	Mary Samuel	Ded	Nashoba
2	John Allen	"	"	Betsy Allen	"	"
3	No1			No2		
4	No1			No2		
5						
6						
7						
8	For two children of No1 (one being child of No2) see NB (Apr 26-06) Card #730					
9	No.4 = "Died prior to September 25, 1902; not entitled to land or money."					
10	(See Indian Office letter of June 20, 1910, D.C. #849-1910)					
11						
12						
13						
14						
15				#1 to 3		
16				Date of Application for Enrollment. 5/29/99		
17				No 4 enrolled Jany 14, 1900		

Choctaw By Blood Enrollment Cards 1898-1914

RESIDENCE:	Nashoba		COUNTY.				Choctaw Roll	CARD No.	
POST OFFICE:	Smithville I.T.		**Choctaw Nation**				*(Not Including Freedmen)*	FIELD No.	2051

Dawes' Roll No.	NAME		Relationship to Person First Named	AGE	SEX	BLOOD	TRIBAL ENROLLMENT		
							Year	County	No.
5876	1 McGee Sissie	43	Named	40	F	Full	1896	Nashoba	9268
5877	2 " Ellen	19	Dau	16	"	"	1896	"	9269
5878	3 " Harrison	17	Son	14	M	"	1896	"	9270
5879	4 " Arsehill	15	"	12	"	"	1896	"	9172
5880	5 " Caroline	12	Dau	9	F	"	1896	"	9272
5881	6 " Mack	10	Son	7	M	"	1896	"	9273
5882	7 " Silas	7	"	4	"	"	1896	"	9274
5883	8 Taylor Archibald	6	G.Son	3	"	"	1896	"	9276
	10								
	11								
	12								
	13								
	14								
	15	ENROLLMENT OF NOS. 1,2,3,4,5,6,7,8 HEREON							
	16	APPROVED BY THE SECRETARY OF INTERIOR JAN 16 1903							
	17								

TRIBAL ENROLLMENT OF PARENTS

	Name of Father	Year	County	Name of Mother	Year	County
1	Bob James	Ded	Nashoba	Eular Ama James	Ded	Eagle
2	Gilbert McGee	"	"	No 1		
3	" "	"	"	No 1		
4	" "	"	"	No 1		
5	" "	"	"	No 1		
6	" "	"	"	No 1		
7	" "	"	"	No 1		
8	Phelan Taylor	1896	Nashoba	No 2		
9						
10						
11			For child of No.2 see N.B. (Apr 26 '06) No 559			
12			No 6 on 1896 roll as Mike McGee No 8 " " " " Archibald McGee			
13			No.6 "Died prior to September 25, 1902; not entitled to land or money"			
14			(See Indian Office letter of June 20, 1910, D.C.#828-1910)			
15						Date of Application for Enrollment.
16						5/29/99
17						

Choctaw By Blood Enrollment Cards 1898-1914

RESIDENCE:	Nashoba	COUNTY.	**Choctaw Nation**		**Choctaw Roll** *(Not Including Freedmen)*	CARD NO.	
POST OFFICE:	Smithville I.T.					FIELD NO.	2052

Dawes' Roll No.	NAME		Relationship to Person	AGE	SEX	BLOOD	TRIBAL ENROLLMENT		
							Year	County	No.
5884	1 Johnson Peter	54	First Named	51	M	Full	1896	Nashoba	6885
5885	2 " Lucy	45	Wife	42	F	"	1896	"	6886
5886	3 " Samuel	11	Son	8	M	"	1896	"	6887
5887	4 " Milsy Ann	7	Dau	4	F	"	1896	"	6889
VOID.	5 Fobb Levicy		Niece	15	"	"	1896	"	4145
	6								
	7								
	8								
	9								
	10								
	11								
	12								
	13								
	14								
	15	ENROLLMENT OF NOS. 1,2,3,4 HEREON APPROVED BY THE SECRETARY							
	16	OF INTERIOR JAN 16 1903							
	17								

TRIBAL ENROLLMENT OF PARENTS

	Name of Father	Year	County	Name of Mother	Year	County
1	Bill Sam	Ded	Eagle	Liza Johnson	Ded	Nashoba
2	Thomas Wall	"	Nashoba	Janice Wall	"	Wade
3	No 1			No 2		
4	No 1			No 2		
5	Wallis Fobb	Ded	Nashoba	Mutsy Fobb	Ded	Nashoba
6						
7						
8			No 3 on 1896 roll as Sair Johnson			
9			No 4 " " " " Milsian "			
			No 5 " " " " Lincy Forbb			
10	No.5 cancelled Oct. 4, 1902: duplicate of No.1 on Choctaw #958					
11						
12						
13						
14						
15						
16				Date of Application for Enrollment.		5/29/99
17						

252

Choctaw By Blood Enrollment Cards 1898-1914

RESIDENCE: Wade   COUNTY.

POST OFFICE: Garvin I.T.

Choctaw Nation

Choctaw Roll
(Not Including Freedmen)

CARD No.

FIELD No. 2053

Dawes' Roll No.	NAME	Relationship to Person First Named	AGE	SEX	BLOOD	TRIBAL ENROLLMENT		
						Year	County	No.
5888	1 Bohanan Elizabeth 61	First Named	58	F	Full	1896	Wade	1046
	2							
	3							
	4							
	5							
	6							
	7							
	8							
	9							
	10							
	11							
	12							
	13							
	14							
	15							
	16							
	17							

ENROLLMENT
OF NOS. 1 HEREON
APPROVED BY THE SECRETARY
OF INTERIOR JAN 16 1903

TRIBAL ENROLLMENT OF PARENTS

	Name of Father	Year	County	Name of Mother	Year	County
1	Kanamontubbi	De'd	Wade	Ahiotitona	De'd	Nashoba
2						
3						
4						
5			No.1 also on 1896 Choctaw census roll as Elizabeth Harrison:			
6			page 131: No. 5396			
7						
8						
9						
10						
11						
12						
13						
14						
15						Date of Application for Enrollment.
16			Date of application for enrollment			5/29/99
17						

RESIDENCE: Cedar COUNTY. **Choctaw Nation** **Choctaw Roll** CARD No.
POST OFFICE: Tushkahomma[sic] I.T. *(Not Including Freedmen)* FIELD No. 2054

Dawes' Roll No.	NAME	Relationship to Person First Named	AGE	SEX	BLOOD	TRIBAL ENROLLMENT		
						Year	County	No.
5889	1 Morris Esias ²⁶	First Named	23	M	Full	1896	Nashoba	8634
15413	2 " McKinly S ¹	Son	2	M	"			
	3							
	4							
	5							
	6							
	7							
	8							
	9							
	10							
	11							
	12							
	13							
	14							
	15							
	16							
	17							

ENROLLMENT
OF NOS. ~~~2~~~ HEREON
APPROVED BY THE SECRETARY
OF INTERIOR MY 9 1904

ENROLLMENT
OF NOS. 1 HEREON
APPROVED BY THE SECRETARY
OF INTERIOR JAN 16 1903

TRIBAL ENROLLMENT OF PARENTS

	Name of Father	Year	County	Name of Mother	Year	County
1	Holsen Morris	1896	Nashoba	Celia Morris	Ded	Nashoba
2	Nº 1			Ida Morris		Choctaw
3						
4						
5						
6	Nº2 Born April 11, 1902. Application first received June 9, 1902. Returned for					
7	information relative to mother. Nº2 Enrolled Feby. 24, 1904.					
8	No.2 is the son of Artiamissia Anderson on Choctaw card #1989					
9						
10						
11						
12						
13						
14						
15				#1		
16				Date of Application for Enrollment.	5/29/99	
17						

Choctaw By Blood Enrollment Cards 1898-1914

RESIDENCE: Wade   COUNTY. **Choctaw Nation**   **Choctaw Roll** CARD No.
POST OFFICE: Lenox   (Not Including Freedmen)   FIELD No. **2055**

Dawes' Roll No.	NAME		Relationship to Person First Named	AGE	SEX	BLOOD	TRIBAL ENROLLMENT		
							Year	County	No.
5890	1 McDaniel, Thomas	30		27	M	Full	1896	Wade	9240
14717	2 " , Melvina	40	Wife	37	F	"	1896	"	9241
5891	3 Potts , Mary	17	S. Dau	14	"	"	1896	"	10290
	4								
	5								
	6								
	7								
	8								
	9								
	10								
	11								
	12								
	13								
	14								
	15	ENROLLMENT OF NOS. 1, 3 HEREON APPROVED BY THE SECRETARY OF INTERIOR Jan 16, 1903					ENROLLMENT OF NOS. 2 HEREON APPROVED BY THE SECRETARY OF INTERIOR May 20, 1903		
	16								
	17								

TRIBAL ENROLLMENT OF PARENTS

	Name of Father	Year	County	Name of Mother	Year	County
1	Washington McDaniel	Ded	Skullyville	Susan Williams	1896	Wade
2	John Pitchlynn	"	Wade	Oklaioke	Ded	"
3	Charles Potts	"	"	No 2		
4						
5						
6						
7						
8						
9						
10						
11						
12						
13						
14					Date of Application for Enrollment.	
15						
16					5/29/99	
17						

Durant I.T. 1/12/03

Choctaw By Blood Enrollment Cards 1898-1914

RESIDENCE: Wade   COUNTY. **Choctaw Nation**   **Choctaw Roll** *(Not Including Freedmen)*   CARD No.

POST OFFICE: Albion I.T.   FIELD No. 2056

Dawes' Roll No.	NAME	Relationship to Person Named	AGE	SEX	BLOOD	TRIBAL ENROLLMENT Year	County	No.
5892	1 Meashintubby Silman 29	First Named	26	M	Full	1896	Wade	8567
5893	2 " Nancy 30	Wife	27	F	"	1896	"	8568
5894	3 " Eastman 8	Son	5	M	"	1896	"	8569
	4							
	5							
	6							
	7							
	8							
	9							
	10							
	11							
	12							
	13							
	14							
	15	ENROLLMENT OF NOS. 1,2,3 HEREON						
	16	APPROVED BY THE SECRETARY						
	17	OF INTERIOR JN 16 1903						

TRIBAL ENROLLMENT OF PARENTS

	Name of Father	Year	County	Name of Mother	Year	County
1	Maly Meashintubby	1896	Wade	Meha	De'd	Nashoba
2	Washington McDaniel	Ded	Skullyville	Susan McDaniel	1896	Wade
3	No 1			No 2		
4						
5						
6						
7						
8						
9						
10						
11						
12						
13						
14						
15					Date of Application for Enrollment.	
16					5/29/99	
17						

Choctaw By Blood Enrollment Cards 1898-1914

| RESIDENCE: Nashoba | COUNTY. **Choctaw Nation** | **Choctaw Roll** | CARD No. |
| POST OFFICE: Smithville I.T. | | (Not Including Freedmen) | FIELD No. 2057 |

| Dawes' Roll No. | NAME | Relationship to Person | AGE | SEX | BLOOD | TRIBAL ENROLLMENT | | |
						Year	County	No.
5895	1 Ludlow Austin 27	First Named	24	M	Full	1896	Nashoba	8000
	2					.		
	3							
	4							
	5							
	6							
	7							
	8							
	9							
	10							
	11							
	12							
	13							
	14							
	15	ENROLLMENT OF NOS. 1 HEREON						
	16	APPROVED BY THE SECRETARY						
	17	OF INTERIOR JAN 16 1903						

TRIBAL ENROLLMENT OF PARENTS

Name of Father	Year	County	Name of Mother	Year	County
1 H.J. Ludlow	1896	Nashoba	Matson Ludlow	1896	Nashoba
2					
3					
4					
5 Husband of Josephine Wilkin 7-2109					
6					
7					
8					
9					
10					
11					
12					
13					
14					
15					
16			Date of Application for Enrollment.	5/29/99	
17					

Choctaw By Blood Enrollment Cards 1898-1914

| RESIDENCE: Wade | COUNTY: | **Choctaw Nation** | Choctaw Roll | CARD NO. |
| POST OFFICE: Talihina, I.T. | | | (Not Including Freedmen) | FIELD NO. **2058** |

Dawes' Roll No.	NAME	Relationship to Person First Named	AGE	SEX	BLOOD	TRIBAL ENROLLMENT Year	County	No.
5896	~~M'Intosh, Louis~~ DIED PRIOR TO SEPTEMBER 25 1902 ¹ 71	~~First Named~~	~~44~~	~~M~~	~~Full~~	~~1896~~	~~Wade~~	~~9243~~
5897	₂ " Jane ³⁷	Wife	34	F	3/4	1896	"	9244
5898	₃ " Alexander ²⁴	Son	21	M	Full	1896	"	9245
5899	₄ " Andrew ⁹	"	6	"	7/8	1896	"	9246
5900	₅ " Annie ⁷	Dau	4	F	7/8	1896	"	9247
~~5901~~	₆ " ~~McKinnon~~ DIED PRIOR TO SEPTEMBER 25 1902	~~Son~~	~~1~~	~~M~~	~~7/8~~			
5902	₇ " Cornelius ²	Son	10mo	M	7/8			
	₈							
	₉							
	10							
	11							
	12							
	13							
	14							
	15	ENROLLMENT OF NOS. 1,2,3,4,5,6,7 HEREON APPROVED BY THE SECRETARY OF INTERIOR Jan 16, 1903						
	16							
	17							

TRIBAL ENROLLMENT OF PARENTS

	Name of Father	Year	County	Name of Mother	Year	County
₁	~~Isaac M'Intosh~~	~~Ded~~	~~Jacks Fork~~	~~Sopha M'Intosh~~	~~Ded~~	~~Jacks Fork~~
₂	Louis Spring	"	Wade	Susan Spring	"	" "
₃	No 1			Mattie M'Intosh	"	" "
₄	No 1			No 2		
₅	No 1			No 2		
₆	~~No 1~~			~~No 2~~		
₇	No 1			No 2		
₈						
₉						
10						
11			No2 on 1896 roll as Jancy M'Intosh			
12			No3 is now husband of No3 Ada Woods, on Choctaw Card #2018 May 17, 1901			
			No7 Enrolled Aug 13, 1901.			
13	No 1 died June - 1901: No 6 died - 1899: Enrollment cancelled by Department July 8, 1904					
14	No.6 died in 1899: Proof of death filed Dec 12, 1902					#1 to 6
15	No.1 died in June 1901: Proof of death filed Dec 30, 1902				Date of Application for Enrollment.	
16	For child of No 2 see NB (Mar. 3-1905) Card No 55				5/29/99	
17						

No.3 Duncan I.T. 1/6/03

258

Choctaw By Blood Enrollment Cards 1898-1914

RESIDENCE: Wade   COUNTY.   **Choctaw Nation**   Choctaw Roll   CARD No.
POST OFFICE: Albion I.T.   (Not Including Freedmen)   FIELD No. 2059

Dawes' Roll No.		NAME		Relationship to Person First Named	AGE	SEX	BLOOD	TRIBAL ENROLLMENT		
								Year	County	No.
I.W. 713	1	Heath, Chester R	59		56	M	I.W.	1896	Wade	14619
5903	2	" Catherine	47	Wife	44	F	1/2	1896	"	5393
5904	3	" Archibald	24	Son	21	M	1/4	1896	"	5394
5905	4	" Aribella	11	Dau	8	F	1/4	1896	"	5395
	5									
	6									
	7									
	8									
	9									
	10	ENROLLMENT								
	11	OF NOS. ~~~ 1 ~~~ HEREON APPROVED BY THE SECRETARY								
	12	OF INTERIOR MAY -7 1904								
	13									
	14	ENROLLMENT								
	15	OF NOS. 2,3,4 HEREON APPROVED BY THE SECRETARY								
	16	OF INTERIOR JAN 16 1903								
	17									

TRIBAL ENROLLMENT OF PARENTS

	Name of Father	Year	County	Name of Mother	Year	County
1	Daniel Heath	Ded	Non Citz	Emily Heath	Ded	Non Citz
2	Ellis Wade	"	Wade	Sarah Wade	1896	Wade
3	No 1			No 2		
4	No 1			No 2		
5						
6						
7			For child of No.3, see N.B. (Apr 26, 1896) Card No. 188.			
8						
9			No1 See Decision of March 2' 04			
10				No4 On 1896 roll as Aribelle Heath.		
11						
12						
13						
14						
15						
16				Date of Application for Enrollment.	5/29/99	
17						

Choctaw By Blood Enrollment Cards 1898-1914

RESIDENCE: Wade
POST OFFICE: Albion I.T.
COUNTY. **Choctaw Nation** **Choctaw Roll** (Not Including Freedmen)
CARD NO.
FIELD NO. 2060

Dawes' Roll No.	NAME		Relationship to Person First Named	AGE	SEX	BLOOD	TRIBAL ENROLLMENT		
							Year	County	No.
5906	1 Noah, Davis S.	32	First Named	29	M	Full	1896	Wade	9617
5907	2 " Margaret	29	Wife	26	F	1/2	1896	"	9618
5908	3 " Alfred	11	Son	8	M	3/4	1896	"	9619
5909	4 " Isabelle	9	Dau	6	F	3/4	1896	"	9620
5910	5 " Irena E	7	"	4	"	3/4	1896	"	9621
5911	6 " Sophia	6	"	3	"	3/4	1896	"	9622
5912	7 " Webster M	4	Son	2/3	M	3/4			
5913	8 " Seth D	3	Son	3mo	M	3/4			
5914	9 " Robert Lee	1	Son	2½ mo	M	3/4			
	10								
	11								
	12								
	13								
	14								
	15								
	16								
	17								

ENROLLMENT
OF NOS. 1,2,3,4,5,6,7,8,9 HEREON
APPROVED BY THE SECRETARY
OF INTERIOR JAN 16 1903

TRIBAL ENROLLMENT OF PARENTS

	Name of Father	Year	County	Name of Mother	Year	County
1	Stephen Noah	Ded	Nashoba	Suffie Noah	De'd	Wade
2	Houston Pebsworth	"	Wade	Catherine Heath	1896	"
3	No 1			No 2		
4	No 1			No 2		
5	No 1			No 2		
6	No 1			No 2		
7	No 1			No 2		
8	No. 1			No. 2		
9	Nº1			Nº2		
10						
11			No 1 on 1896 roll as D.S. Noah			
12			No 6 " " " " Ella "			
13		No.8 Enrolled June 25, 1900				
14		Nº9 Born Dec. 22, 1901; enrolled March 13, 1902				
15		For child of Nos 1&2 see NB (March 3 1905) #857		#1 to 7 inc		
16				Date of Application for Enrollment.	5/29/99	
17						

260

Choctaw By Blood Enrollment Cards 1898-1914

RESIDENCE: Wade	COUNTY.	Choctaw Nation	Choctaw Roll (Not Including Freedmen)	CARD NO.
POST OFFICE: Talihina, I.T.				FIELD NO. 2061

Dawes' Roll No.	NAME			Relationship to Person First Named	AGE	SEX	BLOOD	TRIBAL ENROLLMENT			
								Year	County		No.
5915	1	Alexander, Henry	29	First Named	26	M	Full	1896	Wade		148
5916	2	" Sarah	28	Wife	25	F	"	1896	"		149
Dead	3	" DEAD Alfred		Son	1	M	"				
5917	4	" Enoch	2	Son	2mo	M	"				
	5										
	6										
	7										
	8										
	9										
	10										
	11										
	12	No. 3 HEREON DISMISSED UNDER									
	13	ORDER OF THE COMMISSION TO THE FIVE CIVILIZED TRIBES OF MARCH 31, 1905									
	14	ENROLLMENT									
	15	OF NOS. 1,2,4 HEREON									
	16	APPROVED BY THE SECRETARY OF INTERIOR JAN 16 1903									
	17										

TRIBAL ENROLLMENT OF PARENTS

	Name of Father	Year	County	Name of Mother	Year	County
1	Thos Alexander	Dead	Skullyville	Lizzie Alexander	Dead	Sugar Loaf
2	Tom Frazier	"	Wade	Hannah Frazier	1896	Nashoba
3	No 1			No 2		
4	No.1			No2		
5						
6						
7	No. 3 Died October 23 1899 Evidence of death filed April 6, 1901					
8	No 4 Enrolled April 9, 1901					
9	For child of Nos 1&2 see NB (March 3 1905) #999					
10						
11						
12						
13						
14						Date of Application for Enrollment.
15						
16						5/29/99
17						

Choctaw By Blood Enrollment Cards 1898-1914

RESIDENCE: Nashoba   COUNTY.
POST OFFICE: Smithville, I.T.

Choctaw Nation

Choctaw Roll
(Not Including Freedmen)

CARD NO.
FIELD NO. 2062

Dawes' Roll No.	NAME		Relationship to Person First Named	AGE	SEX	BLOOD	TRIBAL ENROLLMENT		
							Year	County	No.
5918	1 Bohanan, Stayman	65		62	M	Full	1896	Nashoba	1229
5919	2 " Silas	11	Son	8	"	"	1896	"	1230
5920	3 " Simpson	9	"	6	"	"	1896	"	1231
5921	4 " Melvin	6	"	3	"	"	1896	"	1232
5922	5 Thomas DIED PRIOR TO SEPTEMBER 25, 1902		"	1 mo	"	"			
	6								
	7								
	8								
	9								
	10								
	11								
	12								
	13								
	14								
	15								
	16								
	17								

ENROLLMENT
OF NOS. 1,2,3,4,5 HEREON
APPROVED BY THE SECRETARY
OF INTERIOR JAN 16 1903

TRIBAL ENROLLMENT OF PARENTS

	Name of Father	Year	County	Name of Mother	Year	County
1		Dead	Eagle		Dead	Eagle
2	No 1			Lasen Bohanan	"	Nashoba
3	No 1			" "	"	"
4	No 1			" "	"	"
5	No 1			Lutcey "	"	"
6						
7						
8				Lucy Bohanan		
9	Mother of No 5 is No 3 on 7-799					
10						
11						
12	N⁰1 is husband of Silway Battiest Choctaw card #1889 Jany 20, 1903					
13	No.5 died - - 1899: Enrollment cancelled by Department July 8, 1904					
14						
15					Date of Application for Enrollment.	
16					5/29/99	
17	Ludlow I.T. 12/3/02					

262

Choctaw By Blood Enrollment Cards 1898-1914

RESIDENCE: Nashoba   COUNTY. **Choctaw Nation**   **Choctaw Roll**   CARD NO.
POST OFFICE: Smithville, I.T.   *(Not Including Freedmen)*   FIELD NO.   2063

Dawes' Roll No.	NAME		Relationship to Person First Named	AGE	SEX	BLOOD	TRIBAL ENROLLMENT		
							Year	County	No.
5923	1 Push, Dallas	43	Named	40	M	Full	1896	Nashoba	10365
5924	2 DIED PRIOR TO SEPTEMBER 25, 1902 Sallie	48	Wife	45	F	"	1896	"	10366
5925	3 " Elias	20	Ward	17	M	"	1896	"	10380
5926	4 " Falis	18	"	15	"	"	1896	"	10381
5927	5 " Simpson	13	"	10	"	"	1896	"	10368
5928	6 " Harris	13	"	10	"	"	1896	"	10382
5929	7 DIED PRIOR TO SEPTEMBER 25, 1902 Allistan	8	"	8	"	"	1896	"	10383
5930	8 " Williamson	17	Son	14	"	"	1896	"	10367
	9								
	10								
	11								
	12								
	13								
	14								
	15	ENROLLMENT OF NOS. 1,2,3,4,5,6,7,8 HEREON							
	16	APPROVED BY THE SECRETARY OF INTERIOR JAN 16 1903							
	17								

TRIBAL ENROLLMENT OF PARENTS

	Name of Father	Year	County	Name of Mother	Year	County
1	Har-nah	Dead	Nashoba		Dead	Nashoba
2	Jackson P Wade	"	"	Pali Wade	"	"
3	Hickman Push	"	"	Narsey Push	"	"
4	" "	"	"	" "	"	"
5	" "	"	"	" "	"	"
6	" "	"	"	" "	"	"
7	" "	"	"	" "	"	"
8	No1			No2		
9						
10	No 2 died Dec – 1899; proof of death filed Dec 16, 1902					
11						
12	No 7	Dec.	1900; " "	" " Dec 30, 1902		
13	No.2 died Dec-1899: No.7 Dec-1900: Enrollment cancelled by Department July 8, 1904					
14						
15				Date of Application for Enrollment.		
16				5/29/99		
17						

RESIDENCE: Nashoba COUNTY. **Choctaw Nation** **Choctaw Roll** CARD NO.

POST OFFICE: Smithville, I.T. 4/6/05 *(Not Including Freedmen)* FIELD NO. 2064

Dawes' Roll No.	NAME		Relationship to Person First Named	AGE	SEX	BLOOD	TRIBAL ENROLLMENT		
							Year	County	No.
5931	1 Bohanan, Lartin S	45	First Named	42	M	Full	1896	Nashoba	1240
5932	2 " Sallie Ann	34	Wife	31	F	"	1896	"	1241
5933	3 " Annie	12	Dau	9	"	"	1896	"	1243
5934	4 " Frances	10	"	7	"	"	1896	"	1244
5935	5 " Minnie	6	"	3	"	"	1896	"	1245
5936	6 " Missie	5	"	1	"	"			
	7								
	8								
	9								
	10								
	11								
	12								
	13								
	14								
	15	ENROLLMENT OF NOS. 1,2,3,4,5,6 HEREON APPROVED BY THE SECRETARY							
	16	OF INTERIOR JAN 16 1903							
	17								

TRIBAL ENROLLMENT OF PARENTS

Name of Father	Year	County	Name of Mother	Year	County
1 Staymon Bohanan	1896	Nashoba	Lotiann Bohannan	Dead	Nashoba
2 William Beams	Dead	Wade	Hannah Johnson	"	"
3 No1			No2		
4 No1			No2		
5 No1			No2		
6 No1			No2		
7					
8		No1 on 1896 roll as Laiten Bohanan			
9		No2 " 1896 " " Silian "			
		No4 " 1896 " " Fannie "			
10					
11		No6 Affidavit of birth to be supplied. Recd Dec 8/99			
12		but irregular and returned for correction.			
13		Returned corrected and filed Feby 12, 1900.			
		For child of Nos 1&2 see NB (Mar 3-05) #943			
14					
15					
16			Date of Application for Enrollment.	5/29/99	
17 Ludlow IT.					

Choctaw By Blood Enrollment Cards 1898-1914

RESIDENCE: Nashoba	COUNTY.		
POST OFFICE: Smithville, I.T.			

Choctaw Nation

Choctaw Roll (Not Including Freedmen)

CARD NO. FIELD NO. 2065

Dawes' Roll No.	NAME	Relationship to Person	AGE	SEX	BLOOD	TRIBAL ENROLLMENT		
						Year	County	No.
5937	1 Taylor, Thomas J ⁴¹	First Named	38	M	Full	1896	Nashoba	12135
5938	2 Hudson, Rufus ²³	Ward	20	"	"	1896	"	5520
5939	3 " Artimissie ²⁰	"	17	F	"	1896	"	5521
	4							
	5							
	6							
	7							
	8							
	9							
	10							
	11							
	12							
	13							
	14							
	15	ENROLLMENT OF NOS. 1,2,3 HEREON APPROVED BY THE SECRETARY OF INTERIOR JAN 16 1903						
	16							
	17							

TRIBAL ENROLLMENT OF PARENTS

	Name of Father	Year	County	Name of Mother	Year	County
1	James Taylor	Dead	Nashoba	Nancy Taylor	1896	Nashoba
2	George Hudson	"	"	Susan Hudson	Dead	"
3	" "	"	"	" "	"	"
4						
5						
6						
7						
8			For child of No. 2 see NB (March 3 1905) #944			
9						
10						
11						
12						
13						
14						
15						
16				Date of Application for Enrollment.	5/29/99	
17						

Choctaw By Blood Enrollment Cards 1898-1914

RESIDENCE: Nashoba   COUNTY. **Choctaw Nation**   **Choctaw Roll**   CARD NO.
POST OFFICE: Smithville, I.T.   (Not Including Freedmen)   FIELD NO. 2066

Dawes' Roll No.	NAME	Relationship to Person First Named	AGE	SEX	BLOOD	TRIBAL ENROLLMENT		
						Year	County	No.
5910	1 Taylor, Nancy 87	First Named	84	F	Full	1896	Nashoba	12143
	2							
	3							
	4							
	5							
	6							
	7							
	8							
	9							
	10							
	11							
	12							
	13							
	14							
	15							
	16							
	17							

ENROLLMENT
OF NOS. 1 HEREON
APPROVED BY THE SECRETARY
OF INTERIOR JAN 16 1903

TRIBAL ENROLLMENT OF PARENTS

Name of Father	Year	County	Name of Mother	Year	County
1 Wa-tubbee	Dead	Eagle	Sho-na	Dead	Eagle
2					
3					
4					
5					
6					
7					
8					
9					
10					
11					
12					
13					
14					
15					
16			Date of Application for Enrollment	5/29/99	
17					

No. 1 died May 1, 1902; Enrollment cancelled by Dept Dec 6 1896
March 19, 1909 Department requests report
April 2, 1909 Report to Department
June 14, 1909 Department holds case is not analogous to Goldsby Case and
declines to take any action looking to restoration of No 1 to roll

266

Choctaw By Blood Enrollment Cards 1898-1914

RESIDENCE: Nashoba   COUNTY. **Choctaw Nation**   **Choctaw Roll**   CARD NO.
POST OFFICE: Smithville, I.T.   *(Not Including Freedmen)*   FIELD NO. 2067

Dawes' Roll No.	NAME	Relationship to Person	AGE	SEX	BLOOD	TRIBAL ENROLLMENT		
						Year	County	No.
5941	1 Taylor, Thompson ³⁵	First Named	32	M	Full	1896	Nashoba	12159
5942	2 " Mary ³⁹	Wife	36	F	"	1896	"	12160
	3							
	4							
	5							
	6							
	7							
	8							
	9							
	10							
	11							
	12							
	13							
	14							
	15	ENROLLMENT OF NOS. 1, 2 HEREON APPROVED BY THE SECRETARY OF INTERIOR JAN 16 1903						
	16							
	17							

TRIBAL ENROLLMENT OF PARENTS

	Name of Father	Year	County	Name of Mother	Year	County
1	James Taylor	Dead	Nashoba	Nancy Taylor	1896	Nashoba
2	Alex Pesachubbee	1896	"	Liza Pesachubbee	1896	"
3						
4						
5						
6						
7						
8						
9						
10						
11						
12						
13						
14					Date of Application for Enrollment.	
15						
16					5/29/99	
17						

Choctaw By Blood Enrollment Cards 1898-1914

RESIDENCE: Nashoba   COUNTY. **Choctaw Nation**   **Choctaw Roll**   CARD NO.
POST OFFICE: Smithville I.T   *(Not Including Freedmen)*   FIELD NO.   2068

Dawes' Roll No.	NAME		Relationship to Person First Named	AGE	SEX	BLOOD	TRIBAL ENROLLMENT		
							Year	County	No.
5943	1 Taylor, John	49	First Named	46	M	Full	1896	Nashoba	12144
5944	2 " Sarah	51	Wife	48	F	"	1896	"	12145
5945	3 " Battice	22	Son	19	M	"	1896	"	12148
5946	4 " Hampton	19	"	16	"	"	1896	"	12149
5947	5 " Pelina	15	Dau	12	F	"	1896	"	12150
5948	6 " Joanna	12	"	9	"	"	1896	"	12151
5949	7 " Robert	8	Son	5	M	"	1896	"	12152
	8								
	9								
	10								
	11								
	12								
	13								
	14								
	15								
	16								
	17								

ENROLLMENT
OF NOS. 1 2 3 4 5 6 7 HEREON
APPROVED BY THE SECRETARY
OF INTERIOR Jan 16 1903

TRIBAL ENROLLMENT OF PARENTS

	Name of Father	Year	County	Name of Mother	Year	County
1	Jacob Taylor	Dead	Nashoba	Mollie Taylor	Dead	Nashoba
2	Robison Durant	"	Red River	Che-ho-yo	"	"
3	No 1			No 2		
4	No 1			No 2		
5	No 1			No 2		
6	No 1			No 2		
7	No 1			No 2		
8						
9						
10						
11			No 5 on 1896 roll as Pauline Taylor			
12			No 3 is husband of Silsainy Jones on 7-2084 – See sworn statement			
13			of Edmund M. Wilson			
14			For child of No 5 see NB (Apr 26'06) Card #857			
15			No.4 died in April or May, 1900; No.7 died in August 1900; Enrollment			
16			cancelled by Department February 8-1907 (I.T.D. 9101-1907 D.C. 2236-1907)			
17					Date of Application for Enrollment. 5/29/99	

268

RESIDENCE:	Nashoba	COUNTY.	**Choctaw Nation**	**Choctaw Roll**	CARD NO.	
POST OFFICE:	Smithville, I.T.			*(Not Including Freedmen)*	FIELD NO.	**2069**

Dawes' Roll No.	NAME	Relationship to Person First Named	AGE	SEX	BLOOD	TRIBAL ENROLLMENT		
						Year	County	No.
5950	1 James, Allen W 39		36	M	Full	1896	Nashoba	6894
5951	2 ~~Mollie~~ DIED PRIOR TO SEPTEMBER 25 1902	~~Wife~~	~~19~~	~~F~~	~~"~~	~~1896~~	~~"~~	~~6895~~
5952	3 " Agnes 15	Dau	12	"	"	1896	"	6826
	4							
	5							
	6							
	7							
	8							
	9							
	10							
	11							
	12							
	13							
	14							
	15	ENROLLMENT OF NOS. 1,2,3 HEREON						
	16	APPROVED BY THE SECRETARY OF INTERIOR Jan 16, 1903						
	17							

TRIBAL ENROLLMENT OF PARENTS

	Name of Father	Year	County	Name of Mother	Year	County
1	Willis James	Dead	Eagle	Cartise James	Dead	Eagle
2	~~Peter Johnson~~	~~1896~~	~~Nashoba~~	~~Wilsey Johnson~~	~~"~~	~~Nashoba~~
3	No 1			Artie Samuel	1896	"
4						
5						
6						
7						
8						
9	No1 is now the husband of Vicey Hobb on Choctaw Card #958, Oct. 11, 1902.					
	No.2 on 1896 roll as Marlie James					
10	No.2 died Feby 14, 1900, see letter of No1 filed Nov.6,1902 Proof of					
11	death filed Dec 16, 1902 filed March 2, 1903					
	No.1 is guardian of Ella and Hampton Nichols, Choctaw Card #2175					
12						Feby. 4, 1903
13	No.2 died Feb 14, 1900: Enrollment cancelled by Department July 8, 1904					
14	For child of No.1 see NB (March 3, 1905) #1327					
15					Date of Application for Enrollment.	
16					5/29/99	
17	P.O. Ludlow, I.T. 12/27/02					

Choctaw By Blood Enrollment Cards 1898-1914

RESIDENCE: Wade   COUNTY. **Choctaw Nation**   **Choctaw Roll** CARD NO.
POST OFFICE: Talihina, I.T.   (Not Including Freedmen) FIELD NO. 2070

Dawes' Roll No.	NAME		Relationship to Person First Named	AGE	SEX	BLOOD	TRIBAL ENROLLMENT		
							Year	County	No.
5953	1 Wade, Cyrus B	49	First Named	46	M	Full	1896	Wade	13053
I.W. 18	2 " Martha F	33	Wife	30	F	I.W.	1896	"	15166
5954	3 " Ira R	14	Son	11	M	1/2	1896	"	13054
5955	4 " Ivan S	12	"	9	"	1/2	1896	"	13055
5956	5 " Nathaniel D	8	"	5	"	1/2	1896	"	13056
5957	6 " Malcolm D	6	"	3	"	1/2	1896	"	13057
5958	7 " Della E	4	Dau	9mo	F	1/2			
5959	8 " Nellie May	1	Dau	4mo	F	1/2			
	9								
	10								
	11								
	12								
	13								
	14								
	15								
	16								
	17								

ENROLLMENT
OF NOS. 1,3,4,5,6,7,8 HEREON
APPROVED BY THE SECRETARY
OF INTERIOR Jan 16 1903

ENROLLMENT
OF NOS. ~~~ 2 ~~~ HEREON
APPROVED BY THE SECRETARY
OF INTERIOR JUN 13 1903

TRIBAL ENROLLMENT OF PARENTS

	Name of Father	Year	County	Name of Mother	Year	County
1	Alfred Wade	Dead	Wade	A-ho-ya-te-ma	Dead	Wade
2	James Maxey	"	Non Citz	Ellen Maxey	"	Non Citz
3	No1			No2		
4	No1			No2		
5	No1			No2		
6	No1			No2		
7	No1			No2		
8	No1			No2		
9						
10						
11			No 1 on 1896 roll as C. B. Wade			
12			No 2 " 1896 " " M. Florence Wade			
13			No 3 " 1896 " " Ira Wade			
			No.8 born June, 22d, 1901; Enrolled Oct 9th, 1901			
14						
15						
16						
17						

Choctaw By Blood Enrollment Cards 1898-1914

| RESIDENCE: Nashoba COUNTY. | POST OFFICE: Smithville, I.T | **Choctaw Nation** | Choctaw Roll (Not Including Freedmen) | CARD NO. FIELD NO. 2071 |

Dawes' Roll No.	NAME	Relationship to Person First Named	AGE	SEX	BLOOD	TRIBAL ENROLLMENT		
						Year	County	No.
5960	1 Allen, John ⁶⁵		62	M	Full	1893	Nashoba	5
	2							
	3							
	4							
	5							
	6							
	7							
	8							
	9							
	10							
	11							
	12							
	13							
	14							
	15							
	16							
	17							

TRIBAL ENROLLMENT OF PARENTS

	Name of Father	Year	County	Name of Mother	Year	County
1		Dead			Dead	Red River
2						
3						
4						
5						
6		On 1893 Pay Roll, Page 1, No5, Nashoba co., as John Alin				
7						
8		Also on 1896 roll, Page 4 No 168, Wade Co.				
9						
10						
11						
12						
13						
14						
15						
16						
17						

RESIDENCE: Wade   COUNTY.
POST OFFICE: Muse, I.T.

Choctaw Nation

Choctaw Roll
(Not Including Freedmen)

CARD NO.
FIELD NO. **2072**

Dawes' Roll No.	NAME		Relationship to Person First Named	AGE	SEX	BLOOD	TRIBAL ENROLLMENT		
							Year	County	No.
5961	1 Williams, Joseph	29	First Named	26	M	Full	1896	Wade	13101
5962	2 " Motsy	29	Wife	26	F	"	1896	"	13102
5963	3 DIED PRIOR TO SEPTEMBER 25 1902 Wilburn		Son	3	M	"	1896	"	13103
Dead	4 " DEAD Eveline		Dau	6mo	F	"			
5964	5 Vaughn, Ellis	15	S.Son	12	M	"	1896	Wade	12602
5965	6 Williams, Abel	2	Son	5m	M	"			
	7								
	8								
	9								
	10								
	11								
	12 No. 4 HEREON DISMISSED UNDER ORDER OF THE COMMISSION TO THE FIVE CIVILIZED TRIBES OF MARCH 31, 1905.								
	14								
	15 ENROLLMENT OF NOS. 1,2,3,5 & 6 HEREON								
	16 APPROVED BY THE SECRETARY OF INTERIOR JAN 16 1903								
	17								

TRIBAL ENROLLMENT OF PARENTS

	Name of Father	Year	County	Name of Mother	Year	County
1	Aben Williams	1896	Wade	Annie Williams	Dead	Wade
2	Elijah Town	Dead	"	Ishtechi Town	"	"
3	No 1			No 2		
4	No 1			No 2		
5	Caney Vaughn	Dead	Wade	No 2		
6	No 1			No 2		
7						
8						
9		Surname of first four appears on 1896 roll as William				
10		No.6 Enrolled January 22, 1901				
11		No.4 Died September 3 1899. Evidence of death filed April 6, 1901.				
12	No.3 died Oct. – 1901. Enrollment cancelled by Department July 8, 1904					
13		For child of Nos 1&2 see NB (Apr 26-06) Card #660				
14	" " " " "	" " (Mar 3-05) " #745				
15					Date of Application for Enrollment.	
16					5/29/99	
17						

Choctaw By Blood Enrollment Cards 1898-1914

RESIDENCE: Nashoba **COUNTY.** **Choctaw Nation** **Choctaw Roll** (Not Including Freedmen) **CARD NO.**

POST OFFICE: Cove, Arkansas **FIELD NO.** **2073**

Dawes' Roll No.	NAME		Relationship to Person	AGE	SEX	BLOOD	TRIBAL ENROLLMENT		
							Year	County	No.
5966	1 Robinson, Amsiah	35	First Named	32	M	1/2	1896	Nashoba	10798
5967	2 Going, Lizzie	33	Wife	30	F	Full	1896	"	10799
5968	3 Robinson, Elsie	15	Dau	12	"	3/4	1896	"	10800
5969	4 " Jane	13	"	10	"	3/4	1896	"	10801
5970	5 " Lyman	11	Son	8	M	3/4	1896	"	10802
5971	6 " Moses	10	"	7	"	3/4	1896	"	10803
5972	7 " John	7	"	4	"	3/4	1896	"	10804
DEAD	8 " Peter		"	3	"	3/4	1896	"	10805
15573	9 " Mary	4	Dau	1	F	3/4			
5973	10 Going, Lesine	1	Dau of No2	1	F	Full			
	11 No2 is now divorced from No 1 and is the wife of Peter Going on Choctaw Card #524								
	12 No1 has the custody of Nos 6 and 7, other children with No2, March 13, 1902								
	13 No1 on 1896 roll as Amesiah Robinson								
	No5 " 1896 " " Lymon								
	14 No.8 hereon dismissed under					ENROLLMENT			
	15 order of the Commission to					OF NOS. 1,2,3,4,5,6,7, 10 HEREON			
	16 the Five Civilized Tribes of					APPROVED BY THE SECRETARY			
	March 31, 1905.					OF INTERIOR Jan 16, 1903			
	17								

TRIBAL ENROLLMENT OF PARENTS

Name of Father	Year	County	Name of Mother	Year	County
1 Solomon Robinson	Dead	Wade	Elizabeth Robinson	1896	Nashoba
2 Alex Wilson	1896	Nashoba	Sissie Narlett	1896	"
3 No 1			No 2		
4 No 1			No 2		
5 No 1	ENROLLMENT		No 2		
6 No 1	OF NOS. ~ 9 ~ HEREON APPROVED BY THE SECRETARY OF INTERIOR Sep 22, 1904		No 2		
7 No 1			No 2		
8 No 1			No 2		
9 No 1			No 2		
10 Peter Going	1896	Nashoba	No 2		
11 No9 Born in March 1898. Proof of birth filed April 11, 1904.					
12 For child of No2 see NB(Mar 3-05) #1379					
13 No9 Affidavit of birth to be supplied					
14 No. 1 is now husband of Emma Mambi on Choctaw Card #896					
15					Apr 15, 1902
16 No8 Died July 6, 1901 Proof of death filed Oct. 6, 1902				Date of Application for Enrollment.	5/29/99 1 to 9
P O of No 3 is Smithville I T					

12/3/02   No.10 Born Sept. 23, 1901, enrolled Oct. 6, 1902.

Choctaw By Blood Enrollment Cards 1898-1914

RESIDENCE: Nashoba   COUNTY. **Choctaw Nation**   **Choctaw Roll** *(Not Including Freedmen)*   CARD NO.   FIELD NO. **2074**

POST OFFICE: Smithville, I.T.

Dawes' Roll No.	NAME		Relationship to Person First Named	AGE	SEX	BLOOD	TRIBAL ENROLLMENT		
							Year	County	No.
5974	1 Whale, David	29	Named	26	M	3/4	1896	Nashoba	13396
5975	2 " Angeline J	6	Dau	3	F	1/2	1896	"	13397
5976	3 " Edmon	3	Son	7mo	M	1/2			
15414	4 " Elmira	24	Wife	24	F	1/4	1896	Nashoba	15174
	5								
	6								
	7								
	8								
	9								
	10								
	11								
	12								
	13								
	14								
	15	ENROLLMENT OF NOS. 1,2,3 HEREON APPROVED BY THE SECRETARY OF INTERIOR Jan 16, 1903		ENROLLMENT OF NOS. 4 HEREON APPROVED BY THE SECRETARY OF INTERIOR May 9, 1904						
	16								
	17								

TRIBAL ENROLLMENT OF PARENTS

	Name of Father	Year	County	Name of Mother	Year	County
1	Wesley Whale	Dead	Nashoba	Manda Whale	1896	Nashoba
2	No 1			Elmira Whale	1896	Non Citz
3	No 1			Elmira Whale	1896	Nashoba
4	Joseph Watson	Dead	Nashoba	Rosa A Watson	Dead	Non Citizen
5						
6						
7						
8						
9			Wife on card No D.185			
10						
11			No 3 Enrolled Feby 20th, 1900.			
12	No 4 also on 1893 Pay Roll Nashoba County as Elmyra Wheel					
13	No.4 transferred from Choctaw Card #D.185, March 19, 1904					
14			For child of Nos 1&4 see NB (March 3, 1905)			#1&2
15						Date of Appliacation for Enrollment
16						5/29/99
17						

Choctaw By Blood Enrollment Cards 1898-1914

RESIDENCE:	Wade	COUNTY.							
POST OFFICE:	Talihina, I.T.		**Choctaw Nation**					CARD NO. FIELD NO.	2075

Residence: Wade — County: Choctaw Nation — Choctaw Roll (Not Including Freedmen) — Card No. Field No. 2075

Dawes' Roll No.	NAME	Relationship to Person First Named	AGE	SEX	BLOOD	TRIBAL ENROLLMENT Year	County	No.
5977	1 Burney, Charles 27	First Named	24	M	1/2	1896	Wade	988
	2							
	3							
	4							
	5							
	6							
	7							
	8							
	9							
	10							
	11							
	12							
	13							
	14							
	15	ENROLLMENT OF NOS. 1 HEREON APPROVED BY THE SECRETARY OF INTERIOR JAN 16 1903						
	16							
	17							

TRIBAL ENROLLMENT OF PARENTS

	Name of Father	Year	County	Name of Mother	Year	County
1	David Burney	1896	Wade	Elizabeth Burney	1896	Wade
2						
3						
4						
5			For child of No. 1 see NB (Apr 26-06) Card #932			
6						
7						
8						
9						
10						
11						
12						
13						
14					Date of Application for Enrollment.	
15						
16					5/29/99	
17						

Choctaw By Blood Enrollment Cards 1898-1914

RESIDENCE: Nashoba COUNTY. **Choctaw Nation** Choctaw Roll CARD NO.
POST OFFICE: Smithville, I.T. (Not Including Freedmen) FIELD NO. 2076

Dawes' Roll No.	NAME		Relationship to Person First Named	AGE	SEX	BLOOD	TRIBAL ENROLLMENT		
							Year	County	No.
5978	1 Robert, Artie	21	First Named	18	F	Full	1896	Nashoba	10797
	2								
	3								
	4								
	5								
	6								
	7								
	8								
	9								
	10								
	11								
	12								
	13								
	14								
	15								
	16								
	17								

ENROLLMENT OF NOS. 1 HEREON APPROVED BY THE SECRETARY OF INTERIOR JAN 16 1903

TRIBAL ENROLLMENT OF PARENTS

	Name of Father	Year	County	Name of Mother	Year	County
1	Wallace Fobb	Dead	Nashoba	Mutsey Fobb	Dead	Nashoba
2						
3						
4						
5						
6						
7						
8						
9						
10						
11						
12						
13						
14						
15						
16				Date of Application for Enrollment.	5/29/99	
17						

Choctaw By Blood Enrollment Cards 1898-1914

RESIDENCE: Nashoba   COUNTY. **Choctaw Nation**   **Choctaw Roll** (Not Including Freedmen)   CARD NO. FIELD NO. **2077**

POST OFFICE: Cove, Arkansas

Dawes' Roll No.	NAME	Relationship to Person First Named	AGE	SEX	BLOOD	TRIBAL ENROLLMENT Year	County	No.
DEAD	1 Robinson, Elizabeth DEAD		68	F	3/8	1896	Nashoba	10806
	2							
	3							
	4							
	5							
	6							
	7							
	8							
	9							
	10							
	11							
	12							
	13							
	14							
	15							
	16							
	17							

No. 1 HEREON DISMISSED UNDER ORDER OF THE COMMISSION TO THE FIVE CIVILIZED TRIBES OF MARCH 31, 1905

ENROLLMENT OF NOS. .... HEREON APPROVED BY THE SECRETARY OF INTERIOR ....

TRIBAL ENROLLMENT OF PARENTS

Name of Father	Year	County	Name of Mother	Year	County
1 [Illegible] Watson	Dead	Nashoba	Melvina Watson	Dead	Nashoba
2					
3					
4					
5					
6					
7					
8					
9					
10					
11					
12					
13					
14					
15					
16					
17					

No. 1 died Nov. 14, 1901; proof of death filed April 15, 1902

Date of Application for Enrollment. 5/29/99

CANCELLED

Died prior to Sept. 25, 1902

277

Choctaw By Blood Enrollment Cards 1898-1914

RESIDENCE: Nashoba   COUNTY.   **Choctaw Nation**   **Choctaw Roll** *(Not Including Freedmen)*   CARD NO.

POST OFFICE: Smithville I.T.   FIELD NO. 2078

Dawes' Roll No.	NAME	Relationship to Person	AGE	SEX	BLOOD	TRIBAL ENROLLMENT		
						Year	County	No.
5979	1 McCoy Lilian 22	First Named	19	F	Full	1896	Nashoba	6812
5980	2 " Layvinia 2	Dau	2	F	"			
	3							
	4							
	5							
	6							
	7							
	8							
	9							
	10							
	11							
	12							
	13							
	14							
	15	ENROLLMENT OF NOS. 1, 2 HEREON APPROVED BY THE SECRETARY OF INTERIOR						
	16							
	17							

TRIBAL ENROLLMENT OF PARENTS

	Name of Father	Year	County	Name of Mother	Year	County
1	Joseph Jackson	Dead	Nashoba	Seniley Jackson	Dead	Nashoba
2	Elias McCoy		Choc. Card 793	No. 1		
3						
4						
5						
6						
7						
8		On 1896 roll as Lean Jackson				
9		No.1 is the wife of Elias McCoy on Choc. Card 793. Marriage				
10		certificate filed July 7, 1902				
11		No.2 born Oct. 14, 1900 Enrolled July 7, 1902.				
12						
13						
14						
15				Date of Application for Enrollment. 5/29/99		
16						
17						

Choctaw By Blood Enrollment Cards 1898-1914

RESIDENCE: Nashoba   COUNTY. **Choctaw Nation**   **Choctaw Roll**   CARD No.
POST OFFICE: Smithville, I.T.   *(Not Including Freedmen)*   FIELD No. 2079

Dawes' Roll No.	NAME		Relationship to Person First Named	AGE	SEX	BLOOD	TRIBAL ENROLLMENT		
							Year	County	No.
5981	1	Ludlow, Payson 53	First Named	50	M	Full	1896	Nashoba	7989
5982	2	" Sina 54	Wife	51	F	"	1896	"	7990
5983	3	" Nicey 17	Dau	14	"	"	1896	"	7991
5984	4	" Esbie 15	"	12	"	"	1896	"	7992
	5								
	6								
	7								
	8								
	9								
	10								
	11								
	12								
	13								
	14								
	15								
	16								
	17								

ENROLLMENT
OF NOS. 1,2,3,4 HEREON
APPROVED BY THE SECRETARY
OF INTERIOR JAN 16 1903

	TRIBAL ENROLLMENT OF PARENTS					
	Name of Father	Year	County	Name of Mother	Year	County
1	Mak-in-tubbee	Dead	Nashoba	A-le-ho-na	Dead	Nashoba
2	Sam Lowe	"	"		"	"
3	No 1			No 2		
4	No 1			No 2		
5						
6						
7						
8	No 2 on 1896 Roll as Sainie Ludlow					
9	No 3 " 1896 " " Naisey "					
10	For child of No 3 on NB (Apr 26-06) Card #862					
11						
12						
13						
14						
15					Date of Application for Enrollment.	
16					May 29/99	
17						

279

Choctaw By Blood Enrollment Cards 1898-1914

RESIDENCE: Wade	COUNTY.	Choctaw Nation	Choctaw Roll	CARD No.
POST OFFICE: Talihina, I.T.			(Not Including Freedmen)	FIELD NO. 2080

Dawes' Roll No.	NAME	Relationship to Person First Named	AGE	SEX	BLOOD	TRIBAL ENROLLMENT Year	County	No.
5985	1 Coff, Arbis 43	First Named	40	M	Full	1896	Wade	2397
5986	2 " Samehs DIED PRIOR TO SEPTEMBER 25, 1902	Wife	30	F	"	1896	"	2398
5987	3 " Noel 10	Son	7	M	"	1896	"	2400
5988	4 " Martha 7	Dau	4	F	"	1896	"	2401
5989	5 " Edwin 2	Son	7mo	M	"			
	6							
	7							
	8							
	9							
	10							
	11							
	12							
	13							
	14							
	15							
	16							
	17							

ENROLLMENT
OF NOS. 1,2,3,4,5 HEREON
APPROVED BY THE SECRETARY
OF INTERIOR JAN 16 1903

TRIBAL ENROLLMENT OF PARENTS

	Name of Father	Year	County	Name of Mother	Year	County
1	Coff	Dead	Towson		Dead	Towson
2	Dennis Push	"	Nashoba	Limey Push	"	Nashoba
3	No 1			No 2		
4	No 1			No 2		
5	No 1			No 2		
6						
7						
8						
9			Surname appears on 1896 roll as Cobb			
10	No 2 died before sept 25 1902. Enrollment cancelled by Department May 2, 1906					
11						
12						
13						
14					Date of Application for Enrollment.	
15						
16					5/29/99	
17						

Choctaw By Blood Enrollment Cards 1898-1914

RESIDENCE: Wade COUNTY. **Choctaw Nation** **Choctaw Roll** CARD NO.
POST OFFICE: Albion, I.T. *(Not Including Freedmen)* FIELD NO. 2081

Dawes' Roll No.	NAME	Relationship to Person First Named	AGE	SEX	BLOOD	TRIBAL ENROLLMENT		
						Year	County	No.
5990	1 McKinney, Sweny 51	First Named	48	M	3/8	1896	Wade	9221
DEAD	2 " Phillis	Wife	46	F	11/16	1896	"	9222
Dead	3 " DEAD Coleman N	Son	11	M	17/32	1896	"	9224
5991	4 " Sissy 11	Dau	8	F	17/32	1896	"	9227
5992	5 " James J 6	Son	3	M	17/32	1896	"	9226
	6							
	7							
	8							
	9							
	10							
	11 No. 2 and 3 HEREON DISMISSED UNDER							
	12 ORDER OF THE COMMISSION TO THE FIVE							
	13 CIVILIZED TRIBES OF MARCH 31, 1905.							
	14							
	15 ENROLLMENT							
	16 OF NOS. 1, 4, 5 HEREON							
	APPROVED BY THE SECRETARY							
	17 OF INTERIOR JAN 16 1903							

TRIBAL ENROLLMENT OF PARENTS

Name of Father	Year	County	Name of Mother	Year	County
1 Jesse McKinney	Dead	Jacks Fork	Elsie McKinney	Dead	Cedar
2 E-yah-mo-un-tubbee	"	Wade	O-to-ma-hona	"	Wade
3 No 1			No 2		
4 No 1			No 2		
5 No 1			No 2		
6					
7					
8					
9					
10					
11					
12 No 3 on 1896 roll as Cole N McKinney					
13 No 1 " 1896 " " Sweeny "					
No 5 " 1896 " " Jas. J "					
14 No 3 Died August 6, 1899, Evidence of death filed April 16, 1901.					
15 No 2 died January 3, 1900. " " " " May 1, 1901.			Date of Application for Enrollment.		
16 No 1 is now the husband of Susan Pitchlynn Choctaw card #2173					
For child of No.1 see NB (March 3, 1905) #1434			5/29/99		
17					

RESIDENCE: Wade   COUNTY. **Choctaw Nation**

POST OFFICE: Muse, I T

Choctaw Roll *(Not Including Freedmen)*

CARD NO. FIELD NO. **2082**

Dawes' Roll No.	NAME		Relationship to Person	AGE	SEX	BLOOD	TRIBAL ENROLLMENT		
							Year	County	No.
5993	1 Billy, Austin	26	First Named	23	M	Full	1896	Wade	1014
5994	2 " Susan	28	Wife	25	F	"	1896	"	13100
5995	3 " Louisa	5	Dau	2	"	"			
5996	4 " Alice	1	Dau	9mo	F	"			
	5								
	6								
	7								
	8								
	9								
	10								
	11								
	12								
	13								
	14								
	15								
	16								
	17								

ENROLLMENT
OF NOS. 1, 2, 3, 4 HEREON
APPROVED BY THE SECRETARY
OF INTERIOR JAN 16 1903

TRIBAL ENROLLMENT OF PARENTS

	Name of Father	Year	County	Name of Mother	Year	County
1	Jamison Billy	Dead	Wade	Maggie Bill	1896	Wade
2	Sam McCoy	"	Nashoba	Louisa McCoy	Dead	"
3	No1			No2		
4	Nº1			Nº2		
5						
6						
7						
8						
9						
10		No2 on 1896 roll as Susan Wright				
11		Nº4 Born Nov. 28, 1901: enrolled Aug. 25, 1902.				
12		For child of Nos 1&2 see NB (March 3, 1905) #788				
13						
14						
15				#1 to 3		
16				Date of Application for Enrollment.	5/29/99	
17						

Choctaw By Blood Enrollment Cards 1898-1914

RESIDENCE: Nash COUNTY.	Choctaw Nation	Choctaw Roll	CARD NO.
POST OFFICE: Smithville, I.T.		(Not Including Freedmen)	FIELD NO. **2083**

Dawes' Roll No.	NAME	Relationship to Person First Named	AGE	SEX	BLOOD	TRIBAL ENROLLMENT		
						Year	County	No.
97	1 Jones, Robinson 21	First Named	18	M	Full	1896	Nashoba	6801
	2							
	3							
	4							
	5							
	6							
	7							
	8							
	9							
	10							
	11							
	12							
	13							
	14							
	15							
	16							
	17							

ENROLLMENT
OF NOS. 1 HEREON
APPROVED BY THE SECRETARY
OF INTERIOR JAN 16 1903

TRIBAL ENROLLMENT OF PARENTS

	Name of Father	Year	County	Name of Mother	Year	County
1	Rogan Jones	Dead	Nashoba	Nancy Jones	1896	Nashoba
2						
3						
4						
5						
6						
7						
8						
9						
10						
11						
12						
13						
14						
15						
16				Date of Application for Enrollment.	5/29/99	
17						

RESIDENCE: **Nashoba**   COUNTY.   **Choctaw Nation**   **Choctaw Roll**   CARD NO.
POST OFFICE: **Smithville, I.T.**   *(Not Including Freedmen)*   FIELD NO. **2084**

Dawes' Roll No.	NAME		Relationship to Person First Named	AGE	SEX	BLOOD	TRIBAL ENROLLMENT		
							Year	County	No.
5998	1 Jones, Nancy	38	First Named	35	F	Full	1896	Nashoba	6800
5999	2 " Artimissa	17	Dau	14	"	"	1896	"	6802
6000	3 " Silsainey	16	"	13	"	"	1896	"	6803
6001	4 " Rennie	13	"	10	"	"	1896	"	6804
6002	5 " Silway	10	"	7	"	"	1896	"	6805
6003	6 " Rosanna	8	"	5	"	"	1896	"	6806
14891	7 Taylor, Ellis	1	Gr Son	5mo	M	"			
	8						ENROLLMENT		
	9						OF NOS. 7 HEREON APPROVED BY THE SECRETARY		
	10						OF INTERIOR May 21 – 1903		
	11								
	12								
	13								
	14								
	15	ENROLLMENT OF NOS. 1,2,3,4,5,6 HEREON							
	16	APPROVED BY THE SECRETARY OF INTERIOR Jan 16, 1903							
	17								

TRIBAL ENROLLMENT OF PARENTS

	Name of Father	Year	County	Name of Mother	Year	County
1	William McClure	Dead	Nashoba	Isabelle McClure	Dead	Nashoba
2	Logan Jones	"	"	No 1		
3	" "	"	"	No 1		
4	" "	"	"	No 1		
5	" "	"	"	No 1		
6	" "	"	"	No 1		
7	Battice Taylor	1896	"	No. 3		
8						
9	No4 on 1896 roll as Pollyrena Jones					
10	No3 is Wife of Battice Taylor on Choctaw Card #2068 – See Statement					
11	of Edmund M. Wilson Dec. 23, 1902					
12	No.7 born July 29, 1902 Application made Dec. 23, 1902 by					
	Edmund M Wilson Dec 23, 1902. Proof of birth filed Feb. 5, 1903.					
13	For child of No2 see NB (Apr 26-06) Card No. 723					
14	" " " No3 " (Mar 3-05) " 926					
15	" No2 " " " " 1066					
16				Date of Application for Enrollment. 5/29/99		
17	No2 Beach I.T. 4/20/05					

Choctaw By Blood Enrollment Cards 1898-1914

DUPLICATE

RESIDENCE: Nashoba   COUNTY. **Choctaw Nation**   **Choctaw Roll**   CARD No.
POST OFFICE: Tushkahomma[sic] I.T.   *(Not Including Freedmen)*   FIELD No. 2085

Dawes Roll No.	NAME	Relationship to Person First Named	AGE	SEX	BLOOD	TRIBAL ENROLLMENT Year	County	No.
8004	1 Morris, Selina DIED PRIOR TO SEPTEMBER 25, 1902		40	F	Full	1896	Nashoba	8627
	2							
	3							
	4							
	5							
	6							
	7							
	8							
	9							
	10							
	11							
	12							
	13							
	14							
	15							
	16							
	17							

ENROLLMENT
OF NOS. ~~~ 1 ~~~ HEREON
APPROVED BY THE SECRETARY
OF INTERIOR Jan. 16- 1903

TRIBAL ENROLLMENT OF PARENTS

	Name of Father	Year	County	Name of Mother	Year	County
1	John Morris	Dead	Nashoba	Cillen Morris	Dead	Nashoba
2						
3						
4						
5		On 1896 roll a Silancy Morris				
6						
7		No1 died Dec. 1900. Proof of death filed Dec 23, 1902 as				
8		"Salynna" Morris.				
9						
10		No. 1 Enrollment cancelled by Department July 3, 1904				
11						
12						
13						
14						
15						
16						
17				Date of Application for Enrollment	5/29/99	

285

RESIDENCE: Nashoba COUNTY. **Choctaw Nation** **Choctaw Roll** CARD No.
POST OFFICE: Tushkahomma[sic] I.T. *(Not Including Freedmen)* FIELD No. 2086

Dawes' Roll No.	NAME	Relationship to Person First Named	AGE	SEX	BLOOD	Year	County	No.
6005	1 Graham, Charles 17	Named	14	M	1/2	1896	Nashoba	4764
6006	2 " Ellis 16	Bro	13	"	1/2	1896	"	4765
6007	3 " Simon 12	"	9	"	1/2	1896	"	4766
6008	4 " George 11	"	8	"	1/2	1896	"	4767
	5							
	6							
	7							
	8							
	9							
	10							
	11							
	12							
	13							
	14							
	15	ENROLLMENT OF NOS. 1,2,3,4 HEREON APPROVED BY THE SECRETARY						
	16	OF INTERIOR JAN 17 1903						
	17							

TRIBAL ENROLLMENT OF PARENTS

Name of Father	Year	County	Name of Mother	Year	County
1 Steve Graham	Dead	Nashoba	Maley Graham	1896	Nashoba
2 " "	"	"	" "	1896	"
3 " "	"	"	" "	1896	"
4 " "	"	"	" "	1896	"
5					
6					
7					
8		No3 on 1896 roll as Isham Graham			
9					
10					
11					
12					
13					
14					
15				Date of Application for Enrollment.	
16				5/29/99	
17					

Choctaw By Blood Enrollment Cards 1898-1914

RESIDENCE: Wade   COUNTY.   **Choctaw Nation**   **Choctaw Roll** (Not Including Freedmen)   CARD NO.

POST OFFICE: Albion, I.T.   FIELD NO. **2087**

Dawes' Roll No.	NAME	Relationship to Person First Named	AGE	SEX	BLOOD	TRIBAL ENROLLMENT Year	County	No.
6009	1 Meashintubby, Julius 23	Named	20	M	Full	1896	Wade	8576
6010	2 " Nancy 29	Wife	26	F	"	1896	"	4072
6011	3 Fobb, Emma 6	S.Dau	2	"	"			
6012	4 Meashintubby Ida 2	Dau	22mo	F	"			
	5							
	6							
	7							
	8							
	9							
	10							
	11							
	12							
	13							
	14							
	15							
	16							
	17							

ENROLLMENT
OF NOS. 1,2,3,4 HEREON
APPROVED BY THE SECRETARY
OF INTERIOR Jan 17 1903

TRIBAL ENROLLMENT OF PARENTS

	Name of Father	Year	County	Name of Mother	Year	County
1	Wm Meashintubby	1896	Wade	Wilsey Meashintubby	Dead	Wade
2	John Durant	1896	"	Sealy Durant	"	"
3	Sim Fobb	Dead	"	No 2		
4	No 1			No 2		
5						
6						
7			No2 on 1896 roll as Nancy Fobb			
8			No 4 Born Sept. 28, 1900 enrolled June 14, 1901			
9						
10						
11						
12						
13						
14						
15				#1 to 3 inc		
16				Date of Application for Enrollment.	5/29/99	
17						

Choctaw By Blood Enrollment Cards 1898-1914

RESIDENCE: Wade		COUNTY.						
POST OFFICE: Albion, I.T.		**Choctaw Nation**			**Choctaw Roll** *(Not Including Freedmen)*		CARD No. FIELD No. **2088**	

Dawes' Roll No.	NAME	Relationship to Person	AGE	SEX	BLOOD	TRIBAL ENROLLMENT		
						Year	County	No.
6013	1 Burney, Alfred 25	First Named	22	M	1/2	1893	Wade	81
	2							
	3							
	4							
	5							
	6							
	7							
	8							
	9							
	10							
	11							
	12							
	13							
	14							
	15	ENROLLMENT OF NOS. 1 HEREON APPROVED BY THE SECRETARY OF INTERIOR JAN 17 1903						
	16							
	17							

TRIBAL ENROLLMENT OF PARENTS

	Name of Father	Year	County	Name of Mother	Year	County
1	David Burney	1896	Wade	Elizabeth Burney	1896	Wade
2						
3						
4						
5						
6	On 1893 Pay Roll as Alfred Burnie, Page 9, No 81, Wade Co					
7	No.1 is now the husband of Sarah Wright on Choctaw Card #2196 Sept 26, 1901					
8	For child of No.1 see NB (March 3, 1905) #992					
9	" " " " " " (April 26, 1896) #612					
10						
11						
12						
13						
14						
15						
16				Date of Application for Enrollment	5/29/99	
17						

288

Choctaw By Blood Enrollment Cards 1898-1914

RESIDENCE: Wade   COUNTY. **Choctaw Nation**   **Choctaw Roll**   CARD NO.
POST OFFICE: Lenox, I.T.   *(Not Including Freedmen)*   FIELD NO. 2089

Dawes' Roll No.	NAME	Relationship to Person First Named	AGE	SEX	BLOOD	TRIBAL ENROLLMENT Year	County	No.
6014	1 Woods, Stephen ³¹	First Named	28	M	1/8	1896	Wade	13091
6015	2 " Kizzie ³¹	Wife	28	F	1/4	1896	"	13092
6016	3 " Martin ¹¹	Son	8	M	3/16	1896	"	13093
6017	4 " Homer ⁶	"	3	"	3/16	1896	"	13094
~~6018~~	DIE PRIOR TO SEPTEMBER 25, 1902 5 ~~Theodore~~	"	~~1~~	"	~~3/16~~			
6019	6 " Benjamin James ²	"	4mo	"	3/16			
6020	7 " Florence Elizabeth ¹	Dau	3wks	F	3/16			
	8							
	9							
	10							
	11							
	12							
	13							
	14							
	15	ENROLLMENT						
	16	OF NOS. 1,2,3,4,5,6,7 HEREON APPROVED BY THE SECRETARY						
	17	OF INTERIOR JAN 17 1903						

TRIBAL ENROLLMENT OF PARENTS

	Name of Father	Year	County	Name of Mother	Year	County
1	B. J. Wood	1896	Wade	Josephine P Woods	1896	Wade
2	Button Burns	Dead	Non Citz	Lizzie Holson	1896	Sugar Loag
3	No 1			No 2		
4	No 1			No 2		
5	~~No 1~~			~~No 2~~		
6	No 1			No 2		
7	Nº1			Nº2		
8						
9						
10	For child of Nos 1&2 see NB (Apr 26-06) Card #697					
11	~~No2 on 1896 roll as Lizzie Woods~~					
12						
13	No5 Affidavit of birth to be supplied. Recd May 30/99					
14	No6 Enrolled December 21, 1900 ~~Nº7 Born Sept. 18, 1902; enrolled Oct. 9, 1902~~					#1 to 5 inc
15	No.5 died Spring of 1902: Enrollment cancelled by Department July 8, 1904					Date of Application for Enrollment
16						5/29/99
17	Talihina I.T. 10/9/02					

Choctaw By Blood Enrollment Cards 1898-1914

RESIDENCE: Wade   COUNTY. **Choctaw Nation**   **Choctaw Roll** CARD No.

POST OFFICE: Talihina, I.T.   *(Not Including Freedmen)*   FIELD No. 2090

Dawes' Roll No.	NAME	Relationship to Person First Named	AGE	SEX	BLOOD	TRIBAL ENROLLMENT		
						Year	County	No.
6021	1 Cobb, Frank ⁵⁸		55	M	Full	1896	Wade	2392
	2							
	3							
	4							
	5							
	6							
	7							
	8							
	9							
	10							
	11							
	12							
	13							
	14							
	15							
	16							
	17							

ENROLLMENT
OF NOS. 1 HEREON
APPROVED BY THE SECRETARY
OF INTERIOR JAN 17 1903

TRIBAL ENROLLMENT OF PARENTS

Name of Father	Year	County	Name of Mother	Year	County
1 James Cobb	Dead		Amy Cobb	Dead	Skullyville
2					
3					
4					
5					
6					
7					
8					
9					
10					
11					
12					
13					
14					
15					
16			Date of Application for Enrollment.	5/29/99	
17					

RESIDENCE: Wade   COUNTY. **Choctaw Nation**   **Choctaw Roll** (Not Including Freedmen)   CARD No.

POST OFFICE: Talihina, I.T.   FIELD No. 2091

Dawes' Roll No.	NAME	Relationship to Person First Named	AGE	SEX	BLOOD	TRIBAL ENROLLMENT Year	County	No.
6022	1 Paxton, Albert DIED PRIOR TO SEPTEMBER 25 1902	First Named	32	M	Full	1896	Wade	10274
6023	2 " Hettie ²⁸	Wife	25	F	"	1896	"	10275
6024	3 " Minerva J ¹²	Dau	9	"	"	1896	"	10276
6025	4 " Ivaline ⁶	"	2	"	"			
6026	5 " Alismon ⁴	Son	3mo	M	"			
6027	6 " Flora ²	Dau	6wks	F	"			
	7							
	8							
	9							
	10							
	11							
	12 For child of No. 2 see NB (Apr 26-06) Card #844							
	13							
	14							
	15							
	16							
	17							

ENROLLMENT
OF NOS. 1,2,3,4,5,6 HEREON
APPROVED BY THE SECRETARY
OF INTERIOR JAN 17 1903

TRIBAL ENROLLMENT OF PARENTS

	Name of Father	Year	County	Name of Mother	Year	County
1	Cha-lan-tubbe	Dead	Jacks Fork	Mulsey	Dead	Jacks Fork
2	Thos Frazier	"	Wade	Hannah Frazier	1896	Wade
3	No 1			No 2		
4	No 1			No 2		
5	No 1			No 2		
6	No.1			No.2		
7						
8			No 3 on 1896 roll as Minerva Paxton			
9			No.6 Enrolled April 9, 1901			
			No 1 died Feb 12, 1902: proof of death filed Dec 16, 1902			
10	No.1 Died Feb 12, 1902: Enrollment cancelled by Department July 8, 1904					
11						
12						
13						
14					#1 to 5	
15					Date of Application for Enrollment.	
16					5/29/99	
17						

Choctaw By Blood Enrollment Cards 1898-1914

RESIDENCE: Wade   COUNTY. **Choctaw Nation**   Choctaw Roll   CARD No.
POST OFFICE: Talihina, I.T.   FIELD No. 2092

Dawes' Roll No.	NAME	Relationship to Person First Named	AGE	SEX	BLOOD	TRIBAL ENROLLMENT		2092
						Year	County	No.
15415	1 Harris William	24	21	M	1/16			
	2							
	3							
	4							
	5	ENROLLMENT OF NOS. ~~ 1 ~~ HEREON APPROVED BY THE SECRETARY OF INTERIOR MAY 9 1904						
	6							
	7							
	8 Take no further action relative to enrollment of No 1							
	9 Protest of Attys for Choctaw and Chickasaw Nations Jan 23,04							
	10 Protest over rules: see Departmental letter of March 31, 1904							
	11							
	12							
	13							
	14							
	15	ENROLLMENT OF NOS. HEREON APPROVED BY THE SECRETARY OF INTERIOR						
	16							
	17							

TRIBAL ENROLLMENT OF PARENTS

	Name of Father	Year	County	Name of Mother	Year	County
1	C. C. Harris	1896	Non Citz	Sarah Harris	De	Non Citz
2						
3						
4						
5	Admitted by Dawes Commission as a citizen by blood					
6	Case No 1349. No appeal					
7	See his testimony					
8						
9	For child of No.1 see NB (March 3, 1905) #949					
10						
11						
12						
13						
14						
15				DATE OF APPLICATION FOR ENROLLMENT.		
16					5/29/99	
17						

Choctaw By Blood Enrollment Cards 1898-1914

RESIDENCE: Nashoba	COUNTY.				
POST OFFICE: Smithville, I.T.		**Choctaw Nation**			

Choctaw Roll *(Not Including Freedmen)*
CARD No.
FIELD No. 2093

Dawes' Roll No.	NAME	Relationship to Person First Named	AGE	SEX	BLOOD	TRIBAL ENROLLMENT		
						Year	County	No.
D⁶ 1	Smith, Carnes M	Named	54	M	I.W.	1896	Nashoba	15047
2								
3								
4		DISMISSED						
5		JAN 30 1907						
6								
7								
8								
9								
10								
11								
12								
13								
14								
15								
16								
17								

TRIBAL ENROLLMENT OF PARENTS

	Name of Father	Year	County	Name of Mother	Year	County
1						
2						
3						
4						
5		Admitted by Dawes Commission as an Intermarried				
6		Citizen as Dr. J. M. Smith, Case No 1061. No appeal				
7						
8						
9		Names of parents to be supplied.				
10						
11						
12						
13						
14						
15						
16				Date of Application for Enrollment.	5/29/99	
17						

RESIDENCE:	Wade		COUNTY.					CARD NO.	
POST OFFICE:	Albion, I.T.		**Choctaw Nation**			**Choctaw Roll** (Not Including Freedmen)		FIELD NO.	**2094**

Dawes' Roll No.	NAME	Relationship to Person Named	AGE	SEX	BLOOD	TRIBAL ENROLLMENT		
						Year	County	No.
6028	1 Meashintubby, Jackson 27	First Named	24	M	Full	1896	Wade	8570
6029	2 " Lizzie 28	Wife	25	F	"	1896	"	8571
6030	3 " Missie 5	Dau	2	"	"			
	4							
	5							
	6							
	7							
	8							
	9							
	10							
	11							
	12							
	13							
	14							
	15	ENROLLMENT OF NOS. 1,2,3 HEREON APPROVED BY THE SECRETARY OF INTERIOR Jan 17 1903						
	16							
	17							

TRIBAL ENROLLMENT OF PARENTS

	Name of Father	Year	County	Name of Mother	Year	County
1	Wᵐ Meashintubby	1896	Wade	Wilsey Meashintubby	Dead	Wade
2	Ish-ta-che	Dead	Nashoba		"	Nashoba
3	No 1			No 2		
4						
5						
6	For children of Nos 1&2 see NB (March 3, 1905) #766					
7						
8						
9						
10						
11						
12						
13						
14						
15						
16				Date of Application for Enrollment.		5/29/99
17						

294

Choctaw By Blood Enrollment Cards 1898-1914

RESIDENCE: Wade   COUNTY. **Choctaw Nation**   **Choctaw Roll** CARD NO.
POST OFFICE: Lenox, I.T.   *(Not Including Freedmen)*   FIELD NO. 2095

Dawes' Roll No.	NAME		Relationship to Person First Named	AGE	SEX	BLOOD	TRIBAL ENROLLMENT		
							Year	County	No.
6031	1 Woods, John	44	First Named	41	M	1/2	1896	Wade	13079
6032	2 " Sarah	48	Wife	45	F	Full	1896	"	13080
6033	3 " Cyrus	16	Son	13	M	3/4	1896	"	13082
	4								
	5								
	6								
	7								
	8								
	9								
	10								
	11								
	12								
	13								
	14								
	15	ENROLLMENT OF NOS. 1, 2, 3, HEREON APPROVED BY THE SECRETARY OF INTERIOR JAN 17 1903							
	16								
	17								

TRIBAL ENROLLMENT OF PARENTS

	Name of Father	Year	County	Name of Mother	Year	County
1	Horace Woods	Dead	Non Citz	No-wa-te-ma	Dead	Wade
2	"	"	Sugar Loaf		"	Sugar Loaf
3	No 1			Selma Woods	"	Wade
4						
5						
6						
7						
8						
9						
10						
11						
12						
13						
14						
15						
16				Date of Application for Enrollment.	5/29/99	
17						

Choctaw By Blood Enrollment Cards 1898-1914

RESIDENCE: Wade   COUNTY. **Choctaw Nation**   **Choctaw Roll**   CARD No.

POST OFFICE: Talihina, I.T   (Not Including Freedmen)   FIELD No. 2096

Dawes' Roll No.	NAME	Relationship to Person First Named	AGE	SEX	BLOOD	TRIBAL ENROLLMENT		
						Year	County	No.
6034	1 Billy, Charles ³⁸		35	M	Full	1896	Wade	979
6035	2 " Delilah ³⁷	Wife	34	F	"	1896	"	980
6036	3 " Ephriam ¹¹	Son	8	M	"	1896	"	982
6037	4 " Israel ⁷	"	4	"	"	1896	"	984
6038	5 Johnson, Aribella ¹⁵	S. Dau	12	F	"	1896	"	6694
6039	6 Billy, Lucinda ³	Dau	1mo	"	"			
	7							
	8							
	9							
	10							
	11							
	12							
	13							
	14							
	15	ENROLLMENT OF NOS. 1,2,3,4,5,6 HEREON						
	16	APPROVED BY THE SECRETARY OF INTERIOR JAN 17 1903						
	17							

TRIBAL ENROLLMENT OF PARENTS

	Name of Father	Year	County	Name of Mother	Year	County
1	Willis Billy	Dead	Atoka	Selina Billy	Dead	Atoka
2	Silas Benton	"	Wade	Hannah Frazier	1896	Wade
3	No1			No2		
4	No1			No2		
5	Raymond Johnson	Dead	Wade	No2		
6	No1			No2		
7						
8		N⁰1 Died Sept. 24 1902, proof of death filed Dec 24, 1902				
9		The above notation is an error and refers to				
10		Carles[sic] Billy on Choctaw Card #2490. See copy of				
11		letter from Benjamin Franklin of July 21, 1903				
12						
13						
14					#1 to 5	
15					Date of Application for Enrollment.	
16					5/29/99	
17				No 6 enrolled Nov 1/99		

Choctaw By Blood Enrollment Cards 1898-1914

RESIDENCE: **Wade** COUNTY. **Choctaw Nation** **Choctaw Roll** CARD NO.
POST OFFICE: **Talihina, I.T.** (Not Including Freedmen) FIELD NO. **2097**

Dawes' Roll No.	NAME	Relationship to Person First Named	AGE	SEX	BLOOD	TRIBAL ENROLLMENT		
						Year	County	No.
6040	1 Brown, Elizabeth DIED PRIOR TO SEPTEMBER 25 1902	First Named	39	F	1/4	1896	Wade	998
6041	2 Daney, Perry 11	Son	8	M	5/8	1896	"	3343
	3							
	4							
	5							
	6							
	7							
	8							
	9							
	10							
	11							
	12							
	13							
	14							
	15	ENROLLMENT OF NOS. 1, 2 HEREON						
	16	APPROVED BY THE SECRETARY OF INTERIOR JAN 17 1903						
	17							

TRIBAL ENROLLMENT OF PARENTS

Name of Father	Year	County	Name of Mother	Year	County
1 John Young	Dead	Non Citz	Liza Young	Dead	Wade
2 Daniel Daney	1896	Wade	No. 1		
3					
4					
5					
6	No1 died Dec 31, 1901; proof of death filed Dec 12, 1902				
7	No.1 died Dec 31, 1901: Enrollment cancelled by Department July 8, 1904				
8					
9					
10					
11					
12					
13					
14					
15					
16			Date of Application for Enrollment.	5/29/99	
17					

Choctaw By Blood Enrollment Cards 1898-1914

RESIDENCE: Wade		COUNTY.						
POST OFFICE: Albion, I.T.								

Choctaw Nation

Choctaw Roll (Not Including Freedmen)

CARD NO. FIELD NO. 2098

Dawes' Roll No.	NAME		Relationship to Person	AGE	SEX	BLOOD	TRIBAL ENROLLMENT		
							Year	County	No.
6042	1 Harkins, Jonas		First Named	28	M	Full	1896	Wade	5388
6043	2 " Sallie	23	Wife	20	F	"	1896	"	3704
6044	3 " John	5	Son	1	M	"			
6045	4 Edwin, Eliza	5	S.Dau	1	F	"			
15939	5 Harkins, Ada		Dau of No 2	1	F	"			
	6								
	7								
	8								
	9								
	10								
	11								
	12								
	13								
	14								
	15								
	16								
	17								

DIED PRIOR TO SEPTEMBER 25, 1902 *(over line 1)*

ENROLLMENT OF NOS. ~~5~~ HEREON APPROVED BY THE SECRETARY OF INTERIOR NOV 24 1905

ENROLLMENT OF NOS. 1,2,3,4 HEREON APPROVED BY THE SECRETARY OF INTERIOR JAN 17 1903

TRIBAL ENROLLMENT OF PARENTS

Name of Father	Year	County	Name of Mother	Year	County
1 Willis Harkins	Dead	Wade	Jimisie Harkins	Dead	Wade
2 Ah-tok-kubbee	"	Red River	Sibbie	"	Red River
3 No 1			Sillen Harkins	"	Nashoba
4 Daniel Edwin	Dead	Wade	No 2		
5 Unknown			No 2		
6					
7					
8					
9					
10					
11		No 2 on 1896 roll as Silen Harkins – Error			
12		No 2 also on 1896 roll as Sallie Edwin,			
13		Page 78 No 3704, Wade Co.			
14		No 1 died Jan – 1901: Enrollment cancelled by Department July 8, 1904			
15		No 5 born Sept. 15, 1902: application received and No 5 placed on			
16		this card May 1, 1905, under Act of Congress approved March 3, 1905.			
17			Date of Application for Enrollment. 5/29/99		

⮕ 1 to 4

Choctaw By Blood Enrollment Cards 1898-1914

Dawes' Roll No.	NAME		Relationship to Person First Named	AGE	SEX	BLOOD	TRIBAL ENROLLMENT		
							Year	County	No.
6046	1 Town Winchester	28	Named	25	M	Full	1896	Wade	12063
6047	2 " Missie	26	Wife	23	F	"	1896	"	12064
Dead	3 " Susan		Dau	1	"	"			
Dead	4 " Gilbert W.	3	Son	3mo	M	"			
6048	5 " Harry Dukes	1	S. Son	6wks	M	3/4			
	6								
	7								
	8								
	9								
	10 Nos. 3&4 hereon dismissed under								
	11 order of the Commission to the Five Civilized Tribes of July 18, 1905.								
	12 Feb. 16 1906								
	13								
	14								
	15 ENROLLMENT OF NOS. 1, 2 & 5 HEREON		Nos 3&4 dismissed Feb 16, 1906						
	16 APPROVED BY THE SECRETARY OF INTERIOR Jan 17 1903								
	17								

TRIBAL ENROLLMENT OF PARENTS

	Name of Father	Year	County	Name of Mother	Year	County
1	Elijah Town	Dead	Wade	Stagey Town	Dead	Wade
2	Gaines James	"	"	Ke-ah-im-ma	"	"
3	No 1			No 2		
4	No 1			No 2		
5	Henry Dukes	1896	"	No 2		
6						
7						
8						
9		No 5 born Nov. 30, 1901: Enrolled Jan. 9, 1902				
10		No.3 died in summer of 1898: proof of death filed Feb. 16, 1896				
11		No.4 died in winter of 1899-1900: " " " " " "				
12						
13						
14						#1 to 3
15						Date of Application for Enrollment.
16						5/29/99
17	P.O. of No 2 Talihina I.T. Feb-16, 1906			No4 enrolled Nov 1/99		

Choctaw By Blood Enrollment Cards 1898-1914

| RESIDENCE: | Sugar Loaf | COUNTY. | Choctaw Nation | Choctaw Roll | CARD NO. | |
| POST OFFICE: | Wister I.T. | | | | FIELD NO. | 2100 |

Dawes' Roll No.	NAME	Relationship to Person First Named	AGE	SEX	BLOOD	Year	County	No.
6049	1 Push, Susan 24		21	F	Full	1896	Sugar Loaf	9137
6050	2 McCurtain Jackson 6	Son	3	M	"	1896	" "	9139
6051	3 " Allen 7	"	4	"	"	1896	" "	9138
6052	4 Push, Alice 2	Dau	10mo	F	"			
15832	5 " Annie	Dau	1	F	"			
	6							
	7							
	8							
	9							
	10							
	11	ENROLLMENT OF NOS. ~~~ 5 ~~~ HEREON						
	12	APPROVED BY THE SECRETARY						
	13	OF INTERIOR JUN 12 1905						
	14							
	15	ENROLLMENT OF NOS. 1,2,3,4 HEREON						
	16	APPROVED BY THE SECRETARY						
	17	OF INTERIOR JAN 17 1903						

TRIBAL ENROLLMENT OF PARENTS

Name of Father	Year	County	Name of Mother	Year	County
1 Sampson Newell	Ded	Sugar Loaf	Elizabeth Newell	De'd	Sugar Loaf
2 Daniel McCurtain	"	" "	No 1		
3 " "	"	" "	No 1		
4 Sylvester T. Push	1896	" "	No 1		
5 " " "	"	" "	No 1		
6					
7					
8	No.1 is now the wife of Sylvester T. Push on Choctaw Card #2102. See letter				
9	of S. T. Push filed Nov. 7, 1901.				
10	No.4 Born Jan. 13, 1901: Enrolled Nov. 7, 1901.				
11	No.5 was born Sept. 23, 1902: Application received and name placed on				
12	this card March 25, 1905, under provision of act of Congress approved				
13	March 3d, 1905.				
14					
15					
16	P O Talihina I.T June 27 – 04		Date of Application for Enrollment.	5/29/99	
17	Albian Okla				

300

9 781649 680105